The Joan Palevsky Imprint in Classical Literature

In honor of beloved Virgil—

"O degli altri poeti onore e lume . . ."

—Dante, *Inferno*

The publisher gratefully acknowledges the generous support of the Classical Literature Endowment Fund of the University of California Press Foundation, which was established by a major gift from Joan Palevsky.

The Hellenistic Far East

The Hellenistic Far East

*Archaeology, Language, and Identity
in Greek Central Asia*

Rachel Mairs

UNIVERSITY OF CALIFORNIA PRESS

University of California Press, one of the most distinguished university presses in the United States, enriches lives around the world by advancing scholarship in the humanities, social sciences, and natural sciences. Its activities are supported by the UC Press Foundation and by philanthropic contributions from individuals and institutions. For more information, visit www.ucpress.edu.

University of California Press
Oakland, California

First paperback printing 2016

Library of Congress Cataloging-in-Publication Data

Mairs, Rachel.
   The Hellenistic Far East : archaeology, language, and identity in Greek Central Asia / Rachel Mairs.
      p. cm.
   Includes bibliographical references and index.
   ISBN 978-0-520-28127-1 (cloth: alk. paper)
   ISBN 978-0-520-29246-8 (pbk.: alk. paper)
   ISBN 978-0-520-95954-5 (electronic)
   1. Asia, Central—Antiquities   2. Greeks—Asia, Central—Antiqui-
ties.   3. Ay Khanom (Afghanistan)—Antiquities.   4. Bactria—Antiqui-
ties.   5. Excavations (Archaeology)—Asia, Central.   6. Cities and towns,
Ancient—Asia, Central.   7. Garrisons—Asia, Central—History—To
1500.   8. Group identity—Asia, Central—History—History.   9. Asia,
Central—Languages—History—History.   10. Social archaeology—Asia,
Central.   I. Title.
DS328.M24   2014
958'.01—dc23   2014011416

Manufactured in the United States of America

23 22 21 20 19 18 17 16
10 9 8 7 6 5 4 3 2 1

For My Grandfather

CONTENTS

ILLUSTRATIONS

MAPS

FIGURES

ACKNOWLEDGMENTS

The book in which I first read about Ai Khanoum was a childhood gift from my grandparents, but my interest in Hellenistic Bactria began in earnest when I was an undergraduate in the library of St Catherine's College, Cambridge, when I should have been writing an essay on something else. Sir William Woodthorpe Tarn's *The Greeks in Bactria and India* had a title too intriguing and downright bizarre to possibly be ignored. It also left me with more questions than I could even begin to know how to go about answering.

Dorothy J. Thompson has been a supervisor and mentor without equal throughout my vacillations between Egypt and Central Asia. I owe her an immense debt for showing me how one can think critically and creatively about language and identity. Parts of this book originated in a PhD thesis under her supervision at the University of Cambridge.

The Hellenistic Far East does not have any real disciplinary home, but I have been grateful for the welcome given me by various centers of classics, oriental studies, and archaeology, as well as the institutions where I have worked over the past few years. The academic communities of the Institute for the Study of the Ancient World (ISAW), New York University; Merton College, University of Oxford; the Joukowsky Institute for Archaeology and the Ancient World, Brown University; and the Department of Classics, University of Reading, have all provided financial support and terrific opportunities to share and discover new research. My students at Brown gave me the chance to actually teach Central Asian archaeology for the first time. Sören Stark and Lillian Tseng kindly allowed me to participate in their seminar on Cultural Interactions in Eurasian Art and Archaeology at ISAW and to learn more about the archaeology of Central Asian nomads.

Raymond J. Mairs provided an architect's perspective on Ai Khanoum. Participants at numerous conferences over the years have also given me food for thought and have let me test the principle that you can only know if your ideas are actually crazy once you've said them aloud in front of a large, imposing audience.

Thanks also go to everyone who has contributed to my Hellenistic Far East Bibliography, named individually in the acknowledgements to Mairs 2011b and subsequent updates. I will continue to update the bibliography regularly at www.bactria.org (through which I occasionally get requests for logistical support in Afghanistan because of confusion with a similarly named website).

Lynne Rouse gave me the opportunity to excavate and conduct research in Turkmenistan, which was supported by a grant from the British Academy. Carol Mairs, Central Asian traveling companion extraordinaire, put up with the highs (Samarkand), the lows (Konye Urgench), and all the plov a person could reasonably eat.

Frank L. Holt and Matthew Canepa offered superb critique and advice in the preparation of this manuscript, for which I am very grateful indeed. Paul Bernard and Nicholas Sims-Williams provided kind assistance with the Sōphytos inscription and the Bactrian documentary texts. At University of California Press, Eric Schmidt, Maeve Cornell-Taylor, and Cindy Fulton have been supportive and astute editors, and Paul Psoinos an exemplary copy editor.

Thanks for everything must go to my family.

A NOTE ON ABBREVIATIONS

For epigraphical publications, the abbreviations used in the notes to this volume follow those appearing in the frontmatter lists of Simon Hornblower and Anthony Spawforth, eds., *The Oxford Classical Dictionary,* 3rd edition, revised (Oxford, 2003), and H. G. Liddell, Robert Scott, et al., eds., *A Greek-English Lexicon,* 9th edition, with supplement (Oxford, 1968); those for papyri are as given in the *Checklist of Greek, Latin, Demotic and Coptic Papyri, Ostraca and Tablets,* available online at http://library.duke.edu/rubenstein/scriptorium/papyrus/texts/clist.html.

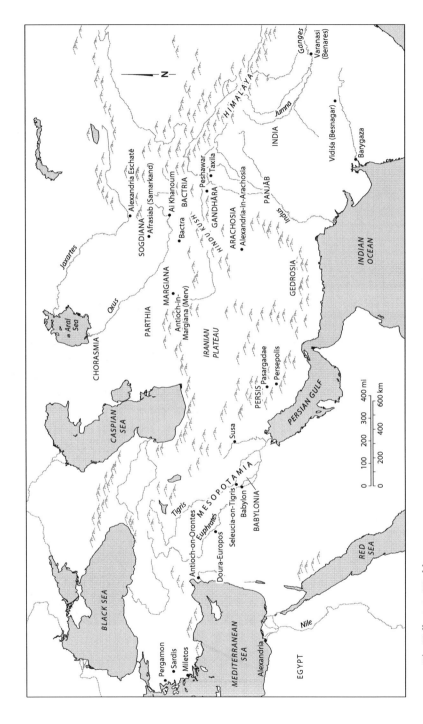

MAP 1. The Hellenistic World.

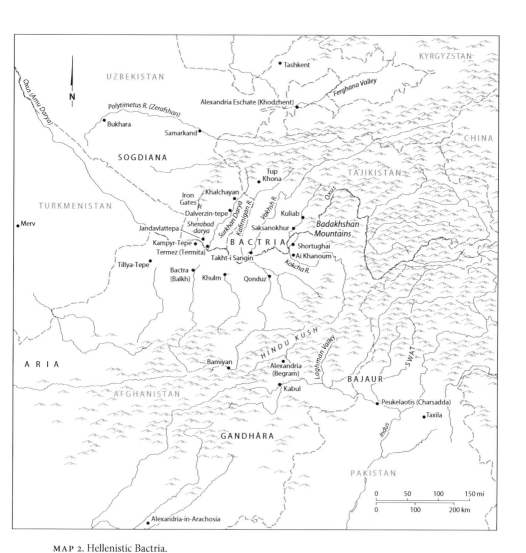

MAP 2. Hellenistic Bactria.

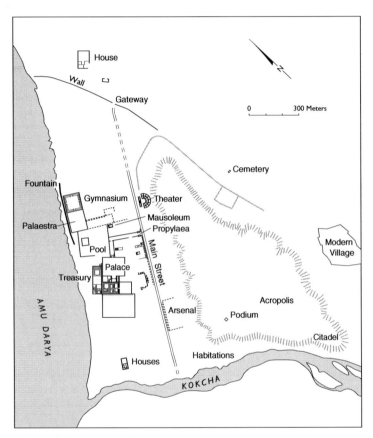

MAP 3. Ai Khanoum city plan.

Introduction

Coins with Indian inscriptions.
Those of the most powerful monarchs,
of Evoukratindaza, of Stratasa,
of Menandraza, of Heramaïaza.
That's how the scholarly book conveys to us
the Indian writing on one side of the coins.
But the book shows us the other side as well,
that is, moreover, the right side,
with the figure of the king. And how quickly he stops there,
how a Hellene is moved as he reads the Greek,
Hermaios, Eukratides, Straton, Menandros.

> —C. P. CAVAFY, "COINS WITH INDIAN INSCRIPTIONS" (1920; TRANS.
> AFTER MENDELSOHN 2012, 334)

A GREEK CITY IN AFGHANISTAN

In 1966, excavators at an ancient city on the river Oxus in northern Afghanistan discovered two short Greek inscriptions.[1] In one, from a gymnasium, two brothers named Straton and Triballos dedicate to Hermes and Herakles. In the second, the more famous inscription, a man named Klearchos states that he has copied down a series of ethical maxims at Delphi and brought them here to be set up in the "sanctuary of Kineas." On the same stone, the surviving portion of a much longer inscription, we find the last of these precepts, which contain instructions for those at different stages in their lives: "As a child, be well behaved; as a young man, self-controlled; in middle age, be just; as an elder, be of good counsel; and when you come to the end, be without grief."

---

1. For the idea of Ai Khanoum as an intrusive "Greek city" in Central Asia, see Frye 1966 and Bernard 1982b. The "two short Greek inscriptions" mentioned in the text were published by the epigrapher Louis Robert in the *Comptes-Rendus de l'Académie des Inscriptions et Belles-Lettres* for 1968. Both will be discussed at greater length in chapter 2.

1

It had long been known from brief references in the works of Greek and Roman historians that Greeks had settled in Central Asia in the aftermath of the campaigns of Alexander the Great, in the late fourth century B.C.E. The city that was being uncovered on the Oxus, however, was the first actual material remnant of such settlement to have been revealed. Its local name was Ai Khanoum ("Lady Moon" in Uzbek). In addition to the shrine of Kineas and the gymnasium, Ai Khanoum contained a fine array of grand public buildings, some of them strikingly Greek in architectural style, others with closer connections to the architecture of Central Asia and the Near East. Ai Khanoum has remained the most important source of evidence for the lives of the Greek settlers of Central Asia and their descendants, but many important questions remain unanswered. Is our impression of the overt "Greekness" of these communities correct? What languages did they speak, what gods did they worship, and what relationship did they consider themselves to have to their Greek ancestral homeland?

The territories with which this book will be concerned cover the easternmost regions crossed by Alexander the Great in his campaigns through the Persian empire, in the late fourth century B.C.E. These were Sogdiana and Bactria in the north, in what is now Uzbekistan, Tajikistan, and northern Afghanistan; Arachosia, now southern Afghanistan; and Gandhāra, in today's northwestern Pakistan. I will discuss some material from other regions also, in particular from Central India, where we have evidence of the presence of Greeks. The common history of these territories makes a catchall term convenient, and I have chosen to use the term "Hellenistic Far East," which is imperfect but is of reasonably common currency.[2]

The history of the Hellenistic Far East is known only in the broadest of outlines. In the 320s B.C.E., Alexander the Great left garrisons of Greek and Macedonian settlers across the territories from Sogdiana to northwestern India.[3] The whole region was inherited by his Seleucid successors, but Arachosia and the Indian territories were quickly lost to the Maurya empire, and by the mid-third century B.C.E. Bactria was effectively independent under a local Greek dynasty, the Diodotids.[4] The Diodotids were overthrown by Euthydemos, whose independence the Seleucid king Antiochos III was forced to confirm at the end of the third century. Euthydemos's son Demetrios spearheaded a Graeco-Bactrian expansion into India, but the realm fragmented into a large number of smaller kingdoms, ruled over by kings who began to strike coins with Greek inscriptions on one side and

2. The term was apparently coined by Hassoulier in 1902, as "Extrême-Orient grec" (on which see Schmitt 1990, 42, and Schlumberger 1960). Canali de Rossi's (2004) compendium of Greek inscriptions from the "Estremo Oriente greco" has brought the term into wider scholarly circulation. I prefer "Hellenistic" over "Greek," for reasons that I hope my discussion of the ethnic diversity and cultural dynamism of the region will make clear.

3. On Alexander in Bactria, see Holt 1988 and 2005.

4. Holt 1999b.

Indian on the other. In the 240s B.C.E., the Greek state of Bactria itself fell, to a combination of nomadic invasions from the north, war with Parthia, and internal dynastic conflict. Some Indo-Greek statelets struggled on in northern India until around the turn of the common era.

The archaeological and epigraphic evidence from the Hellenistic Far East is still patchy and problematic, despite the advances brought by the discovery of Ai Khanoum. In addition to the material from Ai Khanoum, we have a variety of other pieces of historical and archaeological evidence from across the region. (See "Sources," below.) There are a small number of Greek inscriptions from sites other than Ai Khanoum, as well as one important mention of a Greek in a contemporary Indian inscription. There are also more mundane, everyday administrative and legal documents in Aramaic and Greek. There are the coins struck by the kings of a succession of Graeco-Bactrian and Indo-Greek kingdoms. There is evidence (mostly limited in quantity and quality) from archaeological sites across Bactria, Sogdiana, Arachosia, and Gandhāra. In this material, discussed in the following chapters, we will encounter such characters as a Greek ambassador to the court of an Indian king, a man with a non-Greek name writing sophisticated Greek verse, Greek and Bactrian officials working in a royal treasury, and Scythian mercenaries in Greek employ. This record is, however, fragmentary, and it demands to be better contextualized: geographically, historically, and in terms of theoretical approaches to questions of ancient colonialism, ethnic interaction, and identity formation.

Distance, terrain, and political boundaries isolate the Hellenistic Far East geographically from the better-known contemporary empires of the Mediterranean, Near East, and India. Its archaeological record displays a complex combination of material culture forms and stylistic traits, some of which are also found in these neighboring empires, and some of which are not. Scholarly territorial claims over the Hellenistic Far East (see below) appear to have given way to a common perception that the region does not really "belong" in either a classics department or an oriental studies or South Asian studies department—although the remains of Ai Khanoum, and the Greek inscriptions of the region, have on occasion provoked excitement and a certain amount of discussion among classicists. This material is exotic in a double sense. It presents a dramatic confirmation of the presence and persistence of Greek culture in a remote region, Central Asia and the Indo-Iranian borderlands, for a period of some three hundred years after the initial settlement under Alexander and the early Seleucids. Earlier generations of scholars spoke of the notion of a vibrant Greek culture in Central Asia, there to be discovered by adventurous archaeologists, as a "mirage"; but this mirage has turned out to have material substance.[5] The other sense in which the archaeological and epigraphic

5. Foucher and Bazin-Foucher 1942–47, 73–75, 310; Schlumberger 1960, 152; Kuz'mina 1976; Holt 1987.

record of the Hellenistic Far East is exotic is in analysts' constant confrontations with material that will be unfamiliar to them, whatever their scholarly training. Ai Khanoum is exotically, intrusively, Greek in its Central Asian location, but it is also exotically un-Greek in terms of much of the archaeological material recovered from it. This is not Athens, nor even Alexandria, Antioch, or Seleucia. The challenge with such material is to move beyond its exoticism—or sheer oddness—and try to elucidate something of the social and cultural dynamics of the society that produced it, and to relate this society in a meaningful way to its regional hinterland and contemporary states in both the Near East and the Indian subcontinent. Material from the Hellenistic Far East may be novel and interesting, but what do we actually do with it?

These are all questions that I shall explore in the following chapters. This book is not, however, intended to be a general or comprehensive history of the Hellenistic Far East, and there are many topics—perhaps even ones familiar to a general audience—that I will not cover.[6] These include the campaigns of Alexander the Great in the region, the Greek inscriptions of the Maurya emperor Aśoka from Kandahar, coinage of the Graeco-Bactrian and Indo-Greek kings, and questions of political and dynastic history in general. I have selected my material in order to explore several broad research questions. In chapter 1, I ask how the Hellenistic Far East was administered by its rulers, and I discuss the evidence for continuity in administrative practices and personnel before and after the period of Greek rule. Chapter 2 is devoted to a study of Ai Khanoum in which I try to view the city as a living, working community rather than an abstract collection of diverse architectural traits, and to contextualize it within the wider and longer-term evidence for urban settlement in Bactria. Two inscriptions, one made by a Greek in Prākrit and the other by an Indian in Greek, are analyzed in chapter 3. Both inscriptions raise questions about the attachment of individuals in the Hellenistic Far East to the Greek language and culture, and the types of identities that they might try to construct and assert on the basis of this attachment. In chapter 4, I return both to archaeological evidence and to a *longue-durée* approach, examining the period of the fall of Graeco-Bactrian kingdom. I question the traditional viewpoint that the Greek "civilization" of Bactria was destroyed by "barbarian" nomadic invaders from the north.

In this preamble, I aim to set the historiographical scene, to explain how we came to have the textual and archaeological record that we do, and why this record has come to be viewed by scholars in the way that it has. I shall discuss the source material available from the Hellenistic Far East, whether textual or archaeological; the ways in which current debates on culture and ethnicity in the ancient world

6. Mairs 2011b (updated regularly at www.bactria.org) surveys the archaeological and epigraphic data from the Hellenistic Far East, with a full listing of publications on this material.

may help us to approach this source material; and the immediate intellectual and political context of the discoveries in Central Asia of the nineteenth and twentieth centuries.

SOURCES

In his "Coins with Indian Inscriptions," the Alexandrian Greek poet Constantine P. Cavafy (1863–1933) describes his surprise in browsing through a catalogue of Indo-Greek coins and finding some with the names of Greek kings rendered in Indian script. Most of these kings are known only from the numismatic record and do not appear in any ancient historical account. Greek, Roman, Indian, and Chinese written sources preserve little of the history of the Hellenistic Far East in general. (What few sources there are will be considered in chapters 1 and 4.) Until the second half of the twentieth century, the amount of archaeological and documentary evidence available was also extremely limited.

The project with which modern historians of the Hellenistic Far East have therefore traditionally been faced is that of making the best of what there is. The outlooks of scholars (as stated in print) show a combination of pessimism and pluck. We might look at three examples. The German scholar T. S. Bayer (1694–1738) wrote on a range of classical and oriental topics, including Bactria. In his published writings and personal letters he often quoted from the Hellenistic poet Theocritus (an Alexandrian predecessor of Cavafy by over two thousand years): "The Greeks got into Troy by trying. . . . Everything is done by trying!"[7] The French archaeologist Alfred Foucher, who became the first director of the Délégation Archéologique Française en Afghanistan (DAFA) in 1922 (see further below), dug at Bactra without discovering any significant evidence of Hellenistic occupation for some eighteen months. He later wrote that the Greek dynasts of Bactria "have failed in their most basic duty toward our scholarly societies in neglecting to construct in marble temples and palaces engraved with inscriptions."[8] In his *The Greeks in Bactria and India,* first published in 1938, the British historian Sir William Woodthorpe Tarn tackled the historical sources:[9]

> A word must be said here about the sources, though they will sufficiently appear as the book proceeds. They are of course very scrappy. But they were not always scrappy. . . . As there was once a tradition, it is somebody's business to attempt to recover the outline of it.

7. Theocritus, *Idyll* 15.61–62 (quoted, for example, in the preface to Bayer 1730). On Bayer, see Lundbæk 1986; and on his reception, Mairs 2014c.

8. Foucher and Bazin-Foucher 1942–47, 113, on excavations at Balkh of 1925.

9. Tarn 1951, xxi.

In the following chapters, I examine a range of sources and suggest that we can do a lot more than simply "make the best of" what we have. A combination of documentary texts written on leather and ceramics, stone inscriptions, coins, and a wealth of archaeological data, from both excavation and field survey, provide something arguably more valuable than a connected narrative, political history: an insight into the lives, culture, and identities of the inhabitants of the Hellenistic Far East. That we can gain such an insight is thanks to a number of important recent discoveries of inscriptions and documentary texts, as well as ongoing archaeological projects in Afghanistan and Central Asia. Nevertheless, the foundation of our chronological framework for the Hellenistic Far East remains numismatic. Here, too, innovative scholarship of the past couple of decades has allowed us to pinpoint the regnal years of kings and the territorial extent of their kingdoms more accurately, and has also explored the political and cultural messages contained in the images and inscriptions on Graeco-Bactrian and Indo-Greek coins.[10]

The most important step that we can take toward a better understanding of the material from the Hellenistic Far East is, in my view, to restore to it something of its context. I mean this in a regional sense—as part of a wider Hellenistic world, a topic to which I shall return in my conclusion to this volume—and in terms of diachronic perspective, an approach that I will adopt most notably in chapter 1, on the administrative continuity from the Achaemenids to the Greeks in Bactria, and in chapter 4, on the end of Greek rule in Bactria in the mid-second century B.C.E.

It is also important to recognize the apparent cultural contradictions in the archaeological and epigraphic evidence, in particular, and to find more nuanced ways of approaching these than a simple statement that a particular individual or structure is "Greek" or otherwise. Ai Khanoum, the "Greek city in Central Asia,"[11] complements its overtly "Greek" gymnasium, theater, and founder's shrine with other institutions and architectural elements that are overtly "non-Greek." This stylistic disunity is striking to modern archaeologists but must have made some kind of cultural sense to contemporary local populations: the onus is on us to find a reasonable model for the social dynamics of such a society.[12] The Greek epigraphic record of the Hellenistic Far East introduces a range of figures and concepts that we would be unlikely to encounter in more westerly Hellenistic inscriptions: Buddhist ethical terminology,[13] Bactrian

10. Numerous examples may be cited. Holt 1999b examines the coinage and politics of the Diodotids. Bopearachchi (1991, 1993, 1998) has catalogued several important coin collections. His chronology is followed here. The two most recent numismatically based histories of the Hellenistic Far East are Coloru 2009 and Widemann 2009.

11. Bernard 1982b.

12. For some approaches to the urban landscape of Ai Khanoum, see Liger 1979 and Mairs 2013c.

13. Schmitt 1990, 50.

river gods,[14] and Indian emperors.[15] They present us with some odd juxtapositions: a man with an Indian name writing recherché Hellenistic verse with Homeric touches,[16] or maxims from Delphi transcribed in northern Afghanistan.[17] The appearance, more recently, of further material on the international antiquities market has only served to complicate the matter, for such finds—which include Greek[18] and Aramaic[19] documentary texts from Bactria and Greek inscriptions,[20] as well as large numbers of coins[21] and some stunning jewelry with Greek artisans' signatures and weight marks[22]—are almost all without secure provenance.

There is still work to be done. Even with the archaeological work in Afghanistan in the 1960s and 1970s, and more recent excavations north of the Oxus in the Central Asian republics (discussed below), our archaeological picture of the Hellenistic Far East remains fragmentary in the extreme. Bactra (modern Balkh), the capital of the Achaemenid satrapy of Bactria and of the later Graeco-Bactrian kingdom, is still largely unknown, despite promising recent work by the Délégation Archéologique Française en Afghanistan.[23] Across the Hellenistic Far East as a whole, only a few urban sites have been excavated, but many such excavations date to the mid-twentieth century or earlier, and the material unearthed is for various reasons inadequate or problematic, or both.[24] Extensive archaeological field survey has gone some way toward providing a regional context for such sites and has furnished much useful information on the agricultural and economic basis of settlement in the Hellenistic Far East, but here also much remains to be done.[25]

14. Litvinskii, Vinogradov, and Pichikyan 1985; Bernard 1987a.

15. Benveniste 1964.

16. Bernard, Pinault, and Rougemont 2004.

17. Robert 1968.

18. Rea, Senior, and Hollis 1994; Clarysse and Thompson 2007.

19. Naveh and Shaked 2012.

20. Bernard, Pinault, and Rougemont 2004.

21. Bopearachchi and Flandrin 2005.

22. Bopearachchi and Bernard 2002.

23. Schlumberger 1949; R.S. Young 1955; Bernard, Besenval, and Marquis 2006; updates at www.dafa.org.af.

24. Merv: Callieri 1996. Samarkand: Bernard, Grenet, and Isamiddinov 1990, 1992, and subsequent campaigns. Termez: Leriche and S. Pidaev 2007. Herat: Lézire 1964. Old Kandahar: McNicoll and Ball 1996, Helms 1997. Begram: Hackin 1939, 1954. Charsada: Wheeler 1962. Taxila: Marshall 1951, 1960. I include here multiperiod sites where there may be little material from the Hellenistic era and those that have been subject to only very cursory archaeological exploration. Full reference has not been given to the work of the International Merv Project, since material published to date has been predominantly Islamic or Sasanid: see Herrmann, Masson, and Kurbansakhatov 1993 and subsequent reports. Takht-i Sangin does not appear in this list, because little has yet been published on the settlement that surrounded the temple (Litvinskii and Pichikyan 2000, 2002; Litvinskii 2001; Pitschikjan 1992).

25. Gentelle 1989, Lyonnet 1997, Gardin 1998, Stride 2001.

IDENTITY

The region comprising Afghanistan, Central Asia, and the northwestern Indian subcontinent in antiquity was ethnically and culturally diverse. Greek settlers were only the latest addition to an already heterogeneous population, which spoke many languages and practiced a variety of religions. The annexation of the region by a foreign king, Alexander the Great, was also, in a way, nothing new. It had previously been ruled by Persia as part of the Achaemenid empire. What is novel and exciting about the history of the territory taken over by Alexander, from the late fourth century B.C.E. until around the turn of the common era, is the dynamic interaction we can see between the new Greek immigrant community and their neighbors. This interaction is visible in architecture and material culture at sites such as Ai Khanoum. Documents written on animal skin and on potsherds, recovered from excavations or purchased on the antiquities market, also provide us with insights into administrative structures and ethnic landscapes. The ethnic and cultural diversity of the region, in short, becomes very visible in our evidence from Hellenistic Central Asia and northwestern India—and much of this archaeological and documentary evidence has become known to scholarship only recently.

I use the word "Greek" in my title, although "Greek," as will become clear, is not a term I would apply to any individuals, communities, inscriptions, or archaeological material discussed in this book without prophylactic inverted commas. Yet the "Greek question" is one that has dominated scholarly debates on the Hellenistic Far East, as on the wider Hellenistic world. How Greek, in culture, language, and identity (not to mention genetics) were the new kingdoms left in the wake of Alexander the Great's campaigns? Does the use of Greek as an administrative language and a more general lingua franca indicate that it held cultural and political dominance, and that individuals may have sought to associate themselves with it for this reason?

I opened this chapter with a poem by Cavafy, a Greek from Egyptian Alexandria, writing at a time when the city still had something of the ethnic and linguistic diversity of the Hellenistic metropolis. As a Greek of the diaspora, Cavafy becomes emotional when he recognizes familiar Greek names on Indo-Greek coins.[26] Like Cavafy, many modern scholars have struggled to reconcile the Greek and the non-Greek side of the peoples and states of the Hellenistic Far East. As I will discuss at greater length in the conclusion, I view the region as part of a wider Hellenistic world, and concepts and theories that have allowed us to develop more productive approaches to culture and identity in other Hellenistic states are equally applicable to Bactria and the East.[27]

26. On this poem, see further Oikonomides 1984.
27. See Mairs 2010.

Ethnic identity is one of my main preoccupations in this book. By "ethnic identity," I mean not some monolithic, unchallenged, primal identity held by an individual or community but a fluid, situational identity, subject to change across time and space and in different social contexts. (See below on linguistic domains and code switching.) This model of ethnicity is fundamentally that of the anthropologist Fredrik Barth, who noted that a boundary between groups can be delineated in cases when there is little externally observable difference between the languages, cultures, and societies of the groups concerned, and that many different forms of behavior and culture can be given ethnic weight.[28] From a Hellenistic perspective, what this means is that communities may have defended strong ethnic identities even where their material record does not differ greatly from that of their neighbors. It also means, as I will argue in chapter 2, that it is important for us to try to differentiate between what *we* may view as external criteria of ethnic belonging (e.g., the use of Greek architectural forms) and those that were perceived as such by contemporary agents.

The postcolonial turn in classical studies[29] has also brought new ways of approaching the Hellenistic world. The Hellenistic Far East was, of course, a settler society, home to an incoming Greek colonial diaspora and to these settlers' descendants.[30] May the lessons from more recent colonial encounters be brought to bear on evidence from the region? My approach here is more cautious. From the nineteenth century onward, with European colonization of the Indian subcontinent and Central Asia, Alexander and the Greeks of Bactria were viewed as predecessors of the British in India—an identification often claimed with some pride by the British themselves.[31] But there are important differences between the two historical contexts, not least in attitudes toward intermarriage and mixing between ethnic groups and races. I will discuss the more recent history of European archaeological research in the region further below. Other concepts generated from postcolonial studies, such as hybridity and the middle ground, may perhaps be more productively applied to the evidence from the Hellenistic Far East, a subject to which I shall return in my conclusion.[32]

Aside from identity and its construction, the most important theme in this book is that of interaction between communities, and this topic is again a preoccupation that I share with those who work on other regions of the Hellenistic

28. Barth 1969a. There are many, many examples of Barth's work on ethnicity applied to Hellenistic case studies. On ethnicity in the ancient Greek world more generally, see also Malkin 2001 and Jonathan Hall 1997 and 2002.

29. See, for example, Webster and Cooper 1996, Hardwick and Gillespie 2007, and more specifically on the Hellenistic world, Will 1985.

30. Mairs 2008 and 2013a.

31. Mairs forthcoming (3).

32. Mairs 2011c.

world. This interaction may be broken down in several ways: between Greek and non-Greek, between polities, both inside and outside the Greek-ruled states of the Hellenistic Far East, and between settled and mobile populations. This last area will form the main theme of chapter 4, where I explore the myths of a strict nomad-settled divide in Central Asia and of the fall of a settled Greek civilization to nomadic horsemen from the steppe.

LANGUAGE

In most regions, for most of the period considered in this book, Greek was the dominant written language. The earlier use of Aramaic as an administrative language by the Persian empire left some legacy. In chapter 1 I will discuss how, in Bactria, the Persian bureaucracy may have been used as a model by the incoming Greeks. In Arachosia, Aramaic was used by the Maurya emperor Aśoka in a series of edicts to his subjects, alongside Greek, as late as the mid-third century. But the influence of Aramaic faded: it had always been a language of bureaucracy rather than a language of the street. Although many languages must have been spoken in the Hellenistic Far East, Greek remained the only language of literacy after the demise of Aramaic. It was only in a much later period that a local vernacular, Bactrian, was given a written form, and it is significant that it was the Greek alphabet—in the absence of any other available model—that was adapted for this purpose.

The Greek documents and Greek inscriptions discussed in this book are testimony to the enduring importance of the Greek language in the Hellenistic Far East, but they are the tip of the linguistic iceberg. The Hellenistic world as a whole was a profoundly multilingual place. In regions such as Egypt, we have written evidence of the variety of languages used by the population and the range of linguistic registers that a single individual might command. In Bactria we do not, but this absence of evidence should not be taken as evidence of absence. The makers and readers of Greek inscriptions—including those of the Delphic inscription from the sanctuary of Kineas at Ai Khanoum—were probably bilingual or multilingual, and the communities in which they lived must have contained speakers of many languages. This should be borne in mind throughout the following discussion. In one case, considered in chapter 3, we happen to have evidence of how a representative of an Indo-Greek king may have appeared in a different context, in a Prākrit inscription from a Central Indian kingdom. Here we find a man with a Greek name, Heliodoros, who is described as a Greek ambassador and a devotee of an Indian god. This inscription gives some insight into the ethnolinguistic complexity of the region and allows us to speculate about the range of languages—other than Greek—that Heliodoros may have spoken.

Thinking of the Hellenistic Far East as multilingual is useful because it reminds us that the individuals and communities who created the documents and monuments considered in the following chapters did not subscribe to some single, monolithic cultural identity; but it is also helpful from a theoretical point of view. Linguistic analogies have long enjoyed a vogue in studies of cultural interaction more generally. The ways in which languages interact—within individual usage or within a speech community—offer any number of useful models for how cultures and ethnic groups interact. Multilingual individuals only rarely use their languages equally across all speech domains. Instead, they may use one language to speak to their family and another at school, or they may have sufficient competence in one language to talk about technical aspects of their jobs but not to hold social conversations. Speech domains offer an interesting analogy for the patterning of different architectural and artistic styles in a site such as Ai Khanoum, as does the concept of markedness. In linguistics, a marked form is one that differs from a default, more neutral norm: for example, "lion" may be used as a neutral form, whereas "lioness" is marked because it refers only to a female. In chapter 2, on Ai Khanoum, I suggest that it is helpful to question whether forms of public behavior are marked or unmarked. Making a dedication at a temple that does not have a Greek architectural form does not have to be an ethnically marked form of behavior; it may equally be an unmarked default. These considerations have implications for how we consider the ethnic resonance of activities within the public life of Ai Khanoum more generally.

One final linguistic model is particularly useful in analyzing the material from the Hellenistic Far East, that of code switching. Accomplished bilinguals often move back and forth between languages in the course of a single conversation or utterance, and can switch between languages depending upon context or interlocutor. Individuals such as the Greek ambassador Heliodoros are most likely to have been able to manage their behavior in this way, switching fluently between languages and cultures as the need arose. Heliodoros had a professional reason for doing so, but even within communities it is likely that individuals were able to modify the outward expression of their ethnic identity as and when it proved advantageous to do so.

ARCHAEOLOGY IN CENTRAL ASIA

The full story of the modern rediscovery of the Greek kingdoms of Bactria and India, and the painstaking process of piecing together what was possible of their history, has been narrated elsewhere. In recent years, a number of important studies have surveyed the intellectual history of Bactrian studies and provided syntheses and new analyses of the available evidence.[33] The context for this renewed interest in the antiquities of the region is, of course, political. Much of the territory

---

33. Inter alia, Holt 1999b, Coloru 2009, and Widemann 2009.

of the former Graeco-Bactrian and Indo-Greek kingdoms has experienced war or political instability in modern times, just as it did in antiquity,[34] and such instability has both inhibited archaeological research and provided a catalyst for it. In the nineteenth century, British and Russian exploration of Central Asia and investigation of its history took place in the context of colonial expansion. More recently, several decades of war in Afghanistan have resulted in widespread destruction of the country's cultural heritage and the systematic looting of many sites for antiquities to be sold illegally on the international market. But the fact that Afghanistan is in the news has also provoked something of a surge of public and scholarly interest in the country's history and archaeology, and this interest has been sustained by several major exhibitions and television documentaries in Europe, North America, Australia, and Japan.[35] From the early 2000s, foreign archaeological expeditions have once again been active in Afghanistan, and the Afghan Institute of Archaeology has also been conducting fieldwork. The collapse of the Soviet Union and the independence of the Central Asian republics in the early 1990s disrupted archaeological research in the region (among other factors, funding for archaeological projects was not so readily available) but also opened the way for new collaborations between Central Asian and Western archaeologists.

Popular and scholarly interest in the Central Asian past has thus always been excited and directed by political circumstances. The history of European exploration and antiquarian research is already well-trodden ground, a story that has been covered in detail elsewhere, among other places in the works that I have already cited but also in institutional histories of the archaeological missions active in the region, such as the Délégation Archéologique Française en Afghanistan.[36] In what follows, I would like to offer a slightly different perspective on the intellectual history of Graeco-Bactrian studies, one that focuses on the interface between specialist scholarship on the Hellenistic Far East and its dissemination, explication to and reception by wider audiences, both within the academy and among an interested public. I shall also discuss the perspectives brought by scholars to the Hellenistic Far East by their earlier training and political and cultural milieux. After surveying the history of archaeological investigation in the Hellenistic Far East, I turn more specifically toward Ai Khanoum and the excitement that the discovery of this city aroused not just in scholarly journals and learned societies but also in the popular press.

34. Holt 2005 provides a diachronic perspective.

35. See, for example, the catalogues Inagaki 2002, Cambon and Jarrige 2006 (= Hiebert and Cambon 2008), Reiss-Engelhorn-Museen 2009.

36. Olivier-Utard 1997. On European exploration in Central Asia more generally, see Gorshenina 2003.

An Obscure History

Even as late as the first half of the twentieth century, historians were largely justified in their complaints about the poor research prospects of the Hellenistic Far East. Greek coins from Bactria and India had been known to European scholars as early as the eighteenth century, but the region has also traditionally been renowned for its exceedingly low yield of archaeological and epigraphic material and the apparent unwillingness of Greek and Roman authors to transmit much in the way of useful information on its history.[37] It says much that one of our few "historical" references to a Greek king of Bactria—one of Tarn's "scraps" of information— comes in Chaucer's *Canterbury Tales*.[38]

Given this general lack of historical and archaeological data, the Hellenistic Far East has therefore long posed certain challenges to scholarship. As a result of excavations and field survey projects in the twentieth century, and particularly from the 1960s onward, we now have far more evidence at our disposal than could have been hoped for at the time of the first major modern synthetic studies, Tarn's *The Greeks in Bactria and India* (first edition 1938; second, 1951) and A. K. Narain's *The Indo-Greeks* (1957). Although new discoveries have rendered much of the discussion in these books outdated, each still has a useful perspective to offer, and occasionally I shall make reference to their arguments in the following chapters.

Tarn and Narain held rather different views about the political and cultural affinities of the easternmost "Greek" kingdoms, and they outlined these views in very quotable terms. Tarn, a classicist, set out to reclaim Bactria's "lost chapter of Hellenistic history".[39] Narain argued, on the contrary, that "their history is part of the history of India and not of the Hellenistic states; they came, they saw, but India conquered."[40] Upon closer examination, however, this apparent opposition breaks down.[41] Each scholar is right in his own way; but both focus on different regions and chronological periods. The Greek kingdom of Bactria developed along the same lines as the other nascent states of the Hellenistic world: its ruling population, political rhetoric, language, culture, and sense of its own origins are overtly and avowedly Greek. In the northern Indian territories that Graeco-Bactrian kings subsequently conquered, over time, Greek states ceased to exist as political entities, and the Greek language and culture disappeared.

Since the excavations at the city of Ai Khanoum (discussed further below), the Hellenistic Far East has enjoyed a reputation for obscurity of a slightly different sort, inasmuch as it has had a reputation at all: as an occasional source of

---

37. The few such references are collected in the appendix to Holt 1999b.
38. "Knight's Tale" 1297–1301; cf. Boccaccio, *De Casibus Virorum Illustrium* 6.6; Bivar 1950.
39. Tarn 1951, xiii.
40. Narain 1957, 18.
41. Mairs 2006b.

spectacular but problematic material that defies straightforward analysis or cultural categorization. This material, furthermore, has tended not to be much discussed (as opposed to simply cited) in connection with evidence from elsewhere in the Hellenistic world.[42] Two of the central aims of the present work are, first, to move beyond simple synthesis of the available archaeological and textual evidence[43] and ask what we may productively do with it; and, second, to discuss a series of case studies that may be of interest to those who work on other regions of the Hellenistic world and, indeed, beyond.

Russian and Soviet Central Asia

In the late nineteenth and the twentieth century, two nationalities dominated archaeology in Afghanistan and Central Asia: the Russians and the French. North of the Oxus, the context of the first major archaeological investigations was firmly colonial. In the 1860s and 1870s, Russia successively annexed the territories of what would later become the Soviet and post-Soviet republics of Kazakhstan, Uzbekistan, Tajikistan, Turkmenistan, and Kyrgyzstan. To the southeast, meanwhile, the attempts of the British to extend their influence into Afghanistan had resulted only in the establishment of an Afghan buffer state.[44] A number of the soldiers, administrators, scholars, travelers, and journalists who arrived in the wake of the Russian conquest of Turkestan developed an interest in the region's antiquities and conducted amateur archaeological excavations. Russian collectors supported a thriving local market for antiquities and other artworks and crafts.[45] Museums were established in Samarkand (1874), Tashkent (1876), Ferghana (1898), and Ashgabat (1899)—not to mention the vast collections of Central Asian artifacts that made their way via purchase, pillage, or excavation to the great museum collections of Russia and Europe.[46] The "Oxus Treasure," a hoard of Achaemenid-period gold and silver items, was found in 1877 (probably somewhere in the neighborhood of the "Temple of the Oxus" at Takht-i Sangin), transported for sale to India, and eventually ended up in the British Museum.[47] The construction of a road between Samarkand and Tashkent disturbed the ancient site of Afrasiab, and the flood of antiquities onto the market led to the first officially sanctioned Russian

---

42. There are, however, some notable exceptions to this rule, in particular works that treat the survey evidence from the plain of Ai Khanoum alongside the results of similar projects elsewhere in the Near East or in the Hellenistic world: see, e.g., Alcock 1993 and Banning 1996.

43. I have surveyed these in Mairs 2011b.

44. This is not the place for a full discussion of British antiquarianism and the place of the classics in India, on which see, e.g., Hall and Vasunia 2010.

45. Gorshenina 2004.

46. Gorshenina and Rapin 2001, 39.

47. Dalton 1964.

excavations at the site in 1873.[48] Excavations at Afrasiab—a locality that was of great interest because of its identification as the "Marakanda" of the Alexander historians—continued fitfully throughout the 1880s and 1890s. In 1895, the Turkestanskii Kruzhok Lyubitelei Arkheologii (Turkestan Circle of Amateurs of Archaeology: TKLA) was founded in Tashkent, and their research began to be published and circulated in the *Protokoly Turkestanskogo Kruzhka Lyubitelei Arkheologii* (Tashkent, 1896–1916) and other journals.[49]

Systematic professional investigation of the archaeology of Central Asia, however, came only after the Russian revolution and the establishment of the Soviet Union, and in particular with the first major expeditions in the 1920s and 1930s, such as the mission of B. P. Denike of the Moscow Museum of Oriental Cultures between 1926 and 1928. The history of archaeological research at the site of Termez, on the river Oxus, is a good example of how organized, large-scale Soviet interdisciplinary projects dealt with large multiperiod sites and their hinterlands.[50] In the years 1936–38 the Termezskaya Arkheologicheskaya Kompleksnaya Ekspeditsiya (Termez Pluridisciplinary Archaeological Expedition: TAKE) was created under M. E. Masson, who had participated in the amateur excavations at Afrasiab as a teenager, before the revolution. As its name suggests, the project's program was multidisciplinary, and the team included archaeologists, architectural historians, geologists, and orientalists.[51] As with sites on the other bank of the Oxus (see below on the French excavations at Bactra), archaeologists worked under difficult conditions: their movements were monitored and restricted, because they were in a sensitive frontier zone; team members became ill; they had to scramble down steep banks to get drinking water from the river; and food was both limited and monotonous.[52]

Soviet-era archaeologists also worked in a particular intellectual climate, one in which ideological considerations had an impact on interpretations of archaeological material. G. A. Pugachenkova's personal memoir of her participation in the TAKE recalls the resistance at the time to the notion of outside, Hellenistic influence on the material culture of the region and the ideological imperative to focus on local development.[53]

48. Gorshenina 1999, 366.

49. Lunin 1958; Pugachenkova and Germanov 1996; Gorshenina and Rapin 2001, 32–33; Pugachenkova 2001b.

50. Leriche and Pidaev 2008, 13–20.

51. Pugachenkova 2001b, 24.

52. See Pugachenkova 2001a for personal reminiscences and interesting biographical sketches of the personalities of the expedition.

53. Pugachenkova 2001a, 40. Several discussions are available in Western European languages of developments in Marxist archaeology inside and outside the Soviet Union in the twentieth century: Mongait 1961, 233–62 (specifically on Central Asia and Siberia); Bulkin, Klejn, and Lebedev 1982; Klejn 1997; Trigger 2006, 326–44.

From the 1970s onward, there was increasing international collaboration and dialogue with scholars—French and Afghan—working on the region immediately to the south of the Oxus, which continues to the present day in various Central Asian–French collaborative projects. (See further below.) From 1969, a Soviet-Afghan expedition excavated at several sites in Afghanistan, including Dil'berdzhin and Zhigatepe.[54] From 1976 to 1991, a new major project was conducted at Takht-i Sangin, in southern Tajikistan, under B. A. Litvinskii and I. R. Pichikiyan of the Yuzhno-Tadzhikskaya Arkheologicheskaya Ekspeditsiya (Southern Tadzhik Archaeological Expedition: YuTae)—near which the Oxus Treasure was probably found in 1877, and which had been subject to brief investigations by members of B. N. Denike's expedition in 1928, by M. M. Diakonoff in 1950, and by A. M. Mandelshtam in 1956.[55]

This overview has of necessity been brief, confined in the main to sites or projects with Hellenistic material; but several points about Russian and Soviet research in Central Asia bear reiteration. The scale and interdisciplinary character of Soviet expeditions merits mention: expeditions attempted to survey wide areas and took on large, complex multiperiod sites and included specialists in different fields. One of the lasting scholarly achievements of the expeditions of the twentieth century has been the establishment of "archaeological Bactria" as the middle and upper Oxus Basin also, and not just the lands south of the Oxus in northern Afghanistan. The river unites, not divides.

The Délégation Archéologique Française en Afghanistan

A Franco-Afghan convention of 9 September 1922 established the Délégation Archéologique Française en Afghanistan (DAFA), the body that would direct the vast majority of archaeological projects in Afghanistan over the following six decades, until its dissolution in 1982. The DAFA and its archaeologists also organized or participated in a number of major international colloquia, and in particular those that involved collaboration with Soviet scholars.[56] Former DAFA personnel subsequently went on to set up collaborative archaeological projects in other regions of Central Asia, such as the Mission Archéologique Française en Asie Centrale[57] and the Mission Archéologique Franco-Ouzbèke.[58] The DAFA itself was reestablished in 2002 and, among other projects, has returned to excavate at Bactra.[59] The history of Afghan archaeology in the twentieth century is therefore largely that of the DAFA.

54. Published in Kruglikova 1976, 1979, 1984.
55. Litvinskii and Pichikyan 1981, 134–35.
56. Deshayes 1977; Asimov et al. 1985; Francfort 1990; Bernard and Grenet 1991; Leriche et al. 2001.
57. Francfort 1993.
58. Leriche and Pidaev 2001.
59. Bernard 2002; Bernard, Bensenval, and Marquis 2006; Besenval and Marquis 2007; Besenval, Marquis, and Mongne 2009.

The reason why the French were granted the archaeological concession in Afghanistan was largely as a reaction against British dominance in the region. In May 1919, Afghanistan, under the amir Amanullah Khan (1892 1960; reigned 1919–29), launched a surprise attack against the British in India; and in August, thanks in part to British preoccupations in Europe in the aftermath of World War I, managed to negotiate the Treaty of Rawalpindi, which granted Afghanistan autonomy in matters of foreign affairs. The amir was keen to demonstrate Afghan independence from both Britain and Russia. Amanullah very actively solicited foreign aid and cooperation, and his overtures were responded to with enthusiasm. Germany, Turkey, and Italy—but especially France—were among the countries that took an active interest in Afghanistan in this period, providing aid, investment, training, and expertise. Amanullah's drive toward modernization, Westernization, and secularization was commented upon favorably in the European press. The creation of the DAFA must be seen in this context.[60] The convention was instigated by the Afghans and was negotiated as part of a package that included the opening of a permanent French diplomatic mission and a French school in Kabul, the École Amaniya (later the Lycée Esteqlal). The archaeologist Alfred Foucher and his wife and collaborator Eugénie Bazin-Foucher, in fact, arrived before the diplomats—or rather, themselves constituted the first French diplomatic mission. Foucher's reports back to the French Ministry of Foreign Affairs were concerned with diplomatic as much as with scientific matters.[61] Given the sensitivity of the mission, the Fouchers endeavored to travel from India to Afghanistan via Iran, in secret, in order to avoid exciting British suspicion.[62]

The archaeological convention of 1922 gave the DAFA exclusive rights to excavate in Afghanistan for thirty years and established provisions for the sharing of finds between Afghanistan and France. The monopoly was insisted upon by the Afghan and French governments and not by the French archaeologists. Foucher had, indeed, hoped for international collaboration, intending to bring the British-Hungarian archaeologist Aurel Stein to excavate at Bactra and the German Ernst Herzfeld to work at Ghazni.[63] Stein had been trying unsuccessfully to visit Bactra for most of his long career. French diplomatic and archaeological ventures in Afghanistan proved an attractive subject for the popular press. In May 1923, L'Excelsior, an illustrated daily newspaper, carried an article reporting that "un savant français, M. Foucher, est chargé d'opérer des fouilles dans l'Afghanistan."[64]

60. Olivier-Utard 1997, 17–22.
61. See the fascinating collection of archival documents in Fenet 2010
62. Olivier-Utard 1997, 29–31.
63. Bernard 2002, 1290–91.
64. P. Denoyer, L'Excelsior, Monday 7 May 1923, 3.

In 1927, Foucher published an article on the first years of the DAFA.[65] This fairly brief account is still more important because publication of the full account of his Afghan projects, *La vieille route de l'Inde de Bactres à Taxila,* was delayed until the 1940s.[66] Two of the most important themes in both Foucher's preliminary note and the (much) larger publication are: first, his disappointment and frustration that the site of Bactra (modern Balkh) had, despite a grueling eighteen months of excavation, failed to yield any substantial evidence of Graeco-Bactrian remains, or indeed much of anything—a frustration that was all the greater because, second, the visual culture of Hellenistic Bactria was essential to understanding the later Buddhist art of Central Asia and Gandhāra. It is important to note that Foucher had never been under any illusion that the excavation of Bactra would be anything but difficult and that it might not yield much. He was only too aware of the practical problems associated with excavating the site, but the promise and lure of Bactra, the "Mother of Cities," was too great, and his superiors in Paris insisted that he go ahead with the project.[67] Foucher's wish to find the unknown Greek art of Hellenistic Bactria, and to find in it the origins of later Gandhāran Buddhist art was, as it happened, realized by the subsequent DAFA excavations at Ai Khanoum. (See below.) Foucher, however, saw Afghanistan as a "missing link"[68] in more than one sense: chronologically in the development of Buddhist art but also geographically as a zone of transition between the archaeologically better-known regions of India and Turkestan. His thought only later developed in the direction of seeing Afghanistan as a land of invaders and pilgrims rather as a region with its own internal cultural dynamics.[69]

The archaeologists of the first decades of the DAFA worked under very difficult diplomatic and physical conditions. DAFA service had devastating effects on the health, personal finances, and general good humor of a succession of researchers. Finances were almost always tight. Another serious problem was the matter of publications: full archaeological reports rarely appeared in a timely fashion, again because of financial constraints, and also because the researchers returned to the field as quickly as possible after the conclusion of each season. During World War II, the struggles between Vichy France and Free France were played out in microcosm among the French residents of Kabul and their various political masters in France, London, and French overseas territories. Several DAFA archaeologists died in the war (Joseph and Ria Hackin and Jean Carl, all in 1941). Nevertheless, successful excavations were conducted at sites such as Begram, and the results

65. Foucher 1927.
66. Foucher and Bazin-Foucher 1942–47.
67. Olivier-Utard 1997, 59.
68. He uses the English term: Foucher 1927, 118.
69. Olivier-Utard 1997, 77–81.

were eventually published.[70] These too proved of interest to the readers of more widely circulating publications, even foreign journals such as the American magazine *Asia*.[71]

The DAFA's most famous project, the excavations at Ai Khanoum, also suffered from financial constraints and from being in a frontier zone to which access was officially restricted. The many people to whom the discovery of Ai Khanoum has been attributed include the English traveler John Wood[72] and DAFA member Jules Barthoux,[73] but it was King Zaher Shah, who in 1961 was shown the remains of stone columns while hunting in the area, under whose patronage the first DAFA excavations proceeded.[74] In chapter 2, I will discuss what the urban plan, material culture, and inscriptions of Ai Khanoum can tell us about the social and cultural history of its inhabitants. Here, and in chapter 1, I aim to set studies of Ai Khanoum in their historiographical context and then to explore its geographical and historical context as a colonial city in eastern Bactria.

The Excavations at Ai Khanoum

ARCHAEOLOGISTS FIND 2300 YEAR OLD GREEK CITY
IN NORTHERN AFGHANISTAN

The ruins of a large Greek city dating from the third and second centuries B.C. have been discovered in Northern Afghanistan at the junction of the Amu and Kokcha rivers.

The modern name of the place is Ai Khanum.

According to Professor Daniel Schlumberger, Director of DAFA (French Archaeological Delegation in Afghanistan) the importance of the discovery can hardly be overestimated. At least a score of Greek towns are known to have been founded in this region of Asia by Alexander the Great and his successors. . . . Now, for the first time, one of them is available for archaeological excavation and study. (*Kabul Times,* 20 December 1964)

The results of the first excavations at the site of Ai Khanoum, a ten-day preliminary investigation in November 1964, were reported with enthusiasm in the popular press even before their formal presentation at a meeting of the Académie des Inscriptions et Belles-Lettres in Paris on 5 February 1965. The *Kabul Times,* as might be expected, was first off the mark, and its report must have been written only very shortly after the DAFA archaeologists returned from the field. Although the full story was carried on an inside page, the front page of the 20 December

---

70. Hackin 1939 and the posthumous Hackin 1954.
71. Hackin 1940a, 1940b.
72. Wood 1841, 394–95.
73. Tarzi 1996.
74. Schlumberger 1965, 590–91.

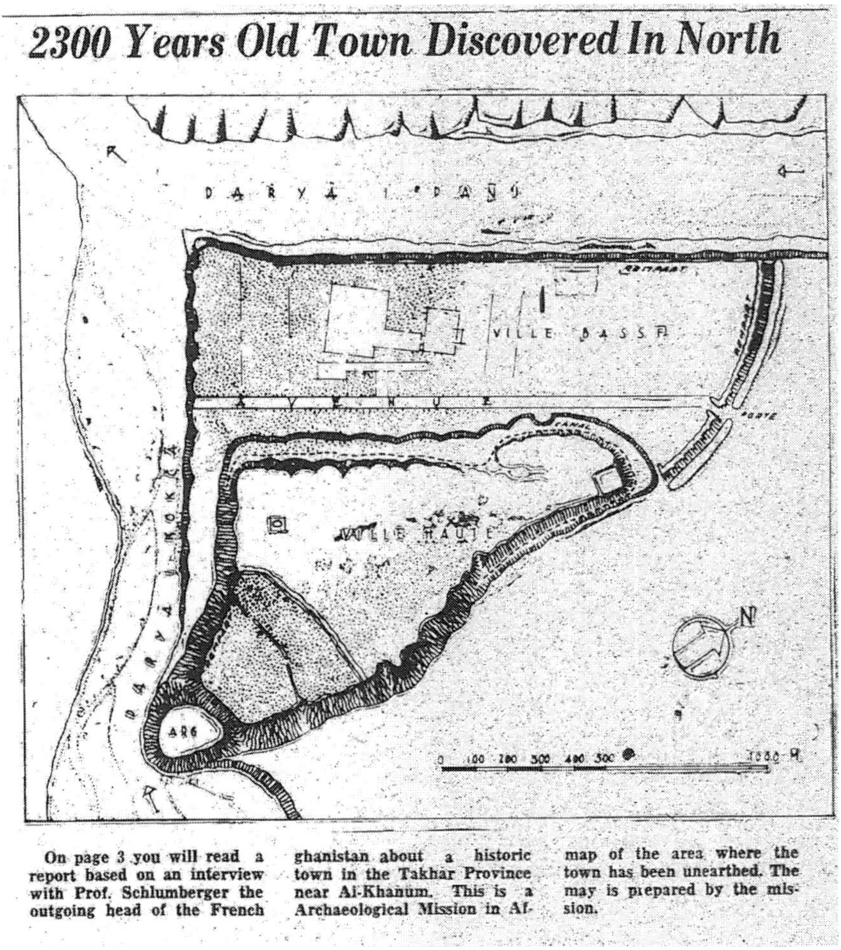

2300 Years Old Town Discovered In North

On page 3 you will read a report based on an interview with Prof. Schlumberger the outgoing head of the French ghanistan about a historic town in the Takhar Province near Ai-Khanum. This is a Archaeological Mission in Af- map of the area where the town has been unearthed. The may is prepared by the mis- sion.

FIGURE 1. The discovery of Ai Khanoum as reported in the *Kabul Times,* 20 December 1964.

edition bore a sketch map of the city, with a "teaser" headline and caption. On 31 December, a story on Ai Khanoum appeared in *Le Monde,* and the following day, in the United Kingdom, *The Guardian* reproduced the information in this article for the benefit of its readers.[75]

75. Among the Anglophone press, the *Guardian* showed the most consistent interest in Ai Khanoum over the next few years, because of the attentive attendance of its Paris correspondent at meetings of the Académie des Inscriptions et Belles-Lettres. This level of interest was not paralleled in the British and American press as a whole. I have searched the archives of the *Times* of London, the *New*

The *Comptes-Rendus des Séances de l'Académie des Inscriptions et Belles-Lettres* (*CRAI*) was quickly established as the favored home for the official field reports on Ai Khanoum,[76] at least until their sheer length forced them to relocate to the *Bulletin de l'École Française d'Extrême Orient.*[77] Schlumberger's initial account in *CRAI* makes a point of underlining the significance of the Ai Khanoum finds for his audience.[78] Ai Khanoum offers a unique opportunity to recover the "histoire perdue" of the Hellenistic Far East, a region previously marked by a lacuna in the archaeological as well as in the historical evidence. Ai Khanoum, unlike the other Greek cities of the region, such as Herat, Kandahar, and Bactra, is not buried under a thousand years or more of subsequent occupation. Already, in this very preliminary publication, the main lines of the city and its institutions had been recognized. Ai Khanoum offers classical archaeologists familiar things in unfamiliar surroundings: "Ces trouvailles, qui seraient banales en Grèce, cessent de l'être dès lors qu'elles sont faites sur l'Oxus."[79] Interestingly, Schlumberger also draws parallels between the Greek colonists of the eastern part of the Achaemenid empire and the Spanish in the Americas,[80] prefiguring more recent scholarly interest in parallels between ancient and modern colonial contexts.

Schlumberger and Bernard's further account of the circumstances of the site's discovery and the "premiers fruits" of the initial prospection of November 1964 in the *Bulletin de Correspondance Hellénique*[81] was able already to say much about the ceramics and the presence—and even local production—of familiar Greek forms previously practically unattested in the region. The presence of a small number of

York Times, and the Washington Post. (The New York Times for 22 October 1972 did, however, carry an obituary of Daniel Schlumberger, director of the DAFA at the time of the first excavations at Ai Khanoum.) The Guardian's Paris correspondent through the period in question was Darsie Gillie, who had reported on several previous occasions on the activities of the DAFA, as presented at the Académie des Inscriptions: see the Guardian (Manchester), 31 January 1953 and 23 July 1958 (presumably that later published as Schlumberger et al. 1958 in the Journal Asiatique); and Gillie 1964. These much briefer English accounts for a general audience appeared in print before the full scholarly publications in the Comptes-Rendus des Séances de l'Académie des Inscriptions et Belles-Lettres (CRAI). See, e.g., Gillie's 1965 report on the meeting of 5 February, which resulted in Schlumberger and Bernard 1965; Gillie 1966 = Bernard 1966, the report on the first season of excavations; Gillie 1969 = Bernard 1969, on the fourth and fifth seasons. See also the Observer, 20 February 1966, with a report on Mortimer Wheeler's comments on Ai Khanoum to the annual meeting of subscribers to the British School at Athens.

76. The excavators, principally Bernard, published a smaller number of articles in Syria (e.g., Bernard 1968, 1970; Leriche and Thoraval 1979) and the Bulletin de Correspondance Hellénique (e.g., Schlumberger and Bernard 1965; Veuve 1982).

77. Bernard et al. 1976, 1980; Gardin and Gentelle 1976, 1979. CRAI continued to publish condensed versions.

78. Schlumberger 1965, 38–39, 45; on Schlumberger's career, see Gelin 2010.

79. Schlumberger 1965, 44.

80. Ibid. 36.

81. Schlumberger and Bernard 1965.

fragments of "Megaran bowl" forms was noted, along with the probability of local production, perhaps aided by imported molds.[82]

Because of a conjunction of circumstances, including financial constraints and the war in Afghanistan, the final volumes of the Ai Khanoum excavation reports were either delayed in publication for some years or have yet to appear.[83] This means that the preliminary publications, such as the articles in *CRAI,* have had a disproportionate impact on how the site is still viewed today. Ai Khanoum has also made appearances in publications for a broader interested public. The popular archaeology magazine *Dossiers d'Archéologie* devoted an issue to "Aï Khanoum, ville coloniale grecque" in 1974.[84] In reporting Ai Khanoum to the outside world, and to wider scholarship, certain ways of presenting the city, and certain ways of conceptualizing cultural and ethnic affairs there, became the standard very early. These then passed into the literature, and some early views have stayed there and refused to budge, even when the excavators may later have reconsidered their conclusions, or new information may have come to light. The most important are, in brief, the notion of Ai Khanoum as an outpost of Hellenism, a "Greek city" in Central Asia; a strong Greek culture, with an element of cultural conservatism in, for example, mosaics; the presence of artifacts that indicate direct connections to the distant Mediterranean world; a division of some sort between Greek and non-Greek facets of the city's architecture and material culture. These facts and themes are not necessarily fallacies, but they recur as tropes, often treated uncritically, in much of the scholarly literature since. I will return to many of these topics in chapter 2.

The notion of Ai Khanoum as a "Greek City in Afghanistan"[85] has been one of the most enduring of such ideas. Ai Khanoum's Greekness was dramatic and unusual, a sensational confirmation of the Greekness of the Bactrian state known from classical historians, the coins of its kings, and even the later Graeco-Buddhist art of the region—all matters that had fascinated European writers since the eighteenth century. Richard Frye's brief report on the first season of excavations at Ai Khanoum in the *American Journal of Archaeology* focused on the Greek: "The top layer of the site is Greek with no Kushan or Islamic strata above the Greek stratum. This promises exciting rewards for future work in the first Greek city found in Central Asia." Significantly—and this will become a common thread in what follows—this excited and, it must be said, not *in*accurate report was written on the basis of very limited information. Given the date of publication and the informa-

82. Ibid. 631.

83. See the critical discussion in Fussman 1996; Foucher's "vieille route" was also subject to considerable delays. The volumes that have been published (1–8) are Bernard 1973, 1985; Guillaume 1983; Francfort 1984; Leriche 1986; Guillaume and Rougeulle 1987; Veuve 1987; and Rapin 1992.

84. Bernard 1974a; see also, on French excavations in Central Asia in the 1990s, inter alia, (Collectif) 1996, Rapin and Rakhmanov 1999, Rtveladze 1999.

85. Frye 1966.

tion contained in the footnotes Frye must have based his account on Schlumberger's very first report in *CRAI* [86] and the oral delivery of the report later published in that journal. [87] Reporting Ai Khanoum to the Anglophone scholarly community in the early years is a matter as much of journalism as of scholarship. What people cite is interesting, and even where one cannot tell directly what sources they have used, the sources from which they reproduce their illustrations are usually telling.

Just after the end of the second full season of excavations, Paul Bernard delivered that year's Albert Reckitt Archaeological Lecture at the British Academy. [88] Its publication, in the *Proceedings of the British Academy,* was lavishly illustrated, with twenty black-and-white photographic plates, in addition to maps and plans. [89] This article remains one of the very few general accounts of Ai Khanoum in English and has had a lasting influence—even though Bernard and the other excavators of the site subsequently modified some of the views presented in it. This is especially true of Bernard's original emphasis on the "Greekness" of the city, on Alexander's settlements in Bactria as "the nucleus of a central Asian Greece." [90] "The overall impression that these two campaigns of digging give us," Bernard wrote, "is that Ai Khanum was first of all a Greek city whose colonists strove to maintain the integrity of the civilization they had brought with them." [91]

Among Bernard's other themes were the problem of the lack of archaeological evidence from Hellenistic Bactria, the difficulties of reconstructing its history from the sparse but tantalizing textual and numismatic evidence, and the disappointment of the excavations at Bactra. Bernard introduced the main features of the city as revealed in the first two full seasons of excavations: the "administrative quarter" (later referred to as the "palace": the function of this structure will be discussed in chapter 2), the shrine of Kineas, with its Delphic inscription, and the gymnasium, also with its own inscription. These descriptions of the inscriptions predate the fundamental study by Louis Robert in *CRAI.* [92] Bernard's emphasis throughout is very much on the Greek artistic and cultural context, and to a lesser extent the Achaemenid, and he insists on the Hellenic cultural identity of the city and its inhabitants. It is essentially from this article that the general scholarly perception of Ai Khanoum as an outpost of Hellenism in Central Asia derives.

86. Schlumberger 1965.

87. Bernard 1966.

88. Schlumberger, Bernard's predecessor as director of the DAFA, had given the Reckitt Lecture for 1961, on the DAFA excavations at the Kushan site of Surkh Kotal and "The Problem of Hellenism in Bactria and India" (Schlumberger 1961).

89. Bernard 1967a.

90. Ibid. 71.

91. Ibid. 91.

92. Robert 1968.

In Mortimer Wheeler's *Flames over Persepolis,* published in the following year, Ai Khanoum takes a starring role in his account of the spread of Greek culture to the East, cast once again as the first material evidence of the Greek kingdom of Bactria and as a remote colonial outpost of Greekness.[93] Wheeler's modern adventure story of the discovery of a lost Hellenistic civilization in Bactria lays emphasis on the natural advantages of the site, Hellenic institutions like the probable theater and gymnasium, Greek inscriptions, and Greek architectural elements such as Corinthian columns:[94]

> In one way and another, this city at Aï Khanum is already, in the early stages of its revelation, a human and historical witness of the first order. It was the work of adventurous and imaginative and above all civilized pioneers on the uttermost fringe of the Eurasian world. The ethics of Delphi were here advertised in its midst, probably at the carefully cherished tomb of the founder. The architecture was skillfully sculptured and gaily coloured, in accordance with Western canons though not without occasional acknowledgment of an Eastern environment; here and there details such as the bolstered, unclassical base of a column, already referred to, or the winged pseudo-palmette of a roof-ornament have been thought to point to Asian, perhaps Achaemenid influence, as indeed they may. With the progress of discovery, such hybrid elements will no doubt assume a clearer measure of importance. But this will remain secondary to the over-all Hellenism of the scene. Greek priests, philosophers, craftsmen may already be inferred. The stamp on a wine-jar or oil-jar which may be of local manufacture refers to an *agoranomos* or market-controller such as is known in Greek cities of the Black Sea and Near East. It is not too much to assume that most of the familiar apparatus of Hellenistic urban life will be revealed here in due course.

But the most influential article on Ai Khanoum in Anglophone scholarship has been the paper "An Ancient Greek City in Central Asia" published by Bernard in the journal *Scientific American* (and subsequently in its French sister publication *Pour la Science*) in 1982.[95] The ancient and modern-day adventure story begins with the opening "A legacy of Alexander's conquest of Persia was a Greek kingdom in what is now Afghanistan. A French archaeological group has spent the past 15 years unearthing one of its cities, Ai Khanum." The maps and illustrations in the article include a map of the Hellenistic world, a city plan of Ai Khanoum, a plan of the administrative quarter, a photograph of the Greek papyrus imprint from the treasury, a comic-mask fountain spout, and a bone figurine from the temple. Ai Khanoum is an "outpost of Greek civilization"; the "Greco-Bactrian mirage" is referenced, and Ai Khanoum's direct contact with the Mediterranean world and its position as "the easternmost extension of Hellenism" are emphasized:[96]

93. Wheeler 1968, 12, 75–87.

94. Ibid. 82–84. In his bibliography, Wheeler cites Schlumberger 1965, Schlumberger and Bernard 1965, and Bernard 1967a and 1967b. He takes his illustrations from the former.

95. Bernard 1982a, 1982b.

96. Ibid. 126.

Our expedition's concept of what might be found at Ai Khanum when the investigation began in 1965 has changed profoundly in the 15 years of excavation. No one expected to find what had obviously been a powerful and wealthy capital city in this remote corner of Central Asia. Nor had anyone anticipated, on the one hand, the Greek settlers' stubborn loyalty to Hellenic culture in most respects and, on the other, their wholehearted acceptance of Eastern practices in such matters as architecture and religious worship. . . . As the Greek colonists on the banks of the Oxus strove to preserve their cultural identity they were also prepared to assimilate the lessons that could be learned from the local civilization.

The presentation of Ai Khanoum is essentially as a colony in the modern European sense, with certain power dynamics between the immigrant, colonial population and the locals. As will be discussed throughout the following chapters, I do not think that the ethnic dynamics of Bactria worked in quite this way, not least because the Greek and Macedonian settlers cannot have maintained any social or matrimonial segregation. On the local Bactrian names among the persons mentioned in the Greek economic texts from the treasury, Bernard suggests that "evidently the new masters of Bactriana found it expedient to retain the native bureaucrats trained by the former rulers of the province. It seems safe to assume that the same reasoning was applied to local workers of more modest statues. A number of modest one-room houses on the acropolis could have been those of local people who were not allowed to settle in the lower town."[97] It is not that I think Bernard is essentially wrong in this regard (chapter 1, in particular, will argue strongly for the kind of administrative continuity here suggested): more that there are issues of ethnic and cultural nuance that we ought to explore further. Nor is it that I think modern colonial parallels should be rejected: more that we should also take on board what such more recent contexts, and the political and cultural dialogue that resulted from them, have to tell us about how groups interact and conceptualize interaction in such situations. If, as Bernard and others have often noted, the architecture and material culture of Ai Khanoum demonstrate a certain cultural conservatism, then we ought to consider whether such conservatism was a deliberate policy of Hellenization or a matter of separation from the Greek world and internal development.[98]

The Twenty-First Century

After its long hiatus during the wars in Afghanistan of the 1980s and 1990s, the Délégation Archéologique Française en Afghanistan was reestablished in 2002 and returned to Kabul. In the intervening years, as I have already noted above,

---

97. Ibid.
98. "In the arts the taste of the colonists remained traditionally Greek, even to the point of perpetuating an outdated Classical style": ibid.

many new French and other international collaborative projects had been established in the countries of the former Soviet Union. As well as traditional excavation, these have increasingly expanded to include field survey projects and exploit new technology such as archaeological geographic information systems (GIS) and Google Earth.[99] More recently, items from the National Museum in Kabul, including material from Ai Khanoum and Begram, have been exhibited in overseas exhibitions in Europe and North America.[100] War has, of course, had a devastating impact on the cultural heritage of Afghanistan. Dramatic events such as the destruction of the Bamiyan Buddhas have attracted the attention of media throughout the world, but a flourishing illicit antiquities market has also developed, trading in material gathered from unofficial excavations at archaeological sites throughout Afghanistan.[101] Several of the documents and artifacts that I will discuss in the following chapters are unprovenanced, and even the private collections in which they are now held are not public knowledge. The position of Bactrian studies at the beginning of the twenty-first century has advanced almost beyond recognition from the state of knowledge at the beginning of the eighteenth. War, politics, and scholarly fashion continue to play a role in the historiography and reception of an obscure topic. The accumulated material of the past three hundred years, as I shall discuss in the following chapters, has confirmed many long-held theories about the political and cultural landscape of the Graeco-Bactrian and Indo-Greek kingdoms, and has raised many new questions.

99. Up-to-date details of such projects and their publications may be found in Mairs 2011b and forthcoming supplements to that volume.

100. The catalogues Cambon and Jarrige 2006 and Hiebert and Cambon 2008 and 2011 reproduce essentially the same material.

101. For a case study of one such find and its trajectory through the international antiquities market, see Bopearachchi and Flandrin 2005.

Administering Bactria

From Achaemenid Satrapy to Graeco-Bactrian State

And from that amazing panhellenic expedition,
crowned with victory, everywhere acclaimed,
famed throughout the world, illustrious
as no other has been illustrious,
without any rival: we emerged,
a new world that was Greek, and great.
We: the Alexandrians, the Antiochenes,
the Seleucians, and the numerous
other Greeks of Egypt and Syria,
and in Media, and in Persia, and all the others.
With their far-flung realms,
with the nuanced policy of judicious integration.
And the Common Greek Language
which we've taken as far as Bactria, as far as the Indians.

—C. P. CAVAFY, "IN 200 B.C." (1931; TRANS. AFTER
  MENDELSOHN 2012, 171–72)

BACTRIA AND ITS RESOURCES

Part of Bactria lies beside Aria toward the north, but most of it lies above and to the east of Aria. It is large and all-productive except for oil. Because of the excellence of the land, the Greeks who rebelled there grew so powerful that they conquered both Ariana and India as well, according to Apollodorus of Artemita. And so they subdued more peoples than Alexander—especially Menander if indeed he crossed the Hypanis River toward the east and advanced as far as the Imaus, for some were subdued by Menander himself, and some by Demetrios the son of Euthydemos, the king of Bactria. They took over not only Patalene but also the rest of the coast, which is called the Kingdom of Saraostos and Sigerdia. In sum, Apollodorus says that Bactria is the jewel of all Ariana; moreover, the Greeks of Bactria

> *extended their empire as far as the Seres and Phryni.*[1]
>
> *. . . that most prosperous Bactrian empire of the thousand cities . . .*[2]

The campaigns of Alexander the Great brought the Greek language and Greek rule to large territories of Central Asia and northwestern India. Cavafy's narrator in "In 200 B.C." uses Bactria and India to indicate the very ends of the earth, the farthest extent of the Hellenistic *oikoumenē,* the inhabited—for which read "Hellenized and civilized"—world. But Bactria has undergone something of a scholarly rehabilitation from the reputation it once held as the "Siberia of the Hellenistic world."[3] Part of this rehabilitation is due to our better understanding of the political and economic ties that bound it to the world of the Near East. Although geographically distant from the centers of the various Near Eastern empires that asserted control over it (the Achaemenid Persian empire, and later the empire of Alexander the Great and his Seleucid successors), Bactria was neither economically nor politically peripheral. It possessed considerable natural resources and occupied a strategic position between the world of Iran and Mesopotamia and the world of the Eurasian steppe.[4] The resources that made Bactria attractive to the Persians and then to the Greeks also meant that it could be used as a power base, whether as a springboard for a satrap's imperial ambitions or for the secession of an independent regional state.

In addition to its agricultural potential with irrigation, Bactria and its southern neighbor Arachosia were sources of manpower. Because of their geographical position, these territories also served as conduits for military forces and war elephants from northwestern India, which might serve under the command of the satraps of Bactria and Arachosia.[5] The region continued to be a source of elephants for the rulers of the Seleucid empire as and when they were able to assert some authority there. In 305 B.C.E., Seleukos I received five hundred elephants under the provisions of a treaty with the Indian emperor Chandragupta Maurya but lost control of Arachosia under this same accord.[6] A Babylonian astronomical diary records the satrap of Bactria supplying war elephants to the Seleucid king in 274/3 B.C.E.[7] In the last decade of the third century B.C.E., Antiochos III conducted an extensive eastern campaign in which he, in the end, made little in the way of territorial acquisitions but did acquire elephants— one hundred and fifty in total—from both the Graeco-Bactrian king Euthydemos and the Indian king Sophagasenos, who ruled in the Kabul Valley.[8]

1. Strabo 11.11.1, trans. Holt 1999b, 183.

2. "Opulentissimum illud mille urbium Bactrianum imperium": Justin, *Epitome of Pompeius Trogus* 41.1.8.

3. Rawlinson 1909, 23.

4. On Bactria's connections to the Achaemenid imperial road network, see Briant, 2012.

5. Arrian 3.8; Briant 1984, 71–74; 1988a and 1997, 180–87.

6. Strabo 15.2.9; Plutarch, *Alexander* 62.4.

7. Sachs and Hunger 1988, 345 no. 273.

8. Polybios 11.34.

The Badakshan Mountains of eastern Bactria were the location of probably the only exploited source of lapis lazuli in the ancient world, as well as deposits of other minerals and precious stones. There does not appear to have been any archaeological investigation of the Badakshan mines to date, but their products appeared as far away as Egypt, as early as the Predynastic period.[9] At Shortughai, an outpost of the Indus civilization was established in around 2200 B.C.E., evidently to control access to the Badakshan mineral resources.[10] As well as serving as a center for management of this resource, Shortughai was also notable for the working of lapis. The treasury at the Hellenistic city of Ai Khanoum contained some 75 kilograms of unworked blocks of lapis at the time of its abandonment.[11] The "lapis factor" is therefore an important constant in the economic history of eastern Bactria.

A combination of archaeological and written sources (both literary and documentary) make Bactria an excellent case study for looking at how an empire might manage such a resource-rich region, incomplete though our knowledge of administrative systems must necessarily remain. Crucially, in order to be exploited effectively Bactria's resources required concerted effort and the mobilization of substantial labor forces. The land had agricultural potential but required irrigation. Lapis had to be mined from deposits high in the Badakshan Mountains. Soldiers had to be recruited or conscripted, and elephants had to be acquired and transported. Although there are only a few excavated sites of the Achaemenid and Hellenistic periods, the extensive field-survey project conducted in eastern Bactria in the 1970s provided data on settlement patterns and land use over a period of several millennia. More recently, a small number of administrative documents written on prepared skin have emerged without secure provenance onto the antiquities market. Three are in Greek and date to the late third or early second century B.C.E. A further group, deriving apparently from a single archaeological context, are in Aramaic and cover the period of the end of Achaemenid rule in the region and the conquests of Alexander the Great.

The sections that follow will discuss what these sources can tell us about the organized exploitation of agricultural and other resources in Bactria by locally based apparatchiks working in the ultimate service of external imperial powers. The presence and efficacy of such administrative structures is manifested in our sources both directly and indirectly—indirectly by the very existence of irrigation systems and mining operations that required concerted collective effort, such as might be made possible by a strong local administrative apparatus; and directly by the information contained in the documentary texts on revenue collection, pay-

9. Bavay 1997.
10. Francfort 1989.
11. Bernard and Francfort 1978, 9; Rapin 1992, 50, pl. 100.2.

ments to officials, and the central management of tasks such as building fortifications. On a more human level, among the Aramaic documents we have preserved
the correspondence between a local governor and his superior, full of terse instructions, reprimands, and lengthy reiterations of previous orders. Resources could be
redistributed locally or channeled to the imperial center, but they could also be
mobilized quickly and efficiently in emergency situations, such as the need to supply the army column of the satrap-turned-king Bessos, in his flight from the army
of Alexander the Great. My focus, in this chapter, is on the *longue durée* of Bactria's
administrative history and on its external relations. Chapter 2 will give a smaller-
scale, more detailed case study of the city of Ai Khanoum for which the discussion
of the eastern Bactria survey in this chapter provides the necessary context. In
chapter 4, the focus will again broaden to consider the relationship, economic and
political, between Bactria and its other neighbors, the peoples of the steppe and
pastoral and nomadic groups in the immediate hinterland of the settled river valleys of Bactria-Sogdiana. Like Bactria's links to the Near East, these connections
are crucial to understanding the region's internal affairs.

The field-survey data, as already noted, gives a valuable perspective on the
longue durée in Bactria. The surviving documentary evidence in Aramaic, on the
other hand, happens to cover an especially interesting microperiod in the administrative history of Bactria, the transition from Achaemenid to Graeco-Macedonian control. This provides an intimate perspective on a phenomenon widely
attested throughout the Hellenistic world, the retention of the existing Achaemenid bureaucracy as a foundation for the administrative structures of the new Hellenistic states.[12] Alexander the Great, it has frequently been argued, was the "last
of the Achaemenids"; the Seleucid empire, too, "in its origin and its constituent
elements, was a branch grafted directly onto Achaemenid stock."[13] The Seleucid
empire provides more copious evidence for exploring such questions of administrative continuity.[14] Even allowing for the different types of evidence available for
the two periods (primarily the Persepolis fortification tablets for the Achaemenid
administration and Greek documents for the Seleucid), there is, as may be anticipated, much similarity between the two systems. The evidence from Bactria may
be more limited, but my conclusions are essentially the same.

One of my major themes in the following discussion will therefore be not the
development and imposition of mechanisms of imperial control but the *retention*
of personnel and institutions,[15] and the efficacy of such a policy in enabling the
incoming regime both to efficiently manage and control resources and (poten-

12. For further regional case studies, see Briant and Joannès 2006.
13. Briant 2002, 2.
14. Aperghis 2004, 263–95, with the two systems directing compared at 289–90.
15. cf. Briant 1985b on the Iranian elite in post-Achaemenid Asia Minor.

tially) to limit political resistance. Maintaining the existing bureaucracy, and keeping on the staff to run it, is not "lazy imperialism"—however calculating the laissez-faire attitude of its practitioners may or may not have been—but a sound political and economic strategy. Crucially for the present study, however, such administrative continuity may mean that control and exploitation of a territory by an external imperial power is less visible in the archaeological and documentary records than may be supposed.

Although I will introduce material—in particular from the archaeological field survey of eastern Bactria—from periods from the Bronze Age through to the Kushan empire, my focus will be on the periods of Persian control in the region, under the Achaemenid dynasty, and of Greek control, under both the external authority of Alexander the Great and his Seleucid successors, and the local control of subsequent independent Graeco-Bactrian dynasts. This corresponds to the latter part of the eastern Bactrian Iron Age, from around 800 B.C.E. through to the conquest of the region by Alexander the Great in 330–329 B.C.E., and the Hellenistic period, which in Bactria effectively ends with the northern nomadic invasions of the mid-second century B.C.E. The new data from the documentary texts now allows us to revisit and reengage with long-standing debates about the nature of the Achaemenid and Hellenistic imperial presence in Bactria.[16] On one side of this debate have traditionally been the archaeologists (and in particular Jean-Claude Gardin), who emphasize the lack of any break in the archaeological record corresponding to an Achaemenid or Hellenistic takeover. On the other side stands the historical approach of Pierre Briant, who draws on historical textual evidence for substantial Achaemenid state intervention in the socioeconomic affairs of Bactria, and for the management of resources and resource-gathering systems such as irrigation. Resolving this debate is not a matter of simple compromise: archaeological and historical sources each obscure some aspect of the "true picture" of Achaemenid Bactria. This historical sources, for example, make no mention of the region's impressive irrigation works.[17] The new documentary texts now also make it clear that the picture of continuity in material culture obscures the very real and effective mechanisms of Achaemenid imperial control.

From around the middle of the sixth century B.C.E., with Cyrus the Great's expeditions in Central Asia,[18] Bactria begins to feature in our historical sources, which are mostly Greek and of whom Herodotos is the most prominent. This Greek historical lens is a problem in approaching the history of the Achaemenid empire as a whole, even though it has recently come to be balanced by an increased attention to contemporary sources—especially epigraphic and documentary—in

16. Briant in Shaked 2004, 6–7.
17. Briant 2002, 752–54.
18. Ibid. 38–40.

other languages.[19] A larger number of Greek and Latin historical works cover the period of the campaigns of Alexander the Great in the 330s and 320s B.C.E. and contain accounts of his military activities in Central Asia and the peoples and terrain he encountered there. The preserved sources draw on contemporary accounts but are later in date.[20] For the period of Seleucid and Graeco-Bactrian rule in Central Asia, we possess far fewer historical sources, and the region's political history in this period must be reconstructed primarily on the basis of numismatic evidence.[21]

For the purposes of the present discussion, I would like to extract a few themes or pieces of pertinent information from these historical sources, which may be compared and contrasted with the archaeological and documentary evidence, or which raise questions that we may turn to this data to answer. The first theme concerns the origin of officials in the Achaemenid satrapal administration. The higher echelons, such as the positions of satrap or local governor, tended to be occupied by a "dominant ethno-class" of Persians, with locals of the various satrapies in lower ranks.[22] There does not appear to have been any attempt on the part of the Persians to spread or impose their religion or language beyond the ethnically Persian provincial elite.[23] What this means in archaeological terms is that we should not automatically expect to see any appreciable presence or influence of Persian material culture in the provinces, whatever the degree of Persian political control. This, of course, is the view from the center: if Persian culture was not actively imposed, aspects of it may still have been adopted and adapted by local populations on their own initiative and on their own terms.[24] The archaeological evidence from eastern Bactria indicates that, in this particular region, any such engagement with Persian culture on the part of local populations was limited.

The second point that I would like to draw out from the historical sources is the degree of authority exercised by local "big men," who might operate within wider imperial power structures but also independently.[25] The agency of local governors or warlords can be seen most clearly in the fierce resistance encountered by Alexander and his army in Central Asia. Many such individuals mounted military opposition or retreated to a fortified hilltop, or both, and had to be rooted out one

19. Sancisi-Weerderburg and Kuhrt 1987; Kuhrt 2007.

20. Heckel and Yardley 2008.

21. Sources collated in appendix D to Holt 1999b; the most recent "numismatic history" of the Hellenistic Far East is Widemann 2009.

22. See the discussion on Egypt in Briant 1988b.

23. Briant 1986, 1987, and 2002, 76–77.

24. For a more detailed outline of how such processes might work, see the considerable literature on Romanization in the Roman empire: e.g., Millett 1990, Woolf 1998.

25. See Briant 1985a, 246–49.

by one, at considerable costs in terms of manpower, provisions, and lost time.[26] In Arrian's *Anabasis of Alexander* these men are usually referred to as *huparchoi* (hyparchs), a Greek term (one may translate approximately as "subrulers") that does little to clarify their precise status but does, perhaps, indicate rather well the extent to which their effective power, in practical, local terms, was out of proportion to their technically subordinate position within Achaemenid power structures. Hyparchs could have been agents for the implementation of imperial policy on a local scale in all sorts of areas, including irrigation schemes or the mustering of troops.[27] As Alexander found, detached from such external obligations, they could also draw on local loyalties and resources to act as independent agents. Yet his policy, where possible, tended toward the incorporation of such powerful local figures: they were to be made to work for him.[28]

At the level of the satrapal government, Bactria itself was also a possible personal power base within the Achaemenid empire or the world of the Hellenistic successor states. The most dramatic example of this use as a power base is the case of Bessos, the satrap of Bactria under Darius III, who after Alexander's defeat of the Persians at the battle of Gaugamela in 331 B.C.E. declared himself king, as Artaxerxes V, took Darius captive, and beat a retreat toward Bactria as a base from which to build his power. In the mid-third century B.C.E., with the independence of the Graeco-Bactrian state, under the Diodotids, from the Seleucid empire, Bactria again showed itself to be a formidable power base, from which a local ruler might challenge the authority of an overarching imperial power. The Aramaic documentary texts offer two particular insights into the potential of Bactria as a regional power base. They document the provisioning of Bessos's supply train and how the resources of Bactria were marshaled in his support. And they present us with the new figures of Akhvamazda, the probable satrap, and his governor Bagavant. Akhvamazda's ownership of personal lands and his administration of these along with affairs of state show the close relationships between local landowners with their own constituencies and the Achaemenid authorities.

26. On Alexander's tribulations in Central Asia, see Holt 1988, Bosworth 1996.

27. Briant 2002, 748–53.

28. Local rulers or high officials who were retained in their positions because they had cooperated or courted Alexander's favor include Taxiles (Diodorus 17.86.4) and Autophradates (or Phrataphernes: Arrian 3.23.7, 3.24.3; Diodorus 8.3.17). The local power struggles behind such appointments might be complex: when Astes, the governor of Peukelaotis (Charsadda in modern Pakistan), attempted revolt, he was replaced by his former subordinate Saggaios, who had gone over to the pro-Alexander Taxiles (Arrian 4.22.8). Even those satraps or "big men" who welcomed Alexander could turn against him once their most compelling reason for doing so—his army—was gone (e.g., Satibarzanes: Arrian 3.25.2; Curtius 6.4.20, 7.3.2). Executive continuity might, however, be an interim measure, and there are several cases where a Persian official was replaced by a Greek or Macedonian upon his death or retirement (e.g., Artabazos, in Bactria, was replaced by replaced by Amyntas: Arrian 4.17.3; Diodorus 8.1.19; Holt 2005, 74–75).

The third, associated, preliminary point to be made from the historical sources is that attempts by outsiders to disrupt the status quo in Central Asia were often resisted violently, such resistance being marshaled by the kinds of local "big men" just discussed. Again, Alexander the Great provides the best example, with his foundation of the new settlement of Alexandria Eschate on the river Jaxartes (the modern Syr-darya) in 329 B.C.E. Although Alexander treated the river as a border with the steppe lands to the north and attempted to consolidate its position as such, this represented a fundamental break with the existing cultural and political state of affairs, where peoples on either side of the river were in constant interaction, and he inadvertently provoked a major rebellion.[29] For an incoming power, there were political benefits to continuity in executive and administrative personnel. The retention of familiar institutions and social structures (even if these are now managed at the top level by different people) could also be very effective in reducing any "shock of the new" and potential for resistance or revolt among the colonized population.

As I have already suggested, this is the most important theme that emerges from our various forms of evidence from Achaemenid and Hellenistic Bactria, whether these be historical, documentary, or archaeological. Rather than a weakness or deficiency, the retention and productive use of existing structures instead of or in addition to introducing new systems of administration and exploitation is a strength, an active and effective strategy in efficient management of resources and imposition of control.

THE EASTERN BACTRIA SURVEY AND THE HISTORICAL SOURCES ON THE ACHAEMENID PRESENCE

In the archaeological record from Central Asia, the Achaemenid period is still poorly represented.[30] There are only a very small number of excavated "Achaemenid" sites, in the sense of sites whose sole or primary period of occupation falls in the period of Achaemenid rule or sites that betray any substantial influence of Persian or Near Eastern material culture. Although the corpus of available evidence is still at present very small, what evidence there is does rather serve to underscore the point made in this and many previous studies that the period of Persian rule in Central Asia is not one of substantial innovation in terms of material culture or systems of land management. This lack of innovation, however, does

29. Briant 1982, 203–30; Holt 1988, 52.

30. Francfort 2005 provides a state-of-the-question survey; a recent Uzbek-Italian project aims to examine sites of the Achaemenid period in the region of Samarkand: Genito et al. 2009, 2010; Abdullaev, et al. 2011; Genito and Raiano 2011.

not suppose lack of imperial control. In addition, it is likely that our lack of substantial and identifiable archaeological remains of the Achaemenid period is, to some degree, to be attributed to accidents of preservation and practical constraints on fieldwork. Almost all the major historical cities of Central Asia (e.g., Bactra, Samarkand, Merv) bear two millennia or more of levels of occupation on the same site; these were generally abandoned only with the Mongol invasions of 1220–21 C.E. The same forces that inhibited investigation of the archaeology of Hellenistic Central Asia until the excavations at the Graeco-Bactrian city of Ai Khanoum—and gave the illusion of its nonexistence as a distinct and innovative period in the region's cultural history—have inhibited the investigation of Achaemenid Central Asia.[31] (See the discussion above in the introduction to this volume.) The Achaemenid levels lie below even the Hellenistic levels of the major sites, and furthermore archaeologists tend not to have gone looking for Achaemenid Bactria to the same degree as they have gone to in looking for Hellenistic Bactria.

Where we can identify something of the character of the Achaemenid presence in Central Asia is in the data derived from archaeological field survey. From 1974 to 1978, an extensive field-survey project in eastern Bactria sought to provide a wider context—both chronological and geographical—for the DAFA excavations at Ai Khanoum.[32] In order to restore to Ai Khanoum something of this context, I have chosen to begin with a discussion of the less well-known field survey before moving on to consider the scholarly celebrity that is Ai Khanoum in chapter 2. Although initially concerned, in part, to identify "Greek" impact and settlement on the "Bactrian" landscape, two factors that quickly became apparent to the personnel of the eastern Bactria survey were the considerable time-depth of settlement and agricultural activities in the region (as far back as the first part of the

31. On the so-called mirage of Greek culture in Hellenistic-period Bactria, see the original, pessimistic, assessment by Foucher following his excavations at Bactra (Foucher and Bazin-Foucher 1942–47, 73–75, 310). Schlumberger argued that Greek Bactria was "not a myth, but only unexplored" (Schlumberger 1960, 152; cf. Schlumberger 1946). The DAFA excavations at Ai Khanoum (1964–78) finally provided confirmation of this. Kuz'mina 1976 and Holt 1987 provide further discussion of the "'Bactrian Mirage' and the Archaeological Reality."

32. The results of this survey program are published in the three volumes of *Prospections archéologiques en Bactriane orientale (1974–1978)* (Gentelle 1989: palaeogeographical data; Lyonnet 1997: ceramics and chronology; Gardin 1998: sites and settlement patterns), with preliminary reports on the project, its objectives, and its methodology in Gardin 1980; Gardin and Gentelle 1976, 1979; Gardin and Lyonnet 1979; and Gentelle 1978. Gardin 1984 provides an introduction to the survey and its methodologies in English. For an overview of the project and a more comprehensive bibliography, see Mairs 2011b, 28–29.

My comments here are restricted to the eastern Bactria survey. Other such survey projects in Central Asia have been conducted in the valley of the Surkhan-darya, a northern tributary of the Oxus (Stride 2004, 2007) and in the Murghab Delta, around the ancient city of Merv (Gubaev, Koshelenko, and Tosi 1998; Salvatori, Tosi, and Cerasetti 2008). These will form part of my discussion in chapter 4.

third millennium B.C.E.) and the remarkable continuity in the maintenance of irrigation systems, with canals tens of kilometers in length following the same courses through many centuries or, indeed, millennia. An initial survey area around the immediate hinterland of the city of Ai Khanoum was expanded in subsequent seasons to a larger area of eastern Bactria, between the foothills of the Badakshan Mountains and the Oxus River (Amu-darya).

Not only was the settlement history of the region long, but its connections with regions far beyond Bactria and Central Asia were long standing. These connections are best illustrated by the team's discovery, in 1975, of the site of Shortughai, 21 kilometers northeast of Ai Khanoum's position at the confluence of the Kokcha and Amu-darya.[33] The settlement at Shortughai, in its first phase (ca. 2200–2000 B.C.E.), was an "outpost" of the Harappan civilization of the Indus Valley, with identical material culture, including ceramics, imported shell and carnelian, a seal depicting a rhinoceros with signs in the Indus script, and even the same standard brick sizes as used in Indus cities. The land around it was irrigated from the river Kokcha by a canal some twenty-five kilometers in length. The "lapis factor" may account in large part for Harappan interest in eastern Bactria at this period—once again, it must be stressed that even Shortughai was not the earliest archaeological site discovered in the region. In addition to beads, unworked pieces and chips of lapis were found at Shortughai alongside the flint microliths and drillhead used to work them.[34] In Shortughai's second phase (ca. 2000–1800 B.C.E.), however, the picture changes entirely. The site becomes integrated into the local eastern Bactrian archaeological culture and yields no further evidence of long-distance connections to the south and east but does display evidence of connections to western Bactria and to the steppe. The constant is Shortughai's intimate relationship to and reliance on its immediate agricultural hinterland.[35]

The precise status of the Harappan settlement at Shortughai (I hesitate to use the term "colony") is subject to debate, as is the nature of its connection to the Indus Valley, and its position on the "lapis route" to the West. But the relevance of this site to my main discussion, on the Achaemenid and Hellenistic administration of Bactria, is very clear. The dramatic changes in material culture between the site's two periods represent some fundamental realignment of its relationship to the civilization of the Indus Valley. Whether we can view this in terms of the mechanisms of imperial control and their withdrawal is uncertain. With or without the overt cultural presence of an external political power, however, the archae-

33. Francfort 1989.
34. Noted in Francfort 1983, 1984a, 1984c, useful overviews in English of the site and its various points of interest and debate.
35. Francfort 1983.

ological evidence indicates no fundamental interruption in occupation, economic exploitation, or agricultural production.

Later settlements in eastern Bactria—the Hellenistic city at Ai Khanoum, which probably overlay an earlier Achaemenid settlement or the grand Iron Age–Achaemenid fortification, the "Ville Ronde," three kilometers to the north at Kohna Qala[36]—come and go in similar landscape, where the intensity of agricultural exploitation may increase at certain periods but the practices and structures that permit this exploitation remain. The question, of course, is whether these structures (in particular irrigation canals) persisted *despite* the region's changing political status, or whether the various outside political regimes were themselves instrumental in setting up and maintaining such structures. In the very early periods of eastern Bactria's archaeologically recorded history, the question is also whether some kind of state, whether local, regional, or external, was necessary for the development of irrigation works in the first place, or whether these works may themselves even have led to the emergence of a state.[37]

The latter question demands a certain level of engagement with the intellectual history, specifically, of Soviet archaeological research in Central Asia as a coda to my broader survey of the question above in the introduction to this work. North of the Oxus (Amu-darya), in the former Soviet Central Asian Republics, discussion of the sociopolitical conditions that enabled the construction and management of large-scale canal irrigation systems has traditionally been framed in Marxist social-evolutionary terms.[38] In brief, the model proposed in most such studies is that the organization of labor required to construct canals on a scale such as that in eastern Bactria supposes a centralized political authority capable of mustering such labor, and moreover that this political authority must have represented an evolution from an earlier, more egalitarian sociopolitical system to a more hierarchical one, which employed slave labor. I would like to make the rather simpler and more modest points that irrigation on this scale requires collectivization and mobilization of substantial labor forces, that a local state or external imperial power might play a role in organizing such labor, and that this state or empire had much to gain from efficient organization of agricultural production. We are not in a position to say much more about these issues in the Bronze Age, but for the Achaemenid and Hellenistic periods we now have the necessary documentary evidence to say something about how, by whom, and at what level (local, regional,

36. Francfort and Lecomte 2002, maps 7 and 8.

37. For an influential work on irrigation and state formation in Egypt, see Butzer 1976.

38. The survey of Francfort and Lecomte 2002 is greatly to be recommended for its synthesis of archaeological field-survey material from across Central Asia and critical discussion of the methodologies and the ideological underpinnings of Soviet scholarly approaches to irrigation in the region. Stride 2009, no. 1834, discusses similar questions for the region around Samarkand.

empirewide) eastern Bactria's agricultural, mineral, and human resources were managed. The information to be gleaned from these documentary texts will be discussed in the sections that will follow. The remainder of this section will be devoted to an overview of the survey data from eastern Bactria, and what this data has taken to signify.

The first point to be made about the canals that supported the settlements of eastern Bactria concerns their size and sophistication. As well as being very long (canals of 20 to 30 kilometers as early as the Bronze Age), they manage changes in elevation of as much as ten meters.[39] By the Bronze Age, the sites associated with these canals already seem to display a hierarchy from smaller agrarian settlements to larger, fortified sites, although it should be noted that it has not always been possible to date such fortifications securely. In the Iron Age, the population increases, as does the number of fortified sites; it may be possible to date this growth more specifically to the latter part of the Bactrian Iron Age, which corresponds to the period of Achaemenid dominance. In the Hellenistic period, the plain of Ai Khanoum appears to have experienced an intensification in irrigation works and an increase in population corresponding to the period of Greek settlement. Although the Achaemenid takeover did not modify the local ceramic assemblage, the Graeco-Macedonian settlement did. Local Hellenistic ceramic forms maintain a very close correspondence to contemporary ceramics from the world of the Mediterranean littoral,[40] just as the Greek inscriptions and documentary texts of Bactria and Arachosia are linguistically and palaeographically indistinguishable from their contemporaries in Hellenistic Egypt. (See further below.) As I have already noted, although the scale and intensity of settlement and irrigation wax and wane (the progression noted here is something of a simplification), there is otherwise no fundamental break in either the material culture assemblage or in the continued use of individual canals.

The Iron Age intensification of settlement and irrigation implies some regional organization in eastern Bactria more developed than previously:[41]

> We can, on the other hand, not advance any statements on the nature of this ... authority, the limits of its authority, or its place in the political apparatus of Central Asia in the same periods; the Persian conquest, finally, does not necessarily signify the end of this relative autonomy: the coherent pursuit of the same programmes of irrigation until their completion under the Greeks leads us to suppose a certain permanence of local politico-administrative structures subordinated to a foreign authority which doubtless discovered very quickly the advantages of maintaining them.

39. For this and what follows, see Francfort and Lecomte 2002, 638–39; Gardin 1998, 106–12; Gentelle 1978, 1989, 91.

40. Gardin 1985.

41. Gardin 1998, 156.

The latter point—that incoming imperial powers might integrate preexisting local systems of administration and land management into their apparatus of government and exploitation—is, I would argue, the most fundamental one. Not only is it supported by the more recently discovered documentary evidence (as will be discussed in following sections), but it offers a point on which we may reconcile the long-standing debates between Gardin and his colleagues versus Briant.[42] I have already outlined the basic thrust of Briant's arguments above. Bactria, he argues, should not be considered in isolation from other provinces, as a "special case" within the Persian empire: the documentary lacuna that had thus far obscured the mechanisms of the Achaemenid administration in Bactria was a lacuna in our evidence and did not prove the nonexistence of an ancient bureaucracy and its paperwork (as has since been confirmed).[43] Long-term continuities may imply not that the Achaemenid state lacked influence on or failed to intervene in the local administration but rather that that state mobilized and used existing structures and systems.[44] Here, it should be noted, Gardin and Briant are essentially making the same point.

One reason why Achaemenid imperial control in Bactria is not especially archaeologically visible is because much of the existing administrative and economic apparatus was retained. The retention of these systems does not imply the lack of impact of imperial control, but it does tell us that one of the ways in which this imperial control operated was to take advantage of existing structures. Where Achaemenid and Hellenistic imperial control does become visible is in the documentary record, to which I now turn.

THE SATRAPAL ARCHIVE:
ADMINISTERING ACHAEMENID BACTRIA

Although documentary texts from Achaemenid Bactria have emerged only very recently, their existence and their contents provide confirmation of what scholars have been arguing for some time: that Bactria, a province of economic and strategic importance to the Achaemenid state, can have been administered only with the same care and using the same administrative registers (the Aramaic and Elamite languages) and tools as other provinces of the empire.[45]

---

42. See especially Briant 1985a; arguments in this and other publications conveniently summarized in Francfort and Lecomte 2002, 659–62.

43. In tandem with the archaeological evidence, Briant (1984, 103) proposes "to consider that certain programmes of the Achaemenid period could not have been realised without the initiative of the satrap of Bactra, who was the primary beneficiary of them in the form of tribute payments."

44. Briant 1985a, 244.

45. Briant 2002, 753. See also Briant 1985a, 244: "What one might call the 'Bactrian documentary void' (the absence of any document emanating from the satrapal authorities) is an obvious handicap.

Now that we do have some documents from the satrapal archives, what do these add to our understanding of the Achaemenid administration of Bactria? The first thing to be said is that the documents currently known contain no references to irrigation or canals but do refer to private and public land under cultivation, the management of such land, and its agricultural products. The archaeological evidence already considered shows that this agricultural production, in Bactria, was made possible by large-scale irrigation works, but the execution of such works is not mentioned in any of the written sources presently at our disposal. Another point for which the archaeological and documentary evidence must be viewed as complementary rather than accumulative is geographical provenance. The best-documented survey regions are eastern Bactria, the area on which I have focused, and the valley of the Surkhan-darya, in north-central Bactria (which will be discussed in chapter 4). The documents, in contrast, most probably come from the satrapal archive in the city of Bactra, in central Bactria. Some of them relate to the administration of the area around the town of Khulmi, just to the east. Nevertheless, as will be discussed, there are numerous places in which the documents provide new information to bring to bear on existing historical questions.[46]

The documents known at present comprise thirty texts on leather and eighteen wooden sticks, all written in ink. The language is Imperial Aramaic, the standard administrative register of the Achaemenid empire and the same as that of other Achaemenid Aramaic documents from Egypt.[47] In terms of script, orthography, and official terminology and formulae, the Bactrian and Egyptian documents are all but identical. Any Iranian loanwords tend to be Old Persian—that is, from the

---

What I would like to emphasise . . . is that no-one can feel authorised to conclude—from an argument a silentio—that Bactria remained marginal and poorly integrated into an Achaemenid whole where the presence of the State apparatus was marked by fairly numerous written signs: the contrast with other Achaemenid lands (Judaea, the Greek cities, Egypt, Babylonia) is in large part mere appearance; as for the Bactrian documentary void, it comes from accidental reasons."

46. For reasons of space, I limit my discussion of the administrative apparatus of the Persian empire as a whole and of the linguistic landscape of Bactria and its neighboring satrapies in the Achaemenid and Hellenistic periods (on which see Mairs 2011b and below, chapter 5).

The evidence from Bactria is rather limited. But in Arachosia, to the south of Bactria in what is now southern Afghanistan, we find a hint that the same kind of multilingual administration was in operation as in other provinces of the Achaemenid empire. The use of Aramaic may be inferred indirectly, both from later, third-century inscriptions at Kandahar and in the Laghman Valley, and from the fourth-century Aramaic documents of neighboring Bactria. It is the presence of Elamite, however, that is truly telling. A couple of fragments of a tablet with the same contents and physical form as those that were kept in the archives at Persepolis (Hallock 1969) were discovered at Kandahar (Helms 1997, 101: catalogue nos. 1399, 1400). It therefore seems likely that the Achaemenid administration in Arachosia and Bactria observed the same functional differentiation between the Aramaic and Elamite languages for different aspects of record keeping as in other regions of the empire. (For further discussion of this question, see Briant, Henkelman, and Stolper 2008; on Aramaic archives: Millard 2003.)

47. The Arshama archive: Driver 1957; Porten and Yardeni 1986–.

language of the imperial center—not from local languages. The provenance of the Bactrian documents is not known, but they almost certainly came from in or near Bactra (modern Balkh), the capital of the satrapy of Bactria, and later also of the Graeco-Bactrian kingdom. Bactra has, unfortunately, not yet been extensively excavated, although material of the Achaemenid and Graeco-Bactrian periods is gradually coming to light.[48] The chronological range of the dated documents is 353–324 B.C.E., with a single outlier dated on palaeographical criteria to the fifth century B.C.E. The texts therefore span the period of the final decades of Achaemenid rule in Bactria through to the seventh regnal year of Alexander the Great. They provide an invaluable record of the administrative and economic affairs of Bactria at a period of political transition.

Internal connections between the documents indicate that they came from a single archive and that this archive was that of the satrap at Bactra. An important subgroup of documents consists of eight letters and two economic notes addressed or otherwise connected to a man named Bagavant, who was the *paḥtā* (governor) of Khulmi, probably modern Khulm, about seventy kilometers to the east of Bactra (Group A). The letters, however, are rough copies—they contain many corrected and uncorrected errors, as well as traces of previous, erased writing—and therefore belong to the archive of the sender, Akhvamazda, not of Bagavant. The content and epistolary style (abrupt, demanding, lacking in courtesy phrases) of the documents indicate that Akhvamazda was Bagavant's superior. His title is not explicitly given, but that he was satrap of Bactria seems intuitive. In addition to the Akhvamazda-Bagavant correspondence, the collection contains many documents that have no mention of either official, reinforcing the notion of a satrapal archive belonging to a bureau that administered the various economic affairs of the province. Another subgroup of documents consists of letters between officials of more nearly equal rank, as may be seen from their forms of address.[49] Two further groups comprise lists of provisions and agricultural products to be distributed to certain persons of groups of people[50] and wooden tallies giving quantities of commodities given on credit, all dated to Year 3 of Darius III: that is, 333–332 B.C.E.[51] Since these texts come from a central satrapal archive, it may be that these goods are being distributed to satrapal agents or employees through a named official agent and are not records of transactions between private individuals. The physical form of the tally sticks is of some interest: two identical texts were written on the interior faces of a split wooden stick, and each party kept one half, so that the details of the transaction could later be verified.

48. See, most recently, Bernard, Besenval, and Marquis 2006; Besenval and Marquis 2007.
49. Naveh and Shaked 2012, no. 219, group B.
50. Ibid. group C.
51. Ibid. group D.

The Achaemenid imperial apparatus exercised considerable direct control over the economic and military affairs of the province. Agricultural produce is gathered, consolidated, and distributed. The kinds of products mentioned include livestock (chickens, geese, horses, camels), harvested grain, and processed foodstuffs such as yogurt, wine, and vinegar.[52] Significantly, the documents differentiate between cattle and sheep roaming free at pasture and those confined in an enclosed, supervised space:[53] an important confirmation of the importance of the pastoral economy in Achaemenid Central Asia and the ability of the state to supervise and profit from it.[54] Such products are both collected and distributed to lists of named individuals and groups, including soldiers. Among the tasks with which Bagavant is charged are the transportation of grain to the satrapal granary, collection of vinegar from one of the satrapal estates to provision a convoy, and fortification of towns. One item of correspondence concerns Bagavant's resistance to an earlier order to build a wall around a town: the crops have not yet been harvested, he protests, and are at risk from locusts. Akhvamazda gives his permission for the work force to complete the harvest before starting on the fortifications.[55] Although as already noted no documents refer to irrigation works and their maintenance, this last-mentioned letter does demonstrate the extent to which the Achaemenid apparatus was able to mobilize and direct labor.

As in the Greek documents that will be discussed in the next section, onomastics gives us some limited but potentially still useful evidence on the ethnic origins or assumed ethnic identities of various officials. The highest officials all have Persian names, as do the "scribes" of the documents—who may in fact also be executive officers rather than simply secretaries.[56] Like the Bactrian Greeks of the Ai Khanoum treasury texts (on whom see further below), these Bactrian Persians may have had deeper roots in the region, whether as long-term residents or as the products of families that had been settled there for some generations and integrated with local communities. Some of the names in the documents do, however, bear traces of local Bactrian influence, in particular theophoric names derived from the deified river Oxus.

Still better evidence for the deep enmeshment of the Achaemenid administrative apparatus and its personnel in local affairs and socioeconomic structures, however, comes from the indistinct dividing line between Akhvamazda's administration of state property and his personal holdings.[57] Bagavant is charged with managing both the satrap's own personal estates (for example, carrying out repairs on buildings there) and state lands, and it is sometimes difficult to tell which cat-

52. Ibid. 33–35.

53. Ibid. 33; cf. Shaked 2003.

54. See also the data from the archaeological field survey of the Sukhan-darya Valley: Stride 2007. I will return to the question of the pastoral economy in chapter 4.

55. Naveh and Shaked 2012, A4 (Khalili IA 1).

56. Ibid. 23–24, 28–29.

57. Ibid. 25.

egory a particular landholding falls under. Although nominally imperial servants, both men clearly also command strong local power bases, and Akhvamazda's own personal economic interests are bound up with his "official" remit and the resources at his disposal. The incorporation of powerful local "big men"—whether men of Persian origin who had built up Bactrian power bases or the scions of powerful local families of longer standing—was, I would argue, one of the great strengths of the Achaemenid administration in Bactria. The ultimate example is Bessos, the satrap of Bactria who acceded to the imperial throne after Alexander's humiliating defeat of Darius III. As Alexander pursued him into Central Asia, Bessos was able to draw on local resources and support. Among the papers from the satrapal archive, we appear to have one document that relates directly to local provisioning of Bessos's army (Naveh and Shaked 2012: C1 [Khalili IA 21], Nov.–Dec. 330 B.C.E.):

> In the month of Kislev, year 1 of Artax[erxes] the King.   (col. 1, l. 1)
> Provisions in Maithanaka for Ba[yasa], when   (l. 2)
> he passed from Bactra to Varnu.   (l. 3)

Artaxerxes was the throne name assumed by Bessos, and it is very tempting to identify the Bessos (Bayasa) of line 2 with the historical Bessos: it is certainly of the right date for this to be possible. He may therefore appear twice in the same document: as the ruling authority by whom paperwork was dated and as the powerful individual who was able to draw on Bactria's administrative apparatus to supply his army.

EARLY HELLENISTIC BACTRIA: BUSINESS AS USUAL?

> On the 15th of Sivan, year 7 of Alexander   (col. 1, l. 1)
> the King. Disbursement of barley <from Vakhshudata, the barley supplier   (l. 2)
> in Ariavant.   (l. 3)
> (Naveh and Shaked 2012: C4 [Khalili IA 17], 8 June 324 B.C.E.)

Six years later, similar documents were being dated by a different king. The Aramaic documents from Bactria cover a period of transition, from the last decades of Achaemenid rule through into the very early years of the new Graeco-Macedonian regime. In a very literal sense, the Aramaic documents do indeed record "business as usual": the continuing regulation of the province's economic life according to existing practices, within existing administrative hierarchies, and written down in the same language according to the same templates. In dating formulae, the Persian kings give way seamlessly to Alexander the Great, the "last Achaemenid." Since the documents currently known come down only as far as the 320s B.C.E., it is at present impossible to say if and when this Achaemenid Aramaic bureaucracy was modified or replaced. At least by the time of the first Greek documentary texts now known, in the late third or early second centuries B.C.E., Bactria was being administered in Greek.

FIGURE 2. Bactrian Aramaic document of 8 June 324 B.C.E., recorded on skin, with regnal year of Alexander the Great. (Khalili Collections, IA 17 recto. © Nour Foundation. Courtesy of the Khalili Family Trust.)

At least initially, as was discussed above, it is also difficult to find any clean break in the archaeological record corresponding to the political changes of the late fourth century. The most attractive hypothesis is to view much of the third century as a lengthy period of transition, in the course of which the Greek colonial presence gradually made itself felt and undertook programs (whether or not these were centrally directed) for the intensification of settlement and exploitation of the agricultural territory in eastern Bactria. It is probable that this was accompanied by a longer period of crossover or transition from an Aramaic to a Greek bureaucracy, with multilingualism and different languages being used for different purposes on different media, but the evidence with which we may examine this transition is unfortunately very sparse. Although there are Aramaic texts from the regions south of the Hindu Kush into the first half of the third century B.C.E., these are public inscriptions by an external political authority (the Indian Maurya empire) and give us only indirect evidence for the continued use of Aramaic to regulate local affairs.[58] But an ostrakon from Ai Khanoum, fragmentary and cryptic though it is, is in fact rather good evidence that administrative functions in

58. Henning 1949; Pugliese Carratelli and Garbini 1964; Benveniste and Dupont-Sommer 1966; Dupont-Sommer 1966, 1969.

Bactria continued to be performed in Aramaic in at least some contexts or at some levels well into the period of Graeco-Macedonian rule. This ostrakon dates to the second half of the third century B.C.E. (It is written on a Hellenistic ceramic vessel of that date.) The text is too badly broken to be read fully, but it appears to record a transaction having to do with grain.[59] It may therefore be compared to some of the Greek "ostraka" from Ai Khanoum discussed in the next section, which give lists of payments to or by named persons.[60] If this ostrakon does indicate some continuity in accounting practices at Ai Khanoum, we should also be alert to the possibility that some of the Greek titles used in the treasury texts may have been borrowed to refer to offices that developed from, or were even identical to, local Achaemenid precursors.

The majority of the Greek texts that will be considered in the next section come from the Graeco-Bactrian city of Ai Khanoum, the site that the eastern Bactrian survey was originally designed to contextualize. I would like to anticipate some of my discussion of this city in the next chapter by examining how the Greek settlers of Bactria—Alexander's demobbed soldiers—and their descendants modified their built environment in the course of the third century B.C.E. and what these renovations may mean.

Ai Khanoum is at present the only extensively excavated major settlement site of the Hellenistic period in Bactria, but its problematic publication history has left many questions about its history and chronology to remain unresolved.[61] The ceramic data from the site, which received lengthier (although still not comprehensive) publication only some time after the excavations ceased, now offers a more reliable chronological framework within which to place various construction programs undertaken at Ai Khanoum.[62] This data also makes it very clear that there was Achaemenid-period occupation on the site, which predated the Graeco-Macedonian "foundation" and its structures.[63]

The most substantial program of renovation at Ai Khanoum took place between ceramic periods IV and V, which, according to current datings correspond to (roughly) 260–220 B.C.E. and 220–200 B.C.E.[64] This mid-to-late third-century date is significant for two reasons. First, it is the period by which Bactria had succeeded in asserting its independence as an autonomous kingdom. And second, it is well after the death of the first or even the second generation of the Greek settlement.

59. Harmatta 1994, p. 390, no. 382.

60. Rapin 1992, 105, 112–13.

61. Fussman 1996. For a bibliography and literature review of the site and its excavation, see Mairs 2011b, 26–28.

62. Gardin 1977, 1985, 1990a.

63. These issues are discussed most extensively in Lerner 2003–4; see also Mairs 2014a.

64. See the schema in Lerner 2003–4, 380: Lerner proposes to shift the chronology several decades later, which would not seriously compromise the arguments presented here.

As well as providing a medium through which the inhabitants of Ai Khanoum could reimage their connections to their Greek colonial origins,[65] remodeling the urban landscape of the city also allowed them to make blunter, more assertive statements of their local autonomy, in the form of grander, more monumental architecture. If not a fundamental break in terms of government and administration, this marked a point when Bactria started to be administered and developed on its own terms rather than as part of a Near Eastern empire, whether this was that of the Achaemenids, Alexander, or the Seleucids. It was not the introduction of a new external imperial power that marked a new direction for Bactria but a change in its status from province, however devolved its provincial administration, to independent kingdom.

ADMINISTERING HELLENISTIC BACTRIA: REVENUE AND TAXATION

From the last dated Aramaic documents of the new (but not bureaucratically innovative) Graeco-Macedonian administration in Bactria in the 320s B.C.E., there is a gap of a century or more until the first preserved Greek documentary texts, of the late third or early second century B.C.E. The two documentary corpora give us rather different kinds of information, and the Greek material is on two different media (skin and ceramic vessels) and from several different locations. Another contrast with the Aramaic documents is that the majority of the Greek texts come from an excavated context and are thus securely provenanced, both to a site (Ai Khanoum) and to a building within that site (the treasury, in the administrative quarter).[66]

The office at Ai Khanoum from which these texts derived (and any additional bureaux that existed within the administrative quarter) were on a scale rather different from that of Akhvamazda's central satrapal archive but perhaps more akin to Bagavant's regional governor's office. Although we cannot precisely identify the territory that Bagavant administered or assess contemporary land usage or other forms of economic exploitation there, the regional eastern Bactrian center at Ai Khanoum may be related to a wider archaeological context, the area of the eastern Bactrian survey, the data from which was discussed above. If the Aramaic documents give us the local viewed from the (Achaemenid) center, the Greek texts of the Hellenistic period give us a more regional perspective on economic affairs.

65. As argued in Mairs 2014a.

66. A small number of other Greek texts on ceramic vessels, similar to the Ai Khanoum treasury texts, have been excavated at other Bactrian sites, but all are either too fragmentary to yield a reading or else bear single names, sums of money, or descriptors of the vessels' contents (Canali De Rossi 2004, nos. 305–9, 313; Mairs 2011b, 39–40).

The city of Ai Khanoum and its excavated remains will be discussed fully in chapter 2; a glance at the city plan will provide enough information for the purposes of the present discussion. The economic texts on ceramic vessels derive from the treasury, a small court surrounded by magazines, accessed off the main courtyard of the palace.[67] The treasury, although an integral part of this complex of buildings, was positioned in such a way as to make it accessible from the outside, directly from the main court, without requiring a visitor to pass through the rooms and corridors to the south. This was perhaps a more suitable location for an office that necessitated frequent comings and goings of people and goods.

Although the treasury also yielded some fragments of literary texts on perishable materials,[68] I shall be concerned here with texts of an economic nature written on ceramic vessels, the majority in ink but a smaller number incised post-firing.[69] The texts were written when the vessels were intact and still in use: that is, these are not "ostraka" in the sense of broken sherds of pottery reused as cheap writing material, although some complete vessels contained more than one piece of writing, with a canceling sign before each superseded text.[70] For the most part, the texts relate to the contents of the vessels, which include coins, olive oil, and incense, and they describe the reception, quantification, and verification of these contents by several named parties. These include individuals with Greek and with local Bactrian-Iranian names: insufficient evidence, as yet, to say much about ethnic relations and identity at Ai Khanoum. Sums of money are counted in either Indian units of currency or Greek drachmas. The best-known text[71] is dated to "Year 24" of an unnamed king, most likely the Graeco-Bactrian king Eukratides.[72] In addition to the regnal year, archaeological and palaeographical criteria and as well the presence of Indian currency date these texts to the first half of the second century B.C.E., after the Bactrian Greek military expansion into northwestern India. I discuss not all these dipinti here, many of them preserving only a few letters, but only those that bear text sufficient to yield useful information.

Typically, these texts are records of transactions relating to coins or commodities that are concluded *dia* (through) or *para* (from) various individuals, whose

67. On the treasury see in general Rapin 1992, and the earlier discussion Rapin 1987. The chronology of the treasury and its texts is reappraised by Lerner 2011, no. 3112.

68. Rapin and Hadot 1987.

69. I give references to these texts according to Canali De Rossi's (2004) compendium *Iscrizioni dello Estremo Oriente greco*, since it is more easily available than the previous combined edition in Rapin 1992, *Fouilles d'Aï Khanoum* vol. 8, and because Rougemont's 2012 volume in the series *Corpus Inscriptionum Iranicarum* was not yet available to me at the time of writing.

70. E.g., nos. 324, 325, 330, discussed below. See also Rapin 1992, 109.

71. Rapin 1983, 1992; Canali De Rossi 2004, no. 329.

72. Bernard 1985, 99–100; Hollis 1996, nn. 18 and 26; see also Fussman 1980 on evidence for an "Era of Eukratides."

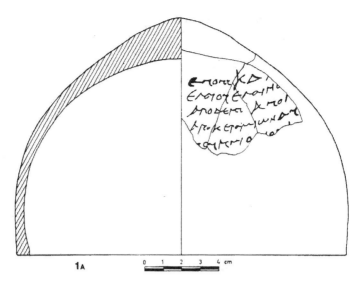

FIGURE 3. Greek economic text on ceramic fragment, from the Ai Khanoum treasury. (© Editions de Boccard.)

official positions, if any, go unremarked.[73] In most cases, the verb "to be counted" (*arithmeisthai*) is probably also to be understood.[74] Otherwise, one or another individual *esphragistai* (sealed),[75] probably to be understood both literally as of the sealing of a vessel and figuratively in the sense of a supervisor "signing off on" the matter. Two such officials may "seal," perhaps as a double-check. We therefore have a record, however brief and perhaps cryptic, of the names of some of the employees of the treasury, where most of these texts were found, as well as their roles in activities there. I summarize these here (with numbers referring to texts as given in Canali De Rossi 2004):

Aryandes: 327 (?), 330 "through."

Hermaios: 325 "counted," 326 "counted," 327 (?).

Hippias: 323 "through."

Kosmos (or Kosmas): 334 "through."

Molossos: 323 "sealed," 328 "through."

Nikeratos: 333 "from," 334 "verified through," 334 "sealed."

73. E.g., no. 323: Hippias, oil.
74. Picard 1984, 679; see further below.
75. No. 323: [Molos]sos and St[raton].

Oxeboakes: 324 "counted," 325 "counted."

Oxybazos: 324 "counted," 324 "sealed," 346 (?).

Philiskos: 330 "from," 331 "from," 332 "from," 347 (?).

Philoxenes: 349 ownership.

Sosipatros: 348 ownership?

Straton: 323 "sealed," 328 "from," 328 "through," 330 "through."

Tarzos: 328 "sealed."

Theophrastos: 332 "sealed."

Timodemos: 325 "from," (?), 341 (?).

Zenon: 324 "from."

The names Kallisthenes, Sinoph[ ]tos, Xatrannos, and Oumanos occur in the list (no. 345), and Kallisthenes perhaps also as one "through" whom a matter was transacted (no. 353).

I qualify the treasury as the location where "most of" these texts were found, because a few similar pieces were recovered from elsewhere in the city. This displacement occurred because the population who occupied the site after its destruction in the mid-second century B.C.E. disturbed the contents of many of its buildings, so that it is not uncommon to find items that would be more at home in a treasury context elsewhere, in particular in the sanctuary of the city's main temple. This is the case with four separate texts on a single vessel recovered from the temple sanctuary, which record cash payments *para* (from) one individual that *ērithmētai* or *ērithmēntai dia*, "have been counted by" or simply "through" two others and "sealed" by a fourth.[76] The sums are in Greek drachmas,[77] or in Indian currencies with names derived from toponyms such as Taxila.[78] Many such Indian coins were discovered at Ai Khanoum.[79] Other, more fragmentary texts of the same formula record similarly substantial payments in Indian currency,[80] as well as cases where the denomination has not been preserved.[81]

76. No. 324: from Zenon, counted by Oxeboakes and Oxybazos, sealed by [the same?] Oxeboakes. No. 325: from Timodemos, counted by Oxeboakes and Hermaios, text broken before name of sealer. No. 330: from Philiskos, through Aryandes and Stra[ton], text broken before name of sealer; a few additional letters are noted in Rapin 1992, p. 98, no. 4d.

77. No. 324: 500 drachmas.

78. No. 325:, *taxaēna*. No. 330: 10,000 *kasapana taxaēna*.

79. See, e.g., Audouin and Bernard 1973; and on the diverse numismatic finds from the treasury, Bernard 1985; Rapin 1992, 106–7.

80. No. 326: counted by [Her]maios. No. 328: from Straton, through Molossos and Straton, sealed by [. . .]bara[..] and Tarzos, 10,000 *kasapana nandēna*. No. 331: from Philiskos, counted by [??], sealed by [??], 10,000 [??]. No. 333: from Nik[eratos], 10,000 [??]. Also, very fragmentary: 10,000 of a sum of money in nos. 337, 338, 339; and probably in drachmas, no. 341: 500 [??].

81. No. 332: from Philiskos, through [??], sealed by Theophras[tos].

These are quite considerable sums of money, suggesting, along with the regularity with which the precise figures of five hundred drachmas and ten thousand Indian coins recur (to the exclusion of any other amounts), that these are transactions of an official nature, not personal payments (for example) of taxes or for purchases. Whatever the ultimate sources of these sums—and the Indian coinage may suggest tribute or taxes exacted from Indian lands conquered by the Graeco-Bactrian kings—what is happening at the treasury is evidently that incoming revenue is being consolidated and recorded, according to fixed divisions. I propose that the regular figures chosen—as well as being convenient, round counting units—have much to do with the practicalities of storage and transportation.[82] What seems less likely—although the possibility must be considered—is that these coins counted and verified (see below) in the treasury were the products of a local mint. Although blank bronze flans attest to the presence of a mint at Ai Khanoum, there is no firm evidence that silver coinage (such as drachmas) was struck there.[83]

The texts already discussed relate to the transaction and supervision of various payments in commodities and coin by a series of individuals. These are the most common formulae among the treasury texts, although there are a couple of exceptions. One, which is written in a more cursive script than the others, may be a more lengthy financial account written on an ostrakon rather than a record of the same type as the texts already discussed.[84] Although this text is fragmentary, clearly it records more than one smaller sum (44 drachmas, 7 drachmas, 8 drachmas, a possible total of 60 drachmas), has the names [He]rmaios and [Ar]y[a]ndes, in the genitive case (which could be taken with either *para* or *dia*), and contains a reference to *tas anaphoras* (revenues). There is also a list of personal names in the genitive case (Kallisthenes, Sinoph[.]tos, Xatrannos, Oumanos), with a possible total number of seventy-four at the foot of the list, suggesting another account

82. On the Attic standard used for Graeco-Bactrian coinage, a silver drachma would weigh ca. 4 g, giving 500 drachmas a weight of 2 kg or a volume of at the very least 0.2 liters. The Indian *karshapana* was a little lighter, at ca. 3–3.5 g, so 10,000 of these coins would weigh 30–35 kg with an absolute minimum volume of 3 liters. These volumes assume, of course, that the coins were packed exceptionally tightly, wherefore a rather larger vessel would of course have been needed. An amphora—on whatever standard we assume to have been in use in the treasury for containing money—could hold much more than this, with as much as 50 kg of silver attested elsewhere in the Greek world (discussed by Rapin 1983, 357–58; the capacity of one inscribed jar found near the main temple was 8.3 liters: Bernard et al. 1980, 15). Assuming that the coins in the treasury were stored in equivalent receptacles, and that silver by weight would have the same value, the discrepancy between the amounts of Indian and Greek currency needs to be accounted for. Perhaps Indian coinage was received in greater amounts, or the figure of 10,000 may not be correct.

83. Bernard 1985, 13–17, 83–84.

84. No. 327.

of sums paid by or through named individuals, with a final total.[85] A different format is followed in a better-preserved text,[86] in which *dokimos* ("approved" or
"assayed") silver, or "legal tender,"[87] is received through Kosmos, *dedokismatai dia*
(verified by) Nikeratos, and sealed by this (explicitly stated) "same" Nikeratos. It
may be that the verification performed by Nikeratos is to be connected with the
presence of more than one currency standard within the treasury.[88]

A small ceramic fragment excavated in the monumental entranceway to the
city's administrative quarter bears a rectangular stamp with an image of an
amphora and the legend *epi agorano[mou] Khaireas* ("during the administration
when Khaireas was *agoranomos*"—although in view of the syntax as restored
Khaireas may not be the same person as the *agoranomos*).[89] Although it cannot be
ruled out that this amphora was an import, it is simpler to propose a local origin,
especially since Bactria was itself a wine-producing region. We therefore have the
probable presence of an official called the *agoranomos* at Ai Khanoum, a figure
known from elsewhere in the Hellenistic world as a regulator of weights and measures, and general supervisor of marketplace commerce.[90]

Wine may well have come from the local area around Ai Khanoum, as may
honey and even olive oil (despite Strabo's claim that Bactria does not produce
oil),[91] but some of the other commodities excavated in the treasury or named in its
texts did not, including incense and cinnamon. The size of the treasury and its
position within the city would not have permitted the storage or regulation of bulk
agricultural produce such as grain. It therefore appears likely that the treasury's
role was more specifically to manage "special" commodities, which were imported,
produced only in small quantities, subject to state control, or produced under a
state monopoly. These commodities were not just received and redistributed as
complete units but were being assayed and repackaged. Some texts record the
transfer and consolidation of contents between partially full vessels.[92] Weights
were also discovered in the treasury.

The notion that the treasury was a clearinghouse specifically for especially
uncommon or valuable goods is confirmed by the archaeological finds of raw
materials from the storage magazines. These contained a very large quantity of
unworked blocks of lapis lazuli, some seventy-five kilograms packaged in a sack

85. No. 345.

86. No. 334.

87. Picard 1984, 683.

88. Rapin 1992, 107; see further Bernard 1979 and Picard 1984 on financial practices and terminology in the treasury texts.

89. Canali De Rossi 2004, no. 322; Schlumberger and Bernard 1965, 636–39, fig. 29.

90. Although his position in Hellenistic and Roman Egypt was somewhat different: Raschke 1974.

91. *Geography* 11.11.1.

92. Nos. 323, 329, 332, 335.

that had decayed,[93] and a much smaller quantity of worked lapis.[94] Other finds included ingots of silver and gold, and of raw glass, semiprecious stones, obsidian, vessels made of glass, metal, stone, and alabaster, and a few smaller worked "luxury items" such as pieces of jewelry containing semiprecious stones.

From the texts, it is possible to say something about the personnel who operated the treasury and their relative positions. This information may be compared and contrasted with that in the Greek documentary texts on skin from Bactria, which I will go on to discuss. The treasury texts appear to come from a comparatively short period of time and involve a rather small range of names. Individuals may appear in more than one text, in different roles, and in more than one role within a single text. In one, Nikeratos both verifies and seals[95]—it is stated explicitly that this is the same Nikeratos—and the like is probably also true in another, where an Oxeboakes both counts and seals.[96] We cannot tell for certain whether the same individual is always concerned or simply two men with the identical name, but the lack of an identifying patronymic or other indication of position in all cases suggests that it was self-evident to the record keepers who within their small bureau was involved (and accountable).

Do officials with Greek or Bactrian names appear in different capacities? The figure "from" whom always has a Greek name; the others may be Greek or Bactrian. Philiskos, whose name is Greek, appears as the agent "from" whom something in transacted in up to four texts. Local Bactrian-Iranian names include the theophoric "Oxus" names Oxeboakes and Oxybazos, a continuity in local naming practices from the Achaemenid period and probably earlier.[97] But it is questionable how meaningful this Greek-Bactrian division is: the corpus of texts is very small, and a name's linguistic origin may not have any direct relationship to its bearer's descent or ethnicity.[98]

This storeroom-bureau, with its own records on the vessels of products and payments themselves, must also have been accompanied by an archive at a higher level of the administration, with accounts on perishable media that have not been preserved.[99] As with the Achaemenid Aramaic documents, we are therefore seeing only a small portion of one office of a much more extensive administrative apparatus, with internal functional as well as hierarchical divisions.

93. Rapin 1992, 50, pl. 100.2.
94. Ibid. 175–76, pl. 78.
95. No. 334.
96. No. 324.
97. A Hellenistic-period Greek inscription from Takht-i Sangin, a temple complex on the north bank of the Oxus downstream from Ai Khanoum, dedicates to the god of the Oxus: Litvinskii, Vinogradov, and Pichikyan 1985; Bernard 1987a.
98. Mairs forthcoming (2), no. 3106.
99. A point made by Rapin 1992, 109–10.

Where we do have contemporary texts preserved on perishable materials, however, is at a lower level of the administration, in the sense of one that relates to regulation of the legal and financial affairs of individuals and their dealings with the state bureaucracy. There are, at present, just three known such Greek texts, on prepared skin, from Bactria. Like the economic texts from the Ai Khanoum treasury—and like, it should be recalled, the Aramaic documents of a century or so before—these documents are written in hands indistinguishable from those of the contemporary eastern Mediterranean world, testifying to their origin and perhaps continued inclusion in a shared bureaucratic system or modus operandi. My interest here is primarily in the data on economic and administrative affairs that may be gleaned from these rather than their (considerable) interest in matters of Graeco-Bactrian chronology. In all cases, it should be recalled that the texts are fragmentary and do not always yield much sense. They certainly do not furnish a coherent map of Bactrian administrative hierarchies.

The first published document was a tax receipt dated to around the first half of the second century B.C.E. [100] It bears a dating formula according to local Greek kings, with a Macedonian month name, and a location in a place called Asangorna.[101] A guardian of the law (*nomophulax*) is the first official named: "Although the placing suggests that he should be an annual magistrate whose name is used for dating purposes, it may be that he is mentioned because of some responsibility he had for the legality of the transaction."[102] Next comes a chain of command stretching upward from a *logeutēs* (tax gatherer), who acted *sumparontōn* (in the presence of) a figure whose name is not preserved, who was *tou sunapestalmenou hupo* (sent out likewise by) two further officials, all *dia* (through, by the agency of) one Diodoros *epi tōn prosodōn* (controller of revenues). The original tax gatherer, Menodotos—the subject of this extended formula—acknowledges receipt from an individual whose name is not preserved of *tē ōnē ta kathēkonta* (payments due in respect of a ["the"] purchase). The precise meaning of this is unclear: the editors of the text suggest that it relates to either a tax concession purchased from the government or a tax payable on a contract of purchase. Toward the end of the document there is a cryptic reference to something to do with a temple or sacred affairs,[103] suggesting that we may here be dealing with financial affairs and state regulation of a temple. All preserved personal names are Greek, with the exception of the patronymic of the taxpayer, which appears to be Iranian.

---

100. Bernard and Rapin 1994; Rea, Senior, and Hollis 1994; Hollis 1996; Rapin 1996b.

101. On attempts to identify these, see Grenet 1996.

102. Rea, Senior, and Hollis 1994, 265; see the latter article in general on the official titles in the document, and also Bernard and Rapin 1994.

103. Bernard and Rapin 1994, 270, translate more confidently as "sacrificial victims."

Despite the many lacunae and uncertainties in this text, the administrative hierarchy is fairly clear. The text most probably derives from a local office of the financial administration, directed by Diodoros the "controller of revenues." Subordinate to Diodoros were a number of "tax gatherers" and other such officials, and they all formed part of a chain of command directing taxation and revenue from individual payers up through increasingly more senior and more centralized bureaux to their ultimate destination in the royal coffers.[104] This, then, is the kind of collection and organization of revenue (albeit just one kind of revenue, from local taxation rather than also from luxury or state-controlled resources and imports) that took place lower down in the administrative pyramid than at the treasury office at Ai Khanoum. It is tempting, furthermore, to trace a fairly direct paper trail from records of individual payments (such as the Asangorna receipt) through to consolidated lists of payments from named individuals (such as nos. 327 and 345 from the treasury, which may record individual payers or the heads of local offices) through to the final packaging of revenue into units of five hundred drachmas, perhaps for shipment to a royal treasury at Bactra. This reconstruction is, of course, hypothetical, and I do not argue that the particular individual documents that I have discussed here stood in this relationship to one another.

The two further Greek administrative texts on skin were published only recently and date probably from the late third to early second century B.C.E.[105] Both are unprovenanced in any meaningful sense, and so it is really impossible to say if they derive from the same source or location as the Asangorna text or each other. The first records the payment of a sum of one hundred drachmas of coined silver and is perhaps a contract or receipt relating to a loan of money. If so, this is one of the only texts relating to the transaction of financial dealings between private individuals within a legal framework. The text is said to have been drawn up in a place named Amphipolis, which, like Asangorna, cannot yet be located securely on the ground. The second text is briefer and more fragmentary still, dates to sometime in the second century B.C.E., and records something (a sum of money?) *ha ekhei Arkhisēs epi phorai* (which Archises has [received] for transport). It also contains a cryptic reference to "stone." As the editors note, it is probably pushing things too far to read this as a reference to lapis lazuli, but the finds from the Ai Khanoum treasury, as discussed above, alert us to the possibility of any form of semiprecious or worked "stone" that could be valued and collected as a commodity.

---

104. Ibid. 287–88.
105. Clarysse and Thompson 2007, who date the Asangorna text also to this period.

FIGURE 4. Greek document, recorded on skin, of the reign of Antimachos. (© Nicholas Sims-Williams.)

CONCLUSIONS: ADMINISTRATIVE CONTINUITY

I would like to be quite cautious in assessing the extent to which all of these texts, even in combination, can be used to reconstruct the workings of the bureaucracy of Bactria in the Hellenistic period, still less the extent to which this bureaucracy was based on its Achaemenid predecessor. As was noted in the introduction to this chapter, the probability is great that the Achaemenid administration of Bactria, like that of other regions of the Achaemenid empire, supplied the template for later Hellenistic administrative structures. Continuity in personnel may be traced only as far down as the early years of the reign of Alexander but is likely to have persisted for much longer. The field-survey evidence, crucially, demonstrates that the essential workings of systems of land management and resource extraction were not interfered with. As was discussed above in the introduction to this chapter, the apparent absence of evidence for the Achaemenid and Hellenistic takeovers in eastern Bactria is in fact rather good evidence for a particular political and economic strategy, the retention of existing personnel and systems of economic production and exploitation in the service of a new political power. The survey data, along with the existence of administrative texts of the fourth and fifth centuries C.E. in the Bactrian language,[106] raise the tantalizing possibility that one day we may even be able to trace something of Bactria's longer-term administrative history.

106. Sims-Williams 2000, 2007.

All this relates only indirectly to the cultural and social history behind these administrative structures. How much investment did the local elites of Bactria retain in the new political system? The historical sources, discussed in the introduction to this chapter, once again bring us down only as far as the early third century B.C.E., showing how local "big men" reacted to the new Graeco-Macedonian regime, whether by rebellion or collaboration.[107] Names, as has already been noted, tell us nothing certain about people's identities or family backgrounds, and so we cannot say much about the social or ethnic origins of the officials named in the Greek documentary texts. To what extent did elites "acculturate" in response to the incoming Greek authority? The material culture of eastern Bactria, as already noted, received a marked influx of Greek or Mediterranean ceramic forms; but pots, notoriously, are not people. The urban sites of Bactria—the inevitable Ai Khanoum but also cities where excavation is ongoing, such as Bactra[108] and Termez[109]—supply plentiful data to begin to answer such questions, but it can be difficult to decide which aspects of these cities' material culture and architectural programs held contemporary ethnic resonance.[110] Sometimes a Corinthian column is just a column.[111] The following chapter will examine how a more holistic approach to Ai Khanoum's urban landscape—considering the institutions of the city in terms of their relationships to one another, and the city in the context of its immediate agricultural hinterland—may begin to furnish some answers to such questions.

107. See also Briant 1978.
108. Bernard, Besenval, and Marquis 2006; Besenval and Marquis 2007.
109. Leriche and Pidaev 2008.
110. Mairs 2007, 2013c.
111. Bernard 1968a.

Ai Khanoum

Let's admit the truth from here on in:
we too are Greek—what else could we be?—
but with loves and with emotions that are Asia's,
but with loves and with emotions
that now and then are alien to Greek culture.

—C. P. CAVAFY, "HOMECOMING FROM GREECE" (1914; TRANS.
MENDELSOHN 2012, 323)

AI KHANOUM AND EASTERN BACTRIA

Ai Khanoum occupies a special place in the historiography of the Hellenistic Far East, as the first major archaeological site to offer the opportunity to look at the architecture, material culture, and wider urban landscape of an actual Graeco-Bactrian community. (See the introduction.) Its supposed Greekness has given it a certain celebrity, but this celebrity—as an anomaly, a remarkable and exotic "outpost of Hellenism"—has not necessarily led to wider, deeper discussions of the site in the classical or archaeological literature. Part of the aim of the previous chapter has been to situate Ai Khanoum in its geographical and chronological context, as the latest in a long series of settlements that allowed external powers to control the resources of eastern Bactria. My intention in what follows is to provide a further level of contextualization—that of the institutions of Ai Khanoum within their urban setting—but also to provide a detailed description of the architecture, inscriptions, and material culture of the site, something that those unfamiliar with the site and its literature may use to orient themselves and direct further research.

Ai Khanoum was perfectly and deliberately placed to manage the resources of the surrounding plain and the mountains to the south as discussed in chapter 1. There were further resources to the north of the Oxus to which the city may have offered the Graeco-Bactrian kingdom access and control.[1] On plans of

1. Bernard 1973, 11, 244–45.

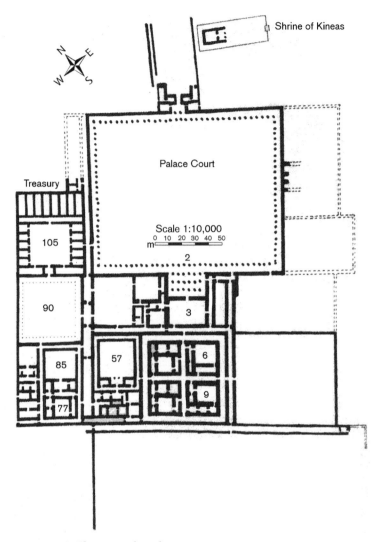

Shrine of Kineas

Palace Court

Treasury

Scale 1:10,000
0 10 20 30 40 50
m

2

105

90

3

85

57

6

9

77

FIGURE 5. Ai Khanoum palace plan.

Ai Khanoum and maps of the city's hinterland, the land on the other side of the Oxus (Amu-darya) is usually presented as blank. The international border between Afghanistan and Tajikistan (formerly the Tajik SSR) means that, whereas Ai Khanoum has been contextualized within its hinterland on the Afghan side of the river, far less is known about the city's relationship with territories on the Tajik side. Further below I shall discuss one southern Tajik site, Saksanokhur, as potentially paralleling the architectural plan of the Ai Khanoum palace. More recent research on Bronze and Iron Age sites in southern Tajikistan, furthermore, offers the potential to situate Ai Khanoum more intimately within the broad zone of mixed agropastoral systems that destabilize the nomad-settled divide across many regions of Central Asia.[2] An important role was also played by economic activities other than primary food production: mining in particular. This is true also of territories to the south. Ai Khanoum's position gave it access along the Kokcha River to the lapis-lazuli mines in the Badakshan Mountains. The sheer quantity of unworked lapis blocks uncovered in the treasury indicates that Ai Khanoum was a major center for gathering and transshipping lapis, whether or not the city also took any more direct supervisory role in lapis extraction.

The city of Ai Khanoum was also designed to exploit the strategic potential of its site, at the confluence of the Kokcha and the Oxus (Amu-darya). Its site incorporated a large, three-sided raised "acropolis" with a high "citadel" at one corner, which dropped down to a large, sloping lower city that, at least until the looting and destruction of the past thirty years, bore substantial architectural remains of the Hellenistic period. Ai Khanoum's size and the grand scale on which its central complexes of public buildings were conceived and constructed contrast with its complete absence from written history. The ancient name is not known, and attempts to ascertain it are, in the present state of the evidence, unlikely to come up with anything more than hypotheses.[3] Yet, from its material culture and inscriptions, we can in fact say rather a lot about the city's (just marginally more than hypothetical) Achaemenid predecessor, its Hellenistic foundation, and the subsequent political and cultural life of the city and its inhabitants. In some inscriptions and monuments, we may attempt to read outright statements of the inhabitants' ethnic identities, cultural affinities, and interpretations of their own civic history. Other, more subtle statements—intentional or implicit—are made by such things as the components and layouts of their houses and public buildings or the media in which they made statues or wall decorations.

The Ai Khanoum that I discuss here is essentially of the first half of the second century B.C.E., the last major architectural phase of the city, implemented in the final decades before its "fall" around 145 B.C.E. "Greek" Ai Khanoum is only part of the site's history. The plain around the city—and perhaps also the site itself—were occupied, irrigated, and economically exploited as far back as the Bronze Age. The citadel at Ai Khanoum displays evidence of occupation from the Achaemenid period through into the Middle Ages. This sequence is not unbroken, but the city's

2. Vinogradova and Lombardo 2002; Good 2010; for further investigation of these issues, see chapter 4.

3. Mairs 2014a.

natural advantages continued to make it attractive: during the most recent war, a gun emplacement was set up on the citadel by the Northern Alliance.[4]

As discussed in chapter 1, there is archaeological evidence of substantial interest in Ai Khanoum and the surrounding area under the Achaemenids; Aramaic texts now show that the Bactrian bureaucracy operated along the same lines as elsewhere in the empire; and several institutions at Ai Khanoum can be explained best as continuing Achaemenid predecessors—whether directly over earlier remains on the site or simply in terms of maintaining wider Bactrian administration and infrastructure. One of my main arguments in this chapter—that much of what is apparently unusual or contradictory about Ai Khanoum is to be explained by positing local Achaemenid precursors—is, as I am very well aware, not possible to substantiate in the present state of the archaeological evidence from the region. Still less is known about the archaeology of Achaemenid Bactria than about the archaeology of Hellenistic Bactria. The field survey and documentary data discussed in the previous chapter, however, make a strong case for a degree of administrative continuity between Achaemenid and Graeco-Macedonian rule. The evidence from Ai Khanoum further supports this case, and it also suggests that key public institutions—administrative centers, temples—continued to operate from buildings whose architectural forms were derived from their Achaemenid precursors. It is in this context that I introduce and discuss possible architectural parallels for the institutions of Ai Khanoum in such Near Eastern sites as Persepolis. Such parallels have been drawn before, but for them to be convincing we must posit a very real political and administrative link.

At the other end of its history, Ai Khanoum had an afterlife (or had afterlives) of sorts, consisting of at least one period of reoccupation in the years immediately following the "fall" of the "Greek" city. During this period, the site was lived in and used in some very different ways from what had gone before. Buildings were given new purposes, residential areas were constructed in formerly public buildings, and material from the earlier phases of the city was moved around. Most references to the post-Greek "squatters" at Ai Khanoum have considered them to be indigenous local peoples reoccupying a thoroughly Greek colonial city, but I do not think that such a stark Greek-native divide can be argued for the period of the active life of the city. Nor does the withdrawal of some cohesive Greek colonial enclave seem like a plausible model, in a region where the preservation of a community of solely Greek culture and descent must have been well nigh impossible. The post-Greek occupants, I suggest, are as likely to have had among them descendants of the city's inhabitants as of any purported disenfranchised native peasantry of the surrounding area.

The generally accepted date for the "fall" of Ai Khanoum is circa 145 B.C.E., and there are good reasons for placing the end of the life of the Greek city in that form—

---

4. Holt 2005, 16, 163.

a decisive break in continuity of population, socioeconomic organization, and political authority—at around this period.[5] The date of 145 hangs on a regnal year 24 of an unknown king in an economic text from the Ai Khanoum treasury. Given the reign length, the only plausible candidate is Eukratides, and this text would thus appear to place the end of the main phase of occupation at Hellenistic Ai Khanoum and the end of Eukratides' reign at around the same date in the mid-140s B.C.E., a period of both internal dynastic strife and external threats to the Greek kingdom of Bactria.[6] The Ai Khanoum treasury text, of course, provides only a terminus post quem, so the first major episode of abandonment and destruction could be dated more liberally, less specifically, to the 140s B.C.E. This period, at Ai Khanoum and in the Hellenistic Far East as a whole, will be discussed at greater length in chapter 4. Although the active life of the city in its current form therefore came to an end— and it seems a rather sudden end—in around 145 B.C.E., it is still less than clear what actually happened at the "fall" of Ai Khanoum.[7] The popular view of Ai Khanoum falling to an invasion of nomads who put an end to the Graeco-Bactrian kingdom as a whole is, as I will discuss, at best only part of the picture.

The period before the "fall," however, was one of growth and prosperity for Ai Khanoum, encouraged by political developments and the Graeco-Bactrian military expansion into northwestern India under Demetrios and Eukratides.[8] Indian material appears at Ai Khanoum, including Indian coins (discussed in chapter 1) and Indian luxury items such as worked ivory.[9] The strategic importance of eastern Bactria seems also to have increased at this period, with both the Graeco-Bactrian conquests in India and population movements and new military threats to the north of the Oxus. The first half of the second century was also a time of political upheaval and factional dynastic conflicts within Bactria itself, and the city's new prominence and prosperity at this time suggest that it played a part in this unrest. It is in this context that we should view attempts to identify Ai Khanoum as the Eukratideia mentioned in classical sources.[10] If such an identification were correct, it would indicate that Ai Khanoum's new prosperity and prominence came from an association with the king and his faction.

As was discussed in the introduction, it is important to understand the history of the site's discovery, excavation, and publication in order to make a realistic assessment of what Ai Khanoum is and is not, as it were, archaeologically "good for." It is at present the only major Bactrian urban center of the Hellenistic period

5. Holt 2012 reviews the evidence and confirms this date.

6. Bernard 1980a, 442–43.

7. Fussman 1996, 247–48.

8. Rapin 1992, 249.

9. Rapin 1996a (in English), excerpted from Rapin 1992 (in French).

10. Ptolemy 6.1.7, Strabo 11.11.

from which we have much archaeological evidence at all. It is the only site in the Hellenistic Far East where we can look directly at a contemporary Hellenistic street plan. At Sirkap (Taxila), the layout of the Indo-Greek city is known only indirectly, through its successor.[11] For these reasons, we do not really have the evidence to judge how representative Ai Khanoum may be either of Bactrian cities or of Greek foundations of the Hellenistic Far East. We may, on the other hand, argue more convincingly that Ai Khanoum is *not* representative of any general pattern of regional urbanism in the Hellenistic period. The duration of the site's Hellenistic occupation, for one thing, was short, from the late fourth century B.C.E. through into the 140s B.C.E. Whatever Achaemenid presence there was at the site, the renovations of the third and second centuries represent the creation of a new city. The latest phases of Ai Khanoum, in particular, are the product of deliberate schemes of urban planning. We may therefore anticipate other cities of Bactria, especially those with much longer periods of occupation, such as Bactra, to display more complex intersections of material culture and architectural forms. Ai Khanoum must be treated qua Ai Khanoum.

Questions of wider interpretation and analysis aside, certain practical problems were faced by the excavators of Ai Khanoum. The sheer size of the city and the monumental scale of its institutions meant that, even if long periods of war and instability in Afghanistan had never intervened when they did, logistical issues— problems of manpower, financial resources, practical constraints on the number and duration of field seasons—would have made it difficult for the "real," "whole" Ai Khanoum ever to emerge. Such problems are sometimes addressed very frankly by the excavators in their published reports. In the mid-1970s, the French Ministry of Foreign Affairs ceased to provide the same level of funding as before, and this budgetary reduction naturally had an impact on the excavations.[12] Erosion along the banks of the Oxus forced the team to concentrate their efforts on the western fortification wall and fountain while they still could rather than on other areas of the upper and lower city that they had planned to explore.[13] The surface terrain of the upper city and its elevation above the plain made it difficult to work there and to remove spoil in any quantity.[14] Faced with the immense size of the gymnasium and its various different periods of occupation and construction activity the excavators decided to dig sondages in several places rather than attempt complete and systematic excavation.[15] Under constraints of time and resources, these were such strategies as were adopted, giving us Ai Khanoum as we know it.

11. Mairs 2009.
12. Veuve 1987, 2.
13. Leriche and Thoraval 1979, 171–72.
14. Bernard in the preface to Leriche 1986, i.
15. Bernard 1978, 423.

The City

Ai Khanoum was built on an immense scale. Its main street, which runs along the foot of the "acropolis" or upper city, is around a kilometer and a half in length, and the longest side of the city's triangular site, along the northern fortification walls of the lower and upper city, stretches for around two and a half kilometers. The level of the upper city was around sixty meters higher than the lower city. Its institutions, too, were built on a colossal scale, with a gymnasium whose two square courts each had exterior sides of around one hundred meters and a theater with a capacity of over six thousand spectators. Ai Khanoum's latest Hellenistic phase, of the first half of the second century B.C.E., was the result of a major, centrally directed architectural program. Traces of the city's earlier layout (or layouts), however, can be seen in places: most visibly in the slightly awkward coexistence of two main axes, an original one parallel to the main street, a later one at an angle to this; and in the way in which the main approach to the palace detours off-axis in order to avoid the shrine of Kineas, one of the very earliest structures in the city, the essential orientation and layout of which was not disturbed despite renovations. This city planning is also very visible in the regular, equally sized units of the southern residential quarter. Stone is used sparingly throughout the city. Unbaked brick is the predominant building material, with baked brick much less in evidence. Constant renovations to the fortifications—necessitated not necessarily by military attack but by the weathering and the wear and tear to which raw mud-brick architecture is vulnerable—also show the resources and planning that went into designing and maintaining the urban fabric of the city.

Part of this planning was directed toward a functional zoning and architectural separation of different districts. The most extensive and most integrated treatment of urban planning and zoning at Ai Khanoum remains, unfortunately, unpublished: Jean-Claude Liger's *maîtrise* thesis of 1979, submitted at the Université de Paris VIII.[16] Despite the fact that this thesis is not widely available, it is worth briefly summarizing (and giving credit to) its contents and major arguments. Of particular interest is Liger's view that the spatial separation of various institutions and the establishment of strict routes of circulation relate to some form of social or ethnic segregation, or both, perhaps analogous to that in more recent colonial contexts. Such a modern, segregationalist colonial model is, of course, contradicted by the very visible interaction of different styles and techniques in the architecture and material culture of the site—and by the fact that the predominantly male Greek and Macedonian military settlers cannot have maintained strict social and matrimonial segregation from the locals, even if they had wanted to.[17] Nevertheless, in general, Liger identifies a clear distinction between a lower city—which

16. Liger 1979.
17. Discussed in Mairs 2011c, 179–82.

is broadly and overtly Greek and of high socioeconomic status, with fine monumental architecture—and a less developed and less impressive upper city, which is Bactrian and of low status. Whether these arguments, from an unpublished thesis, have made it directly into the subsequent literature is difficult to say, but similar arguments and views of the ethnic and cultural implications of Ai Khanoum's urban landscape have been made consistently over the intervening three decades.[18] My discussion of the social and ethnic implications of Ai Khanoum's design and use will follow in the sections below on individual aspects of the city's life and layout, with a briefer discussion here of the main lines of the layout of the urban landscape and access to particular zones. I will consider several of these complexes and categories of institution separately in what follows: the city's administrative buildings and focal points of civic identity; residential areas, both neighborhoods and suites within larger structures; temples and other cult sites, including burial places; the city's defensive structures; two centers of social and cultural life, the gymnasium and theater, which have particular associations with Greek identity (with a brief note on Greek literate culture at Ai Khanoum); and finally the city's water-management facilities, including drainage systems, fountains, and bathhouses.

The main buildings of the lower city show up very well on the few published aerial photographs, and their outlines may still be seen on Google Earth images (coordinates: 37°9′46.30″ N, 69°24′45.86″ E). The early sketch-plan of the city published in the *Kabul Times* in December 1964 also shows that the layout of the palace and the main street were clear on the ground before major excavations even began. (See the introduction.) There are areas, such as the southern residential quarter, where other unexcavated structures are or were quite visible from the air, but there are others where nothing is visible at all. With the proviso that much of the city's immense surface area was never subject to even exploratory excavations, the amount of apparently empty space is striking. The entire zone to the north of the gymnasium, inside the city wall, appears not to have been built on. Schlumberger describes the walls as floating around the built city "comme un vêtement trop large" and proposes that this enclosed space may have been kept empty for a good reason: as a place for mustering troops or as a refuge within the walls for the population of the surrounding plain in times of instability.[19] No later publication mentions any structure in this sector. One may also suggest that apparently "empty" spaces may not in fact have been empty (a proposition discussed further in chapter 4). They may have been occupied by construction in materials other than traditional brick or stone (tents, wood-and-daub shelters), or they may have

18. E.g., Holt 1999b, 45, on ethnic and class divisions between residents of the lower and the upper city, followed by Burstein 2012, 99.

19. Schlumberger 1965, 43.

been used for activities that did not necessarily require permanent buildings (gardens; open-air marketplaces, perhaps periodic; military training). The possible Achaemenid models or parallels for the central architectural complex at Ai Khanoum will be discussed in the next section, but in the matter of the general urban plan, too, Achaemenid analogies may be useful. The plans of Pasargadae and Susa, for example, offer a similar illusion of "emptiness," but these "empty" spaces may have been filled with lighter constructions or else used in ways (e.g., for gardens or recreation) that occupied them without leaving architectural remains.[20] The Ai Khanoum upper city, likewise, was largely free of structures; and here, as will be discussed below in the section on the city's defenses, this impression has been verified through the sinking of test pits. The acropolis, given its height, could not have been irrigated, although it is possible that the space was used as pasture for cavalry horses or livestock.[21] One gets the sense that the urban plan of Ai Khanoum was designed as much to enclose space as to bear intensive and extensive urbanization and that it may never have supported the level of population its size may initially suggest. This is also apparent within the central complexes: the gymnasium and above all the palace or administrative quarter have multiple very large walled enclosures. The main temple has a large sanctuary, and the arsenal and an unidentified public building to the south also have sizable courtyards. Ai Khanoum, viewed from the air, exhibits a remarkably open plan. Its open spaces may indeed have been designed to contribute to its grandeur in the same way as the monumental size of its public buildings. It may also be argued that—given the natural layout of the site, with the position of the acropolis drawing a natural boundary between its northern point and the Oxus, where the city's northern walls were constructed—the architects of Ai Khanoum had no choice other than to construct it on so grand a scale.

On the ground, however, a person moving through the city would have encountered multiple points where access was restricted, contrasting with several places where side passages or shortcuts allowed some individuals to bypass the major routes of circulation. An entire district of the city was set back from the main street through a monumental gateway,[22] in contrast to other buildings that faced directly onto the street (the theater, main temple, unidentified public building, arsenal). This district contained the entrance to the administrative quarter or palace, the two intramural mausolea, and probably also to the gymnasium. In practical terms, the gatehouse and stairway were necessary to manage a change in elevation, a drop of four to five meters below the level of the main street.[23] The propylaea, which

---

20. Boucharlat 2001.
21. Lerner 2003–4, 377.
22. Guillaume 1983.
23. Bernard et al. 1980, 7; Guillaume 1983, ix.

separated the street from the central district, are likely also to have served to restrict access to different buildings and zones of the city, or at the very least to create a visible, monumental expression of the city's zoning.

Within the palace or administrative quarter (I will return to terminological questions below), there were many points at which access was restricted. The main courtyard led back to a series of more private chambers: a columned entrance hall, open to the courtyard; a reception room behind a door; an inner suite of rooms, linked by corridors, in which several groups of people might work or be received without having to encroach on one another's spaces or even be visible; and finally, in the southwestern corner, residential units. Two long corridors, each with several doors, led directly from the main courtyard to the innermost rooms, allowing direct access to certain people, presumably high officials or residents. The ways in which these features aided the working life of the administrative center will be discussed in the next section.

The treasury, which in the last phase of the palace was located to the west of the main courtyard, also had several entrances, with different degrees of closure or protection. A passageway (with no doors) led into a columned courtyard in the interior of the complex, which itself was linked both to one of the inner residential units and to one of the multidoored corridors. Another entrance, however, led across a narrow corridor directly onto the great court, and this was designed to be closed, with a limestone threshold and setting for a wooden door. This entrance may have been intended for employees coming to work from outside the administrative complex and for deliveries of the many commodities stored and inventoried there. In addition, there were blocked-up entranceways in the exterior, western wall of the treasury, which remained in active use only for a very brief period during the unit's construction and would have been used for access by workmen and to bring in construction materials.[24]

Northwest of the palace, between the great court and the gymnasium, lay a walled enclosure with a pool, of which only the southern and western limits have been excavated. It had at least one entrance, in the western wall, which led onto a street that ran north to south along the city's fortifications on the bank of the Oxus. The enclosure had no direct link to the gymnasium, but both had entrances onto the street by the Oxus, in theory allowing people to pass between the two structures. It may therefore be interpreted as having some connection with the gymnasium, as a source of water for athletes' ablutions. Alternatively, it may be compared to the gardens with water features associated with other Hellenistic palaces. (See below.) Or, more prosaically, it could have been used to corral water beasts of burden.[25] These would have had to enter the central administrative zone along the

24. Rapin 1992, 20–22.
25. Ibid. 20.

Oxus street or by some other route, since the passage through the propylaea from the main street had steps.

The street by the Oxus led between the gymnasium (and whatever, if anything, lay north of it) and a southern residential district of large houses. Here, too, it is possible to make some suggestions about how social and ethnic factors influenced urban zoning at Ai Khanoum. Although residents of this wealthy quarter of the city must have provided at least some of the gymnasium's constituency, however, it is best to remain open-minded about "who" (ethnically, culturally, linguistically) these people were and whether the gymnasium also drew attendees from else-where.

The southern neighborhood was not the only residential area of the city, although it is the one with the largest houses and most regular street-plan. There were smaller concentrations of more humble dwellings (of shorter duration) on top of the acropolis and against its southern slope. Outside the northern walls was another large house, and of course the agricultural hinterland of the city bore a sizable population (chapter 1). Some public buildings (the palace, the unidentified public building) also had residential units, which may lead us to particular conclu-sions about the function of these buildings.

Much about the city's urban plan, however, remains unknown and is now unknowable. The public buildings along the southern part of the main street have been only partly excavated. A long depression between the buildings on this street and the palace may or may not contain a possible stadium. The large open courts in the far southern part of the palace are still of unknown function and must prob-ably have had some entrance from the main street. As Liger notes,[26] such an entranceway would have been necessary to access this area on horseback or with pack animals, since the main entrance through the propylaea had a staircase. Such logistical questions are useful in thinking about how the city functioned in practi-cal terms. As well as the architecturally visible restrictions on access and line of sight, differences in elevation across the site—not just between the upper and lower cities but within these—must have considerably impacted how space was used and perceived.

The Central Complex

Overview.   The lower city at Ai Khanoum is dominated by a complex of buildings known in publications on the site as the palace or administrative quarter. This complex, as has already been discussed, lies off the main street behind a monu-mental gateway, which serves both to mark this district off and to manage a sig-nificant change in elevation. The main complex is composed of a large peristyle

26. Liger 1979, 38.

courtyard and an attached building, divided up into blocks that had different functions: offices and meeting rooms, residential units, baths, and the treasury, which was discussed in chapter 1. The central question is what type of administrative or political authority this structure housed: a palace on an Achaemenid or Hellenistic model, which was the seat of a representative of royal authority, or a more neutral administrative quarter, whose functions and functionaries we cannot identify with confidence. I argue for the former, on the basis of distinctive features and potential analogies to be outlined below. There is, furthermore, much to be gained from considering the whole quarter behind the propylaea—palace, treasury, mausolea, gymnasium, open-air pool—as a single supercomplex. Although, as will be discussed, the palace complex at Ai Khanoum shares many features and functions with various Achaemenid and Hellenistic palaces, there are also elements that are quintessentially Graeco-Bactrian. One of the most important of these is the use of peripheral corridors to isolate individual units of a building from each other. This was a distinctive feature of local Hellenistic-Bactrian architecture, as can be seen also from the houses inside and outside Ai Khanoum, and to a lesser extent in another structure excavated at Saksanokhur, a site to the north of the Oxus.

In its construction materials and provision for climatic conditions, too, the Ai Khanoum palace is very much a building of Central Asia.[27] The walls were preserved in places up to a height of two to three meters. Construction was predominantly in raw mud-brick, with more sparing use of baked brick (especially for elements such as the foundations of walls) and very little stone (a soft white limestone) for items such as columns, door thresholds, and the foundations of some walls. Stone was not available locally, but there are several possible quarry sites upriver from which stone could have been transported by water.[28] Wood, which was found carbonized by fire in several places, was used as an inner support for walls (and also for clay and stucco statuary) and for roof beams. Roofs were tiled, with different styles of antefixes in such shapes as palmettes. The orientation of the courtyards of various structures—the palace and the houses—was dictated by the climate, to turn their backs on rain-bearing winds coming from the southwest. In the palace, where the rooms of the interior were lit by windows high in the walls, orientation may also have been influenced by a desire to catch the sunlight at different times of day. A drainage system, with pipes and open-air basins, took rainwater from the main court and channeled it out toward the river through a channel under the treasury, among others.[29]

27. Bernard 1973, 7–17.

28. Bernard (1973, 11, 244–45) regards the most likely source as around 30 km upstream on the right bank of the Oxus, in the Parkhar anticline by the Qizil Su River.

29. Ibid. 35–36.

Most of the rooms of the palace—or at least most of those excavated—lay in a complex to the south of the great court. This complex contained a number of rooms probably for official business (reception rooms, offices) and a residential area. The internal configuration of the palace was such that rooms were divided into individual smaller units by a system of corridors, which had the effect of isolating them from each other and restricting direct access. There are, however, several long corridors that allow a person, in theory, to pass from the great court right into the innermost chambers of the palace without passing through the formal reception areas or the reception rooms and offices of the interior.[30] These were constricted by a series of doors and were evidently intended only for individuals with special permission. One such corridor, which passed from the great court along the eastern side of the palace's interior units, passed all the way through to the back of the palace to another massive open-air court. A further, smaller, open court lay to the east of this corridor. Unlike the great court, these courtyards did not have colonnades. They have not been fully excavated, and it is difficult to say much about their function, but the larger southern court, at least, seems to have communicated with other structures or yards to the south. Bernard suggests that they may have been used for stationing troops,[31] and there are of course numerous other possible functions.

The main entrance to the palace building is in the middle of the southern side of the peristyle great court and takes the form of a columned porch, set three rows of column deep behind the peristyle. This kind of porch is often designated in the literature as an *iwan*,[32] a term taken from the later architecture of Persia and Central Asia, indicating a high, roofed entrance hall, completely open on one side. The columned iwan, as will be seen, is a common feature of Graeco-Bactrian architecture.

Behind the iwan, through a slightly off-center doorway, was a large hall (room 3).[33] It had no internal supports (or at least none in imperishable materials) but probably cannot have been open to the elements: it had no system of drainage, such as that in the open-air great court, and had a decorative scheme that would quickly have deteriorated if exposed to too much sun or rain.[34] This decoration comprised wooden half-columns against the walls, with clay sculptural decoration, now in fragments, including small lion heads (ca. 7–8 cm across), their manes and muzzles painted in yellow and their features in black. The walls themselves

30. Bernard 1971, 386–88.

31. Ibid. 388.

32. Although there are more current systems of transliteration from Persian, for ease of reference I retain the spelling used in the publications cited here.

33. Bernard 1973, 50–53.

34. Ibid. 54–55.

were covered in painted daub, with geometric designs in red, yellow, and white, with black lines and dots against a lighter background.

Behind the iwan and the first main hall, the architectural plan of the building becomes increasingly complex and sophisticated. This complexity is not the product of a gradual, unplanned evolution in the building's form but is a deliberately organized architectural scheme, implemented in the grand renovation program of the last phase of Ai Khanoum. This plan is characterized by a network of long corridors that isolate individual units from each other. Doors between corridors and rooms are almost always offset, so that there are few direct axes—direct lines of movement and sight—outside the corridors themselves, and even where there are no remains of an actual door, access was indirect. The columned iwan (2) and hall (3) are themselves separated by a large door with a stone threshold, with cavities in the masonry where the mechanism of a wooden door would have fitted. Some pieces of ivory were found in the vicinity, indicating that the door was decorated with this material.[35] These doors between units and corridors were very real points of restriction, which could be locked rather than just closed.[36]

The internal configuration of the innermost area of the palace is such that it is divided into four main units: two apparently official, for reception or administration, and two residential. Directly behind the iwan and main hall—but not in direct communication with them—is a square block composed of two nearly identical pairs of units, separated by a cross-shaped corridor. The whole block could be isolated from its peripheral corridors by wooden doors with stone thresholds.[37] Each of these units contained a reception unit to the east (identified thus because of the size of the rooms and their fine decoration) with one large room and two or more antechambers, and to the west an "office unit" with a smaller central room and greater number of subsidiary chambers. Each unit had a vestibule with a hearth for heating.[38] The units nestled like Russian dolls within their peripheral corridors. To get from the main hall behind the iwan to the (spatially very close) reception rooms, a person would have to cross no fewer than three of these isolating corridors.

The main rooms (6 and 9) of the reception units were decorated with stucco and clay statues on wooden armatures, including in room 9 at least fifteen human figures of different proportions and in room 6 one or more human figures, two to three times life-size, as well as a horse. The colors are vividly preserved on some fragments of these statues: vermilion, pale pink, brown-black, and a goldish yel-

35. Ibid. 51.
36. Rapin 1992, pls. 58, 59, 114, for illustrations and photographs of lock-and-key mechanisms found in the treasury.
37. Bernard 1973, 64.
38. Ibid. 74–75.

low, evidently aiming for some kind of naturalism.[39] These sculptures, in their artistic style and technique of workmanship, are visibly the forerunners of the later art of the Kushan empire, such as the figures of Khalchayan, a site in northern Bactria.[40] The rooms bore a similar kind of decoration, with half-columns in wood, as room 3, the hall behind the iwan, with the difference that they had stone pilasters. Many of these pilasters were reworked and reused blocks, as can be seen from the traces of old mortar on them. These half-columns were topped with stone capitals in high relief, painted in black, red, green, and yellow, on a whitewashed background.[41] Further stone fragments in one of the rooms appear to come from two arched niches somewhere in the east wall, perhaps above the level of the pilasters, to let in light.[42] The decoration scheme was elaborate, brightly colored, and visually striking.

The other rooms of the reception units separated them from the internal corridors of the square block. The entrances were offset, so that there was no direct line of access or sight, but show no evidence that they had doors. Each of the two antechambers accessed a different arm of the cross-shaped corridor. The antechambers would work well as waiting or meeting rooms. What the double system of entrances, vestibules, and corridors also means is that, should it have been desirable, two separate groups of people may have been kept waiting at the same time, and that these groups may moreover have been dealt with and may have entered and left without the other group seeing them. Bernard suggests that the reason for having two parallel reception-office complexes was that each was intended to the use of a different official in the palace administration, perhaps two kings of a co-regency or a local governor assisted by a military commander or royal official.[43] It is not necessary, however, to posit a bipartite political system: it may simply have been convenient to have more than one such suite of rooms.

Because of the disturbance of material in the period of the reoccupation of the city in the latter part of the second century B.C.E., it is difficult to say much more about the function of these rooms during their working lives. But some of the rooms in the palace look like excellent places to keep people waiting and potentially to keep several groups of people waiting separately. In its final phase, which is what we have, this is a very carefully thought-out space and must represent a renovation carried out in full awareness of what this space was needed to do, and what problems its earlier incarnations may have had. Another clever aspect of the space is how it can be approached in two ways: along the main axis, with its

39. Bernard 1967b, 319; 1968b, 269–71; and 1973, 68–69, 189–93.
40. Pugachenkova 1965; Nehru 1999–2000.
41. Bernard 1973, 63–67.
42. Ibid. 68.
43. Bernard 1974b, 291–92.

impressive reception and waiting rooms, or through routes designed to circumvent this for everyday users of the building.

To the west of the office and reception units, the two adjacent residential complexes are both divided and linked by the same large north-to-south corridor, with several internal doorways, that runs down the western side of the great court. The larger unit, to the east, has its own court and iwan, and is separated from the smaller, to the west, by a peripheral isolating corridor. It is tempting to identify these as men's and women's quarters, but we really know too little about the social structure of Ai Khanoum and Hellenistic Bactria in general to make such assumptions. These residential units are comparable in plan to the private houses of Ai Khanoum. The units are self-contained, but with connections to the corridors and, indirectly, the official rooms. One of the larger rooms of the western block (77) was decorated with a clay relief, fragments of which indicate that it may have been a series of busts, some of them female.[44] Both units had bathing complexes with pebble mosaics and the same layout as baths elsewhere in the city.[45] The existence of a bath complex under the portion of the palace immediately to the south of the great court may indicate that the palace had some residential function even at the time of its construction or that it contained public baths.[46] To the north of the western residential unit (but, as typically, separated from it by yet another corridor) was an internal peristyle courtyard, and to the north of this was the treasury.

The treasury building in its preserved form, the unit to the southwest of the great court and directly to the north of the western residential unit, was an innovation of the final phase of the palace. In the preceding phase, it was located elsewhere, probably in the unexcavated rooms off the east side of the great court.[47] Like other parts of the palace, the remains of the treasury show how access was managed and restricted. There were several blocked-up entranceways in the western, external wall, used for access of workers and materials during construction and subsequently blocked up.[48] To the south, where a passageway leads into a peristyle courtyard, which further gives access into the innermost apartments of the palace, there is no evidence of provisions for closing. The only other entrance to the treasury was to the east, into the great court, but this was indirect—across an intervening isolating corridor—and had a doorway with a stone threshold and for a wooden door.[49] Employees or others with business in the treasury could thus be permitted entry from the great court. The jobs that these employees did in the

44. Bernard 1976a, 291.
45. Ibid.; Bernard 1975, 173–80.
46. Bernard 1971, 389.
47. Rapin 1992, 11.
48. Ibid. 21–22.
49. Ibid. 20.

treasury have already been discussed in chapter 1. Some of the tools of their trade were preserved in the treasury: seals, writing materials (inkwells and pens), lamps, weights, and measures.[50] One of the storerooms may have been a library: it was here that the two literary texts were found.[51]

This, then, was the main palace building. Traces of additional buildings were visible at the time of excavation, to the east of the main court.[52] Further along the main street, immediately south of the temple sanctuary, was another large public building—with a courtyard and an adjacent residential unit—which was not fully excavated or published, and the function of which remains uncertain.[53] It may well have been linked, architecturally or functionally, or both, to the palace. I will consider several other structures as hypothetically belonging to the same super-complex before returning to the architectural scheme of the palace and what this may tell us about the building's function.

Two mausolea, small two- or three-roomed shrines with burial vaults atop platforms, within their own walled enclosures, lay to the north and south of the palace complex's entrance street. The southern mausoleum, at least, appears to have connected directly with this street, whereas too little is known of the enclosure wall of the northern one (at any rate according to the published plans) to say whether the same is true for it. The southern mausoleum, the shrine of Kineas, has been widely discussed, perhaps more than any other structure at Ai Khanoum.[54] This is because it was the findspot of one of the very few Greek inscriptions from Ai Khanoum, and because we may identify the person in whose honor it was constructed.

This is the inscription that I mentioned in the opening paragraph of the introduction. It states that one Klearchos copied down the famous sayings of wise men from Delphi and brought them here to be set up in the *temenos*—sanctuary—of Kineas. On the left-hand side of the inscription, there is preserved a small sample of these wise sayings. The preserved portion of the inscription was the socketed base of a larger stone text, which survives only in small fragments, only one of which bears further legible text:[55]

50. Ibid. 131–37.

51. Rapin and Hadot 1987, Lerner 2003.

52. These are sketched in Rapin 1992, pl. 6.

53. Bernard 1980a, 451–52; Bernard et al. 1980, 46–50.

54. See the fundamental studies of the inscriptions (Robert 1968) and of the architecture (Bernard, Le Berre, and Stucki 1973); recent discussions include Lerner 2003–4; Mairs 2007, 2014a.

55. Text: Robert 1968; Canali De Rossi 2004 (*IK Estremo Oriente*), 182–84. For an edition of the inscription with the complete text of the Delphic maxims—almost all of it in the square brackets used by epigraphers to mark reconstructed text—see Canali De Rossi 2004 (*IK Estremo Oriente*), 183.

... speak well of everyone; be a lover of wisdom. . . .

These wise sayings of men of old, the maxims of renowned men, are enshrined in the holy Pytho [i.e., at Delphi]. There Klearchos copied them conscientiously, and he set them up here in the sanctuary of Kineas, blazing them from afar.

As a child, be well behaved; as a young man, self-controlled; in middle age, be just; as an elder, be of good counsel; and when you come to the end, be without grief.

The vault beneath the shrine contained several burials in sarcophagi, one of which had provisions for liquid offerings to be made from the room above, through a conduit, directly into the coffin—which we may then suppose to be that of the Kineas of the inscription. The early date of the shrine (it is one of the few structures at Ai Khanoum whose earliest phases have been traced back to the late fourth century)[56] and its veneration of a named figure within the city walls suggest that Kineas was regarded as the founder of the Greek city of Ai Khanoum. The positioning of the vault's additional burials indicates that they belonged to different phases of the shrine's construction:[57] successive generations of a family or, alternatively, a series of magistrates or high officials, themselves successors in a different sense to Kineas? In addition to libations made from the chamber above the burial vault, in Phase III of the structure the northern and western outer walls of the shrine had two long niches, perhaps for additional offerings.[58] These would have been clearly visible from both arms of the street leading to the palace courtyard.

The connection to a wider Greek world that the inscription claims, or to which it aspires, through the reference to the Delphic maxims has naturally provoked much comment. The inscription is one of several features—the gymnasium and theater, the other Greek inscriptions, literary and documentary texts—commonly invoked in support of the notion that Ai Khanoum is a "Greek city in Central Asia."[59] Louis Robert suggested that the Klearchos of the inscription should be identified with the historical Klearchos of Soloi, a pupil of Aristotle who wrote extensively on Eastern philosophies; but this is of course a hypothesis—albeit an attractive one—and ultimately unverifiable.[60]

The northern mausoleum yielded no such inscription identifying its occupants. Like the shrine of Kineas, it contained multiple burials interred over a period of time. These were within a vault made of stone, a material used only infrequently at Ai Khanoum—the structure is conventionally known as the "hérôon au caveau de

---

56. For further discussion see Lerner 2003–4.
57. Bernard, Le Berre, and Stucki 1973, 93–94.
58. Ibid. 92.
59. Bernard 1982b.
60. Robert 1968; Lerner 2003–4. Narain 1987 also doubts Robert's identification with Klearchos of Soloi.

pierre" (*heröon* with stone vault).[61] The occupants of this vault have not been identified (some are women and children), but there is, I argue, a case to be made that they are members of a ruling family of some sort at Ai Khanoum—whether this be royal or a lineage of governors or "big men"—and further that we should associate this group of people in some way with the residential units within the palace.[62] This shrine to a prominent family, along with the palace's residential units, is part of the reason why I have chosen to designate the palace as such and to suppose that the government of Ai Khanoum and its district was in the hands of a high official whose position was kept in the family, so to speak, for more than one generation.

It is worth making an aside to briefly discuss the other burial places at Ai Khanoum, which are outside its walls.[63] By the time of excavation, modern cultivation had encroached sufficiently that little remained of the cemetery under the northern slope of the acropolis. The one excavated mausoleum had a format very different from those inside the walls. It consisted of partially subterranean vaulted chambers with a solid brick superstructure, which did not bear any shrine or building. It contained two types of burial: in sarcophagi and in jars, the latter perhaps representing secondary inhumation of older remains from tombs that had been reused or destroyed. The jars bore names and identifying captions in Greek: "of Lysanias," "of Isidora," "of the (male) little one and the (female) little one," "of Kosmos."[64] Two longer Greek inscriptions found in the extramural cemetery have recently been published, but they are, unfortunately, too fragmentary to yield much connected text.[65] A stone relief depicting a youth in classical style was also found nearby. Of ostensibly Greek burial in Hellenistic Bactria we really know little else.[66] A fragmentary Greek funerary inscription on a ceramic plaque was found at the site of Zhiga-tepe in the Bactra oasis, belonging to a man named Diogenes and—if the proposed restorations are correct—with a reference to Hades.[67] But this is without further architectural context.

Functional and Architectural Comparanda.   The central complex is referred to in the initial reports on the excavations at Ai Khanoum as either the "palais" or the more neutral "quartier administratif." The former comes to predominate, and I

---

61. Francfort and Liger 1976; see also, briefly, Grenet 1984, H9.

62. Suggested in Mairs 2006a, 77–82, and briefly in Mairs 2014a; Canepa 2010a, 8–10, identifies the structure as a royal mausoleum.

63. Bernard 1972, 608–25.

64. Canali De Rossi 2004, nos. 360–62.

65. Rougemont 2012, nos. 136, 137.

66. See the discussion in Mairs 2007.

67. Zhiga-tepe: Pugachenkova 1979, Pidaev 1984. The inscription: Canali De Rossi 2004, no. 304; Kruglikova 1977, 425 fig. 16; Pugachenkova 1979, 74–75; Litvinskii, Vinogradov, and Pichikyan 1985; (Vinogradov) ibid. 104–5; Bernard 1987a, 112–13.

also refer to the central complex of public buildings at Ai Khanoum as the "palace," because it appears to fulfill some of the same functions as other "palaces" in the Achaemenid empire, the Near East, and the Graeco-Macedonian world and to have certain common formats that reflect these shared functions and, potentially, also architectural inspiration. Like some other regional palaces,[68] that at Ai Khanoum need not necessarily have been the seat of a royal family for any or all of its active life, but it did contain residential accommodation for some prominent local family, perhaps that of a regional governor.

Comparisons are most frequently drawn with the palaces of the Achaemenid empire—and there are indeed certain similarities—but there are also many ways in which the Ai Khanoum palace is different. The structures of the Persepolis terrace,[69] for example, do not really work as a comparison, and there is no reason why they should. If we are to look for the origins of Ai Khanoum's architecture in the Achaemenid empire (as I think we ought to do) and in terms of administrative functions, Persepolis is simply the wrong place to look. Its construction (in the late sixth century B.C.E.) and active life are far earlier than the Ai Khanoum palace. Its functions are also very different: Persepolis was the capital of an empire, the seat of an emperor, and it fulfilled important ceremonial functions. Its reliefs depict subject peoples bringing tribute to the Great King, and part of the complex appears to have been designed to house a "harem." The Ai Khanoum palace gives the same impression of wealth and grandeur, and shares a layout of grand courts surrounded by complexes of official and residential units. Such grandeur and "size for the sake of size" could, of course, be a political statement in themselves.[70] But on finer levels of detail the comparison between Ai Khanoum and Achaemenid *royal* palaces such as that at Persepolis breaks down.[71]

The most important differences between the layout of the Ai Khanoum palace and its potential Achaemenid royal comparanda are:

1. The use of the distinctive isolating corridors to separate units within the building. In the Persepolis platform complex, corridors are, indeed, used not just to communicate between rooms but to section off different areas. This is most visible in the apartments of the "harem." But the isolating corridors of Hellenistic-Bactrian palatial and residential architecture are used more widely and systematically than potential comparanda in Achaemenid palaces.

68. For example, some of those discussed in Nielsen 2001a.

69. Schmidt 1953.

70. Veuve 1987, 104.

71. Similar points may be made for the palace of Darius I at Susa: see most recently Amiet 2010; on the development of Achaemenid palaces, see Stronach 2001.

2. The feature of the open court with an iwan, with the main building-complex lying behind this, in contrast to the courtyard surrounded on all sides with buildings—as found, for example, at Persepolis.
3. The Ai Khanoum palace lacks any equivalent of the "apadana" features or hypostyle halls found in several Achaemenid palaces (e.g., Persepolis, Susa). There is a preference instead for open-air spaces.

There are possible practical reasons for these differences, but they also reflect differences in function. The idiosyncratic features of the Ai Khanoum palace have the potential to tell us something about social structures and organizations, or simply ways of doing business, that were peculiar to Bactria and may have been inherited from preexisting Achaemenid or Seleucid systems of organization. As will also be discussed in the next section, on domestic architecture, many of the excavated public and private buildings at Ai Khanoum reflect a distinctive Graeco-Bactrian idiom, which may be argued to have had its roots in Achaemenid Bactria or still earlier. I will shortly discuss local Bactrian comparanda, of the Hellenistic and Kushan periods, but I turn first to a place where I think we may look more productively for architectural and functional comparanda for the Ai Khanoum palace than in imperial centers such as Persepolis and Susa: in the regional administrative centers or gubernational seats of the Achaemenid and Hellenistic empires.

However hazy its architectural origins, there is much to be gained from regarding the Ai Khanoum central complex as a palace in the Achaemenid or Hellenistic sense, a building with a particular set of functions that acts as an administrative and ceremonial center for an area, whether a local district or an entire empire. I follow Inge Nielsen's practical definition of a palace as a building that combines an official and a residential function, whether as the seat of a king or a governor or other local official; and I note that the Ai Khanoum palace fulfills most of her functional and featural criteria for identifying a palace.[72]

The most important question is not how closely it adheres to some model floor plan for an Achaemenid or Hellenistic palace (and it really does not conform closely to any excavated Achaemenid or Hellenistic example) but how far the features of the Ai Khanoum palace demonstrate that it was designed to fulfill the same functions.[73] Nielsen's decision to include Ai Khanoum in her study of Hellenistic palaces demonstrates how much is to be gained from discussing Ai Khanoum as one would any other case study in a wider discussion of the Hellenistic world. I am in broad agreement with her analysis, which views the Ai Khanoum central complex as in origin the seat of a Seleucid governor and later the palace of

72. Nielsen 1994, 11, 14.

73. See Kopsacheili 2011 for a useful comparative discussion of Hellenistic palaces and their Achaemenid and Macedonian antecedents.

a local dynast. I propose in addition, however, that the original Hellenistic palace at Ai Khanoum either was built directly on the site of an Achaemenid predecessor or at least drew on local Achaemenid architectural and administrative models.

If one includes the adjacent mausolea, gymnasium, and pool enclosure, the Ai Khanoum structure fulfills most functions of other Hellenistic palaces.[74] Comparison with such other palaces, furthermore, offers precedents for the co-occurrence of these features at Ai Khanoum and explanations of the political significance that their adjacency to this complex may have had. It is significant that the palaces of the Hellenistic world often incorporated places of recreation and education—and of culture-specific Greek forms of recreation and education, as in gymnasia and palaestrae. If we identify the pool enclosure that lies between the main palace and the gymnasium as a garden, then this could be paralleled by the large parks surrounding Hellenistic palaces, or the courtyard-gardens that may have been contained within them, for which the *paradeisoi* of Achaemenid palaces offered models.[75]

One of the Greek words used for such a garden is *alsos*,[76] a term that occurs in an unprovenanced Greek inscription supposedly from Kuliab, in what is now southern Tajikistan.[77] A man named Heliodotos dedicates an altar to Hestia, for the sake of the kings Euthydemos and Demetrios, in the *alsos* of Zeus. Without further information on its provenance, it is impossible to say what kind of archaeological context this inscription came from, or whether it may even have come from Ai Khanoum—which is not impossible—or whether its Greek description accurately represents the site and practices that it claims to. What is significant for the purposes of the present discussion is that, already in the very late third or early second century B.C.E., decades before the final architectural program at Ai Khanoum, we find a garden dedicated to a Greek deity being used as a place for an individual's demonstration of political loyalty. A garden space such as the one in the central complex at Ai Khanoum could be used as a theater for all sorts of religious and political acts and performances.

Moving on from matters of function, a specific Hellenistic architectural comparison sometimes invoked for the Ai Khanoum palace is that of the Seleucid-period "citadel-palace" at Doura-Europos, on the bank of the Euphrates in what is now eastern Syria.[78] The second phase of this latter is roughly contemporary with the last major phase of the Ai Khanoum palace, in the second quarter of the second century B.C.E. There are some superficial resemblances, somewhat compro-

74. Nielsen 1994, 124–29; cat. no. 19: 280–82.
75. Nielsen 2001a, 167–68.
76. E.g., Strabo 17.1.8 on the *alsos* of the palace at Alexandria in Egypt.
77. Bernard, Pinault, and Rougemont 2004, 333–56; Mairs forthcoming (1).
78. Downey 1986.

mised by the fact that only part of the structure at Doura has been excavated. The principal point of comparison is a subcomplex, probably residential, that lies to the south of a courtyard and communicates with it only indirectly across an intervening corridor. But this is really as far as the comparison can be taken. If there is indeed a connection between the Doura citadel-palace and the complex at Ai Khanoum, then it is indirect. Like the temples at Doura, which share a similar superficial similarity to the Ai Khanoum temples,[79] the forms are at most cousins, common descendants of Achaemenid traditions. Tracing these potential connections, however, is made difficult because we lack knowledge of the earlier phases of these buildings.

Where we do find the closest and most compelling architectural comparanda for the Ai Khanoum palace (and also domestic architecture) is locally, as may be expected, where several excavated structures of the Hellenistic and Kushan periods are visibly phrased in the same Graeco-Bactrian architectural vernacular. Perhaps the most compelling such comparison is to be made with a structure at Saksanokhur, in southern Tajikistan, thirty-five kilometers northeast of Ai Khanoum as the crow flies.[80] A citadel with a fortified palace (and possibly also cult) structure and a nearby artisans' quarter were excavated in the 1960s and 1970s, while excavations at Ai Khanoum were going on to the south. The excavators of each site made reference to the other in their publications,[81] and comparisons were made both with the architectural plans of the two palaces and with individual elements such as stone column bases and capitals. Saksanokhur is the closest and most compelling relative of the Ai Khanoum structures. It reinforces the idea of a local Hellenistic-Bactrian architectural *koinē,* which evolved in part from Achaemenid and Seleucid models, one that we may differentiate even from that of the Indo-Greek kingdoms.[82] Coins, ceramics, and other finds date the active life of the Saksanokhur building from the second century B.C.E. (i.e., the late Graeco-Bactrian period in this region) into the Kushan period, the second to third centuries C.E. Unfortunately, these dates mean that it cannot elucidate much about the origins and development of a "Graeco-Bactrian school."

The excavated structures at Saksanokhur were only a small part of a much larger site, most of which had been leveled and plowed over in more recent times. What survived was the highest point of the settlement, with the "palace-temple complex." As at Ai Khanoum, the buildings are mostly constructed of rammed earth (Persian *pakhsa*) and mud brick, covered with adobe or plaster, with only

79. Downey 1988; Mairs 2013c.

80. Published in Litvinskii and Mukhitdinov 1969 and Mukhitdinov 1968; see also Litvinskii 1998, 54–56.

81. Bernard 1970a; Litvinskii and Mukhitdinov 1969.

82. Fussman 1993b, 95–96.

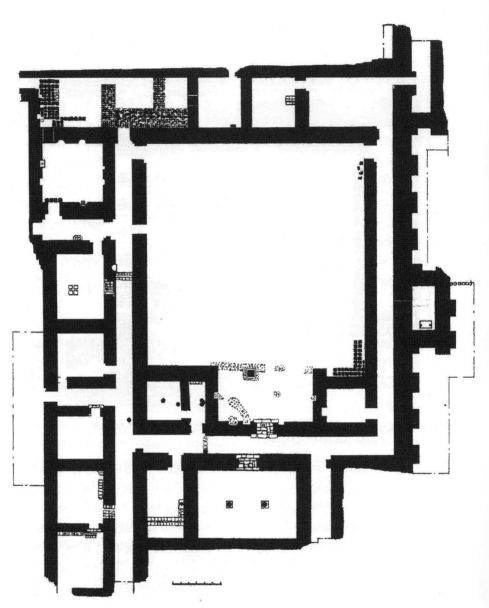

FIGURE 6. The Saksanokhur palace. (North at top; © Deutsches Archäologisches Institut.)

some elements in stone, such as column bases and capitals. Two Corinthian capitals are similar in design to those from Ai Khanoum. At least one of the rooms had painted wall decoration.

In building materials and in design, the Saksanokhur palace is clearly related to the palace and residential buildings at Ai Khanoum. A large central courtyard (27.7 × 27.7 m) had at its southern end a columned iwan through which a person might pass into a peripheral corridor and thence into an internal columned hall. The peripheral corridor surrounded the courtyard on its western and eastern sides; to the north was a line of rooms, none of which opened onto the courtyard itself. There was no direct line of approach or sight to the courtyard from outside. Several individual blocks of two or three rooms were insulated from the courtyard by the peripheral corridor. Again as at Ai Khanoum, lines of movement around the complex were deliberately made indirect, and there are no straight axes; the entrances between the iwan, the inner corridor, and the columned hall are offset by around a meter.[83] On the eastern side, the exterior wall of the building was exposed; this was fortified with buttresses and, at least in the earlier period of the building's functioning, a tower.

The complex had impressive reception rooms as well as private residential quarters. It was fortified and stood on the highest point of the settlement. Fragments of large ceramic vessels found in two of the rooms indicate that they were storerooms. Whether the complex had an additional cultic function is more controversial. Boris Litvinskii and Khurshed Mukhitdinov argue that it did,[84] but Boris Staviskij sheds doubt on the excavators' identification of "altars" in several of the rooms and points out that they may (like the fireplaces at Ai Khanoum) have simply been used for heating.[85] In any case, the Saksanokhur palace serves many of the same functions as the palace at Ai Khanoum and is built according to a similar plan, using similar materials and forms of architectural decoration.

In its floor plan at least, the Saksanokhur palace is therefore far closer to the Ai Khanoum palace and houses than any of the potential comparanda from the West already discussed. Given the two sites' chronology, of course, the Saksanokhur palace cannot have been the model for the Ai Khanoum palace, but rather vice versa. If the two sites had any overlap in their periods of occupation, that must have been at most a few decades in the mid-second century B.C.E.[86] Even if this does not give us the model for the Ai Khanoum palace (for reasons discussed in this and the preceding chapter I take this to have been in the Achaemenid-period architecture of Bactria), it does show that the Ai Khanoum model was one that

83. Litvinskii and Mukhitdinov 1969, 174–75.

84. Litvinskii and Mukhitdinov 1969.

85. Staviskij 1986, 220–21.

86. On the dating of Saksanokhur as largely post-Graeco-Bactrian, see also Francfort 1977, 274–75.

continued to have an influence and to be diffused beyond the site itself. Once again, the most productive approach is to look at Ai Khanoum in a local context. The fact that Saksanokhur continued to be occupied through into the second and third centuries C.E., the period of the Kushan empire, also shows the existence of some long-standing local architectural tradition;[87] furthermore, Saksanokhur provides an example of the kind of long-term administrative and socioeconomic continuity argued in chapter 1. This is an actual physical institution that continued to function in some way across political changes.

My discussion of Saksanokhur leads on naturally to a consideration of domestic architecture, which will be covered in the next section. But in analyzing the function of the Ai Khanoum palace, it is important not to artificially separate out the domestic from the official architectural context. The existence of residential suites within administrative buildings—like the presence of family crypts with provisions for cult offerings in the central neighborhood of the lower city—has the potential to tell us something about the manner in which Ai Khanoum was governed, at least in the last decades of its existence. Both are suggestive of one or more families' holding significant political power in Ai Khanoum, perhaps a dynasty of local governors, or of the city's having at some point become a seat of royal authority. Although a site, in a region, of prime strategic and economic importance, Ai Khanoum was not (at least initially) a royal capital. But the evidence does, I think, point in the direction of its having been the seat of a Graeco-Bactrian governor, and perhaps previously an Achaemenid governor, managing the region from and resident in the palace. The mausoleum with a stone vault, likewise, is a possible candidate for the burial place of a powerful local family. The potential for administrative continuity here (as discussed in chapter 1) already destabilizes any notion that we may have of Ai Khanoum as a purely Greek colonial creation, whether politically or culturally.

DOMESTIC ARCHITECTURE

In addition to the residential units within the palace, large houses with similar layouts were found both inside and outside the city walls. Like the palace, these have often been compared with and contrasted to residential structures elsewhere in the Near Eastern or the Mediterranean world. Although there may be some connection to common Near Eastern architectural traditions, describing the houses of Ai Khanoum in terms of, for example, Persepolis or Olynthos is misleading. They are best treated as local forms of Hellenistic Bactria and as to some extent responses to the local environment.

Much of the southern part of the lower city, to the south and west of the main public buildings on and off the main street, was occupied by large private houses

87. See, e.g., Pugachenkova 1990.

laid out in regular rows. Only one has been excavated, but the placement and plans of the others are visible on aerial photographs.[88] The excavated house consists of a rectangular walled enclosure with an open-air courtyard in the northern half and roofed accommodation in the south. The house proper opens off the courtyard though a small, columned iwan-porch, in a way similar to the complex behind the great court of the palace. This porch is part of a three-room inner complex of (presumably) reception rooms, separated off from the surrounding rooms by a surrounding corridor. Like similar residential units elsewhere in the city, whether independent houses or suites within other multipurpose buildings, the house contained fireplaces for heating and purpose-designed bathrooms. Although this house does not follow (for example) a Mediterranean model of rooms surrounding a central courtyard, comparisons are possible with the palace at the nearby site of Saksanokhur, discussed in the preceding section.[89] I am, as I have already noted, skeptical about how much any comparison with the house plans of other sites in the Hellenistic world—Delos, Olynthos—can productively achieve. I would, however, like to highlight some common features of Graeco-Bactrian domestic architecture, keeping their implications for now ethnically and culturally neutral. One may note several points in which Ai Khanoum's houses and palace follow common plans and are adapted to common needs: a north-facing direction, for protection from prevailing winds and rains; fireplaces for heating, and bath complexes; and, perhaps most important, a modular structure in which individual suites of rooms of different purposes are separated from each other by corridors that allow specific areas to be isolated or bypassed. Although not so elaborate as the layout of the public and private spheres of the palace, the layout of the house in the southern residential quarter also allows certain areas to be secluded from others.

Just outside the city's northern walls another house was excavated, which had a similar layout and orientation and incorporated many of the same features.[90] Over half the enclosed area was occupied by an open courtyard, with a small columned porch communicating between this and the inner rooms, which were themselves separated or linked by a network of corridors. Inside the outer wall the entire complex was surrounded by a corridor, which, to judge from the remains of carbonized wood, appears to have had a roof. The house had fireplaces for heating and bathrooms kitted out like those elsewhere in the city: with facilities for heating water, systems of pipes and drains, and floors in impermeable materials slanted for drainage. The remains of a similar construction were identified around three hundred meters to the northeast of the house but not excavated.[91] A sondage was also

88. Leriche 1986, pl. 9; on the house see Bernard 1968b, 272–76; 1969, 321–26; and 1970a, 312–13.
89. Ibid.; Litvinskii and Mukhitdinov 1969.
90. Bernard 1974b, 281–87.
91. Ibid. 285.

opened at a farmstead further out into the agricultural plain, around five kilometers from Ai Khanoum.[92]

In addition to the suites within the palace that were discussed in the preceding section, a residential unit was also contained within the unidentified, only partly excavated large public building on the main street just to the south of the temple.[93] This unit contains the same bathroom and kitchen configurations as elsewhere but, given our lack of knowledge of the function of this building as well as our fragmentary view of how the residential unit connects to it and fits into its floor plan, it is difficult to draw up hypotheses about its residents. It is worth proposing lower-status (caretakers) as well as higher-status (resident functionaries) options for these.

Some kind of residential zoning was in operation in the city, with separate districts for larger and for more humble residences. As already noted, aerial photographs show that the large house of the southern residential quarter had neighbors laid out in rows on a similar plan, and the extramural house had at least one neighbor, more distant from the city. Groups of much smaller houses occurred in at least two other places in the city. There was a neighborhood between the slopes of the acropolis and the Kokcha, occupied toward the end of the life of the Graeco-Bactrian city and perhaps later.[94] On the acropolis, another group of smaller houses had a brief period of occupation in around the second quarter of the third century B.C.E.[95] Such quarters may represent occupational in addition to or instead of socioeconomic zoning, given the military function of the acropolis and the need for habitations for guards or soldiers. We should be cautious in regard to what if any ethnic implications in addition to professional ones we may wish to impute to these.

Within the larger houses, one obvious solution to the "problem" of the isolating corridors is to posit some kind of gendered segregation or seclusion within the household. Identifying women's spaces is difficult even in excavated houses where domestic artifacts remain.[96] At Ai Khanoum, we can at least state that house layouts would have made such seclusion possible. They may, however, simply reflect a general desire to separate private, family space from outside visitors and more public activities.

Besides the comparison from Saksanokhur already discussed, there are other indications that this Bactrian domestic-architectural *koinē* persisted after the fall of the Graeco-Bactrian kingdom, for whatever practical or cultural reasons. As will be discussed in chapter 4, the "nomad conquests" of the mid-second century

92. Bernard 1978, 461.
93. Bernard 1980a, 451–52; Bernard et al. 1980, 48–50.
94. Bernard 1978, 462–63.
95. Bernard 1980a, 458–59; Bernard et al. 1980, 71.
96. E.g., Olynthos: Cahill 2002, 152–53.

B.C.E. do not represent a complete cultural or administrative break, and thus such continuity is neither impossible nor improbable. At the site of Dil'berdzhin, in the Bactra oasis, a large (84.0 × 57.5 m) house of about 100 B.C.E. displays some of the same features as the residential units from Ai Khanoum and Saksanokhur.[97] It is laid out on a straight axis, with a central court leading onto two main reception rooms to the south. This central unit is surrounded on three sides by a corridor offering access to further suites of rooms, themselves subdivided in places into smaller apartments. The comparison is too general to be pushed further, but the point remains that it is important to stress local comparanda for the structures of Ai Khanoum—including those from earlier and later periods—rather than to prioritize those from the Near Eastern and the Mediterranean world.

TEMPLES AND RELIGIOUS LIFE

The temples and dedicatory inscriptions of Ai Khanoum have perhaps attracted more scholarly attention than any other feature of the site. My focus here will be seeing how we may provide an overall, integrated picture of the religious life of the city; on setting straight some common assumptions about the gods worshipped at Ai Khanoum; and on integrating the religious features of the city better into its overall urban landscape. Religion cannot, of course, be separated out from other practices: the intramural and extramural burial places have already been discussed, and a dedicatory inscription from the gymnasium, to Hermes and Herakles, will be dealt with in the next section.

Three structures at Ai Khanoum have been identified as the site of formal religious cult: a temple in a walled enclosure, accessed off the main street in the lower city; another temple by the side of the road where it leaves the walled city to the north; and an open-air raised podium on the acropolis.[98] The non-Greek character of these structures and of many of the artifacts recovered from them is striking and raises numerous questions about the cultural identity of the people who used them. Yet, as I will argue, the nature and diversity of cult practice within these religious institutions can be approached in a manner more productive than is possible through the conventional dichotomy of Greek versus non-Greek.

The city's main temple, the so-called Temple with Indented Niches, and its sanctuary constitute one of the most strikingly non-Greek sections of the city.[99]

---

97. The *bol'shoi dom*: Kruglikova and Pugachenkova 1977, 5–47; Pugachenkova et al. 1994, 328 fig. 5; this comparison is also drawn by Fussman 1993b, 95–96.

98. The Ai Khanoum temple buildings are included in (inter alia) the wider studies of Downey 1988, 63–76; Bernard 1990; Hannestad and Potts 1990; Boyce and Grenet 1991, 165–79; and Shenkar 2011.

99. The finds from the temple are published in Francfort 1984b, but for the architecture, the preliminary reports must still be consulted: Bernard 1969, 327–55; 1970a, 317–37; 1972, 625–29; and 1974b, 295–98; Bernard and Francfort in Bernard 1971, 414–31.

The main temple building, square in shape, stood on a raised platform. Its outer walls were punctuated by the distinctive stepped niches that give it its modern name. These niches, as I will discuss, connect the temple to architectural traditions from the Near East. Inside, an antechamber led back to a tripartite *cella*. Within the enclosure wall, the sanctuary contained two smaller subsidiary chapels. Both are on a plan that we may view as more recognizably Greek, with columned vestibules. A number of different artistic styles occur in the equipment from the temple, ranging from ivory furniture in a Greek or Hellenistic style to objects in which Persian or Central Asian motifs are present. Although it is worth noting that all the necessary raw materials would have been available to local craftsmen, two examples of plaster moldings demonstrate one mechanism by which motifs may have been propagated over a long distance in the Hellenistic world: a rare point of access to the ways in which ideas and artistic forms may have been physically transmitted.[100]

Analysis of the temple sanctuary, of the objects of worship, and of the activities conducted in the sanctuary is complicated by the fact that the spatial distribution of the objects found in the temple and in its sanctuary was created largely by the occupants of the city after its "fall," around 145 B.C.E.[101] It is possible, however, that some items were neglected for their lack of obvious value (as compared with, for example, metals and precious stones) and left in situ: these may include the ivory furniture found in the temple building and the northeastern part of the sanctuary and small limestone pedestals that may have served as altars or provided supports for burners.[102]

Most discussion of the temple centers around two related problems: the identification of the main cult deity and the origins of the architectural form of the shrine itself. As is indicated by the limestone pedestals, a number of forms of cultic activity took place within the sanctuary. At the rear of the temple platform, ceramic vessels were upended to make libations to the earth. The remains of stucco and clay sculptures of human figures, larger than life-size, were found in the vestibule; these may represent additional objects of worship or simply depict donors or royal figures.[103] In the southern sacristy of the inner tripartite shrine, a medallion depicting the goddess Cybele was found cached between two jars: it shows signs of having been violently torn off an original wooden support.[104] The only indication of the image that occupied the central chamber of the inner shrine, however, comes

100. Francfort 1984b, 31–37; Mairs 2014b.

101. See Francfort 1984b, 107–18, and the distribution maps of particular categories of objects in the same volume.

102. Ibid. 17–18, 81–84.

103. Bernard 1969, 329.

104. Francfort 1984b, 93–94.

in the fragments of an acrolithic statue of a larger-than-life human figure. Part of a stone foot is preserved, with a thunderbolt motif on the sandal that has formed the basis for identifying the cult statue as a Zeus, perhaps to be equated with the "Thundering Zeus" of Diodotid coinage.[105] What has also been suggested—I think plausibly—is that an identification as a Zeus does not tell the full story of the god of the Temple with Indented Niches and that some or all of the temple's constituency may also have known this god as a Mithra or other local or Iranian deity.[106] It should be emphasized, however, that, whatever may appear in print, the central deity of the temple has not been conclusively identified and that all we have are hypotheses. There were, for example, no inscriptions found at the temple.

The second problem in analyzing the form and functions of the Temple with Indented Niches is the basic architectural plan of the building itself, which is commonly referred to as Mesopotamian in inspiration and has been compared with the later temples of Doura-Europos. What does this similarity actually signify? What may it have meant to the people who used this temple, and can we find a way of reconciling it with the temple's local Bactrian context? As I have argued elsewhere, the analogies that have been drawn between the form of the temple and Mesopotamian traditions are valid only in the sense that Mesopotamian influence on the Ai Khanoum niched temple has been mediated through an Achaemenid official context (Mairs 2013c). I argue that if or when more becomes known about Achaemenid Bactria, more about the institutions and material culture of Hellenistic Bactria will begin to make sense.

In comparison with the niched temple, less is known of the city's two other identified cult sites, the temple outside the northern gate and the podium on the acropolis. The extramural temple was constructed according to an architectural program similar to that of the intramural niched temple.[107] It stood on a raised platform, had niches in its exterior walls, and in its first phase had a tripartite inner *cella*. Two wings were added later, with additional chambers. The extramural temple, unfortunately, yielded hardly any artifacts, and we can say little about the cult practiced there or any similarities that it may have had with the niched temple inside the city walls or divergences from it.

The podium on the southwestern corner of the acropolis stood within a small walled enclosure. It stood about two and a half to three meters in height, was oriented to the cardinal points, and had a stair on its western side, suggesting that it was oriented for sacrifice or some other cult toward the rising sun.[108] This stepped

105. See, e.g., the catalogue of Diodotid coinage in Holt 1999b, appendices A and B.
106. Grenet 1991.
107. Bernard 1974b, 287–89; 1976a, 303–6; and 1976b, 272.
108. Described briefly in Bernard 1976a, 306–7, and 1990, 54; Downey 1988, 75. The full discussion in Boyce and Grenet 1991, 181–83, draws on unpublished material.

podium has been set within an Iranian tradition of open-air cult practice on high places. Furthermore, additional evidence from the region enables us to place this structure in the very local Achaemenid context that I have suggested is so crucial for an understanding of the Ai Khanoum palace and Temple with Indented Niches. A structure at Pačmak-tepe in the lower Surkhan-darya Valley provides a good local parallel for the Ai Khanoum stepped podium.[109] This structure is a three-tiered podium of rammed earth, oriented to the southeast, with only a light super-structure. Its dimensions are comparable to those of the stepped podium at Ai Khanoum. It is dated by ceramics to the fifth or fourth century B.C.E., which would offer a context for the Ai Khanoum podium within a local Bactrian Achaemenid context as well as a wider Iranian one.

I began by posing—among other questions—that of how we may conceptually situate the cult sites of Ai Khanoum within the wider urban landscape. I argue that it is important to consider them less as "non-Greek" exotica and more as function-ing institutions, integrated into a city whose inhabitants moved on a daily basis among buildings whose architectural format and decor incorporated influences from across ancient Central Asia, the Near East, and the Mediterranean world. This diversity in material and visual culture need not have compromised an indi-vidual's or a community's ability and desire to assert a particular ethnic identity if they should wish to. What I argue that the archaeological evidence from Ai Kha-noum reveals is a city where public assertions of civic identity took place within a very Greek framework, but individuals might exhibit variation in their behavior in other spheres. Because Greek identity was asserted so strongly in areas such as the gymnasium or at the *temenos* of Kineas, any ethnic resonance in activities such as temple dedications or offerings toward the rising sun might easily be neutralized. To return to the linguistic analogy that I used in the introduction, we may say that this behavior was not ethnically marked but was a "default setting," a common practice of worship not held to have any ethnic weight. It is possible, of course, to read a measure of cultural insecurity into this, but it is important to recognize that our sensitivity to such things as artistic style or religious practice may introduce a conflict between culture, political status, and ethnic identity where the agents themselves may not have perceived any.

Within the sanctuary of the Temple with Indented Niches, we should also be careful not to segregate our analysis of the various religious practices attested—the site was clearly used for a variety of practices: formal and informal, ceremonial and everyday. Whether or not a person engaged in more than one form of religious activity in the course of a visit to the temple—or whether he or she might perform more than one form of religious activity but for different purposes on different occasions—he or she cannot have been unaware of the other uses to which the

109. Pidaev 1974, 33–38.

temple complex was put. Although access to the main temple building, and further to its *cella* and sacristies, may well have been restricted, the sanctuary courtyard was an open space, with the potential for religious activity to be performed openly. A certain amount of tunnel vision may have been in order, with the possibility of ignoring activities in which one was not actively engaged, but it would have required an unreasonable degree of denial and deliberate obtuseness for an individual to mentally appropriate the temple as purely a temple of Zeus or anything else. Whether we suppose that anyone in fact did so is intimately linked with our perception of how individuals in the city negotiated their own ethnic identity. If, as I argued in the introduction to this volume (and will argue again in the conclusion), it was possible for individuals to adopt a wide range of ethnic indicia—and the arenas in which identity was publicly expressed thereby became charged with political and social significance—then we may imagine that the performance of religious activity in the temple sanctuary was a selective business, not wholly promiscuous but subject to manipulation and variation depending upon the individual or the occasion.

DEFENSES

Ai Khanoum had impressive natural defenses: these were one of the principal attractions of the site. The city was surrounded on two sides by rivers, with high, steep banks. Its upper city stood around sixty meters above the level of the plain and afforded a line of sight across the nearer and farther banks of the rivers.[110] At the far southeastern corner of the acropolis was a still higher citadel. The only weak point lay to the north, and here the city was protected by the most formidable of its extensive and imposing man-made defensive structures, a wall and a defensive ditch some twenty meters across and five meters deep. The northern wall had towers, with larger ones at the gateway, where the main street entered the city, and at its northwestern corner, where it reached the river Oxus. This wall continued along the northern side of the acropolis. Elsewhere, along the river banks, the city was protected by less impressive but still formidable ramparts, without towers. The upper city had its own internal defenses, including a fortresslike structure at its northwestern corner, situated so as to protect the walls of the lower city, and a deep ditch separating the citadel. The city's arsenal, which has been neither fully excavated and nor fully published, stood on the eastern side of the southern part of the main street. As well as containing stores of working arms, metallurgical debris suggests strongly that workshops for making arms were located here.[111]

110. See the summary of the fortifications in Leriche 1986, 1–2.
111. Bernard 1980a, 452–57; Bernard et al. 1980, 51–63.

The fortifications provide some of the most interesting and extensive documentation of the history of the site before and after the Graeco-Bactrian city. Their basic format was preserved even when other structures inside the city walls were completely razed and rebuilt. Fortifications, of course, retained their function and importance even when other institutions might change or lose theirs. As discussed in chapter 1, it is here that we find the most decisive evidence for Achaemenid use of the site. The citadel, in particular—the highest, most impregnable part of the fortifications—displays a record of occupation from the Achaemenids right through to the Timurids.[112]

Within a more restricted chronological window, the fortifications show several destruction events and renovation projects over the course of the life of the Graeco-Bactrian city.[113] Mud-brick architecture requires constant maintenance—a problem across the site as a whole, as will be discussed in the section on water management at Ai Khanoum, below—and so not all damage and rebuilding is necessarily to be associated with military attack. At the citadel, for example, it is difficult to say whether the collapse of the latest Greek period of the wall was due to an attack or to simple degradation.[114] Some traces of specifically military activity do, however, remain in various periods of the city's occupation: evidence of sapping in the northern wall and a fire in the wall by the Oxus;[115] stone projectiles, some as much as twenty kilograms in weight, in the citadel;[116] spear points and arrowheads in the northern wall.[117]

The problem, of course, is in trying to tie these attacks and renovations to an absolute chronology (establishing which is a contentious matter in itself for Ai Khanoum) and, further, to associate them with known historical events.[118] A series of assaults on its fortifications marks the end of the Graeco-Bactrian city at Ai Khanoum. As already discussed, textual and numismatic finds from elsewhere in the city date this to the end of the reign of Eukratides, around 145 B.C.E. This was a period when the Graeco-Bactrian kingdom was menaced both by external threats and by internal dynastic strife, and it is tempting to tie one or all of these to the fall of Ai Khanoum.[119] I will discuss this period more fully in chapter 4, but I provide a summary of my discussion here. To the north, population movements, attested in

112. Ibid. 64, 70–74; Leriche 1986, 9–11, 24, 71–72.

113. See, e.g., the summary in Lerner 2003–4, 395–97, or Leriche 1986, 54–57, for a detailed account of renovations in one place in the lower city wall.

114. Ibid. 23.

115. Ibid. 75.

116. Ibid. 77, 114–15.

117. Ibid. 118.

118. Ibid. 67, 82, and Lerner 2003–4, 397–99. Different datings and attributions of a single destruction event may be taken as a case in point; the problems are discussed in general by Leriche 1986, 79–84.

119. See the concise and critical discussion ibid. 83–84.

both Chinese and Greek sources,[120] as well as by archaeological finds, began the series of migrations and military conquests that would establish groups such as the Yuezhi in the region, among them the ancestors of the later Kushan rulers of Bactria.[121] Bactria was also involved in a conflict with Parthia, although this will naturally have affected the west of the kingdom more than the east.[122] And finally, the reign of Eukratides came to an end with internal dynastic struggles and political fragmentation. All these factors led to the collapse of the Graeco-Bactrian kingdom, and although they provide a general political and military context, it is difficult to find specific evidence for the role played by any of them in the fall of Ai Khanoum. Above all, the end of the Graeco-Bactrian-period city of Ai Khanoum was not a simple matter of the invasion of supposed barbarian hordes from the north. The main assault suffered by the northern wall of the city at this period included the use of siege equipment, difficult to reconcile with the notion of attack by nomadic mounted warriors.[123] In a wider sense, the traditionally proposed nomadic conquest of Bactria was not a matter of complete destruction. Some continuity was maintained, given that the Kushan rulers of Bactria later developed a literacy based on Greek script. So, as discussed in the conclusion to chapter 1, some kind of administrative continuity was maintained across conquest and regime change.

The destruction and abandonment of the Graeco-Bactrian city at Ai Khanoum itself was in any case not complete and decisive. There was a period of reoccupation of the city (the "occupation post-grecque" or "occupation tardive") in which many of the city's institutions were adapted to different uses and their contents moved around or disturbed. Although this period is most often interpreted as a takeover of the site by new populations, local to the area but non-Greek, there is no reason why these reoccupants of the site should not have had some relationship to the city and its immediate hinterland, or why they may not have numbered among them some survivors of its fall. The urban landscape was being used in different ways, and the city's essential social and political infrastructure had clearly been completely destroyed, but this may reflect precisely the collapse of such an order, not the arrival of absolutely new populations. The real death of the city is actually marked by a citywide fire that put an end to the fairly brief period of the immediately post-Greek occupation.[124]

---

120. Strabo 12.8.2.

121. Treatments of these events include Bernard 1987b; Lyonnet 1991, 1998; Posch 1995. On the Yuezhi, see Benjamin 2007.

122. See, e.g., Justin, 41.6, Strabo 11.11.2.

123. Leriche 1986, 83.

124. Ibid. 78; ibid. 69 for a chronological table of destructions and renovations across the city's fortifications dated to ca. 125 B.C.E.

GREEK LITERARY AND INTELLECTUAL CULTURE

The written material from Ai Khanoum—inscriptions and documentary texts—provides the greatest insights into the cultural life of the city, and it is furthermore possible to contextualize this material within the urban landscape. The palace treasury contained a small library. The gymnasium, a quintessentially Greek cultural and civic institution, also served as a focus for intellectual activities. And the city also boasted a large theater, in classic Greek semicircular form, set into the side of the acropolis.

Room 107 of the treasury was the findspot of the only Greek literary texts preserved in the city.[125] A philosophical dialogue, originally written on papyrus, was preserved in the form of an ink imprint left on compacted earth.[126] Two fragments of a text written on parchment were also recovered. Little text was preserved, but what there was, was enough to indicate that it was composed in iambic trimeters and to suggest identification as a dramatic text.

This dramatic text is one of several indicators that Greek drama was performed at Ai Khanoum. One of the spouts from the fountain in the western Oxus wall was in the form of a comic mask, water pouring through its open mouth.[127] The theater itself was set into the side of the acropolis, with the seats facing toward the main street.[128] It has not been completely excavated, but enough has been excavated to reveal a typical Greek theater form, with tiered rows of seats, a semicircular orchestra, and a stage with backdrop building. Like many of the institutions of Ai Khanoum, the size of the theater seems excessive. It could seat around six thousand people, more than can possibly have lived within the city itself. It therefore served a population in the wider region, and may have served as a venue for periodic festivals.

The gymnasium stood immediately inside the western Oxus wall, separated from it by a street.[129] Its position within the city's urban schema and its connections to other complexes are not entirely clear, and in particular little is known about the areas immediately to the north and east of the gymnasium complex. The road inside the western wall connected it to districts to the north and the south. It is difficult to establish the precise relationship of the gymnasium to the pool enclosure. There is no direct connection between them—although a person might pass between them indirectly, from the southern door of the gymnasium to the western entrance of the pool enclosure—and they are oriented along different axes. But their proximity and the lack of bathing facilities in the latest phase of the gymnasium imply some connection.[130]

---

125. Rapin and Hadot 1987.
126. Reedited by Lerner 2003.
127. Leriche and Thoraval 1979, 196–98.
128. Bernard 1978, 429–41.
129. Veuve 1987.
130. Ibid. 40–41.

The final phase of the gymnasium, Phase II,[131] is dated by the excavators toward the end of the second quarter of the second century B.C.E.[132] and, like the palace, is the product of a wholesale destruction and rebuilding of an earlier structure.[133] Logistical and financial problems made it difficult for the excavators to get a clear idea of the phases that preceded this, but their layout was rather different; the only constant was the open water-channel, which ran east to west across the southern court.[134] Phase III[135] contained a rotundalike building of unknown function in the southern part of the complex,[136] as well as a bath complex similar to those elsewhere in the city, and other buildings in the southwestern part of what would later be the pool enclosure.[137] Phase IV,[138] earlier still, contained a more extensive bath complex.[139]

Phase II[140] consisted of two connected quadrilateral courtyards. The northern courtyard was a square with sides of around one hundred meters. It contained columned porticos in the middle of each wall, and a corridor ran around immediately inside the outer walls. This corridor had few access points, and perhaps served for promenading.[141] A Greek inscription was found on the base of a statue bust of a bearded man set into the back wall of the northern porch.[142] This was a brief dedication by Straton and Triballos, sons of Straton, to the gods of the gymnasium, Hermes and Herakles.[143]

The southern courtyard (ca. 120 × 100 m) consisted of a simple enclosure wall with access to the northern section, set out to serve as an outdoor exercise place. This area was the findspot of two stone sundials.[144] These attest to the intellectual as well as the sporting activities that typically took place in gymnasiums, and they may also have served the purpose of regulating time for gymnasium activities.

THE GIFT OF THE OXUS

Bactria almost was the Oxus, in the sense that Egypt was the Nile.

—W. W. TARN, *THE GREEKS IN BACTRIA AND INDIA*, P. 102

131. I.e., Bernard 1978, État I.
132. Veuve 1987, 103.
133. Phase I represents the reoccupation of the site.
134. Veuve 1987, 2, 23–41; Bernard 1978, 425, 429.
135. I.e., ibid., État II.
136. Veuve 1987, 49–50.
137. Ibid. 51–52.
138. I.e., Bernard 1978, État III.
139. Veuve 1987, 53–56.
140. Ibid., pl. 4.
141. Ibid. 33.
142. Bernard 1976a, 296.
143. Canali De Rossi 2004, no. 381; editio princeps: Robert 1968, 417–21.
144. Veuve 1982.

The canals built and maintained in the agricultural plain around Ai Khanoum (chapter 1) fed a branch canal that ran along the foot of the acropolis, between it and the main street. It was from this canal, rather than directly from the rivers (the banks at the city being too high), that the city drew its water supply. A network of open channels and of ceramic pipes provided water and drainage to various institutions. An elaborate fountain by the Oxus channeled spring water through waterspouts and into the river.

Quite apart from its location at the junction of two rivers, the Oxus (Amu-darya) and the Kokcha, water plays a prominent role at Ai Khanoum. The rivers themselves were essential for irrigation, and also for transportation. Although, as already discussed, the predominant building material at Ai Khanoum was baked or unbaked mud brick, there were some stone elements, in a soft white limestone. Stone was not available locally, but several possible quarry sites were located upriver in the mountains, from which the most practical route was by water.[145] The rivers or their valleys may also have allowed easier access to the mines in the Badakshan Mountains.

The topography of city, its construction materials, and the local climate meant that water might also be destructive. Its movement through the city, and across changes in elevation of several meters in the lower city alone, was carefully channeled. Constructions in raw mud-brick needed constant maintenance, and when this maintenance was interrupted—as was the case after the fall of the city—rain and runoff from higher ground could cause serious damage.[146] In the case of the city's fortifications, several phases of repairs were revealed via a section through the wall, and in some places[147] it can be difficult to tell whether severe damage is due to military attack or to weathering and erosion. Along the banks of the rivers, the city's fortifications were less impressive than along the northern side of the city, in large part because the rivers themselves acted as a line of defense. But here too the river could compromise what defenses there were: by the Oxus, the excavation of the remains of the defenses and the fountain were essentially rescue excavations, erosion and the collapse of the banks having been sped up by the intensification of irrigation activities in the plain near the city; by the Kokcha, almost any trace of defensive structures had already been washed away by the time of excavation.[148] The problems of unbaked mud-brick architecture and destructive runoff may have been taken into account by the city's architects, as in the replacement of the stepped base of the earlier phases of the niched temple with a more solid, blocklike platform less vulnerable to weathering.[149]

145. Bernard 1973, 10–11.
146. Propylaea: Guillaume 1983, 26–27.
147. E.g., the citadel: Leriche 1986, 23.
148. Ibid. 2, 27.
149. Bernard 1970a, 325–27.

The curious lack of substantial reoccupation of the site may also in large part have to do with reasons connected with water or with the lack of a strong central power to control and manage water: the destruction or neglect of the city's main canal and, in much more recent times, conditions favorable to the breeding of mosquitoes and as a result endemic malaria.[150]

The position of the main canal, by the base of the acropolis, meant that it became something of a water feature in the theater. In earlier phases, it ran right across what was to become the orchestra, and in later phases it was rechanneled around the curved side, crossed by little footbridges to reach the aisles of the seating area.[151] Other facilities were less decorative: the great court of the palace had an extensive drainage system, with buried ceramic pipes and open-air basins to catch runoff from the tiled roofs. This water was then channeled out of the courtyard in pipes, including one that ran across the treasury building.[152] Lack of such drainage facilities may be used to argue that particular areas were roofed in.[153]

Bathing facilities have been identified at several places throughout the city. The most common layout was a suite of two or three adjoining rooms, with pebble-lined floors tilted at an angle for better drainage, and with channels and drains. These were often adjacent to kitchen facilities and shared a common heat source or else had their own hearths. Baths were located in all the city's residential buildings, whether independent or part of larger complexes.[154] Most of the pebble-mosaic floors bore no distinct pattern, with the exception of the bath in the inner residential unit of the palace, which had mosaics decorated with abstract figures (a star), floral patterns, and marine creatures.[155] The use of this technique, in which designs are picked out in white pebbles against a field of dark red ones, is viewed by some as another instance of the cultural conservatism or classicizing tendency of Graeco-Bactrian material culture in a period when mosaics in the Mediterranean world had come to use the technique of square-cut tesserae.[156] Although such conservatism would be in keeping with interpretations of some of the sculpture from the site as classicizing, practical reasons should also be noted: the ready availability of river pebbles and a possible lack of direct contact with or knowledge of evolving Greek techniques. Among the finds from the temple sanctuary (which, it should

150. Schlumberger and Bernard 1965, 602.
151. Bernard 1978, 434–39.
152. Bernard 1973, 35–36; Bernard et al. 1980, 11; Rapin 1992, 24.
153. Bernard 1973, 54–55.
154. Southern residential house: rooms 14 and 17, Bernard 1970a, 312. In an earlier phase under what was later designated room 20 of the palace, to the southwest of the great court: Bernard 1971, 389–405. Likewise in the residential complex within the later phase of the palace: Bernard 1975, 168. The residential unit in the unidentified public building: Bernard 1980a, 451–52; Bernard et al. 1980, 48–49.
155. Bernard 1975, 175–80, and 1976a, 291–92.
156. Burn 2004, 102–6.

be recalled, were not necessarily originally used there) was an iron strigil.[157] It is worth emphasizing that, in addition to the more showy, public gymnasium and theater, this was one very domestic area in which traditional Greek activities were found.[158]

Curiously, one facility that did not have a bath complex in its latest phase was the gymnasium—in which I include the large open enclosure with a pool to its south. In Phases IV and III (the earliest strata) there were bath facilities, with the same pebbled floors as those elsewhere in the city,[159] but these were not maintained when the entire complex was razed and rebuilt according to a completely different format. There are several features: an open channel, a pool, and a nearby fountain, which may or may not have carried on their function of allowing athletes to wash. From its earliest phases, the southern court of the main gymnasium had an open channel that ran east to west, and this is a constant throughout all phases.[160] It is really impossible to say for certain whether this may have been used for athletes to wash or was simply a drain or water feature. The gymnasium was located right by the street inside the Oxus fortifications, outside which an elaborate stone fountain installation (around 6.5 meters below the level of the adjacent street) channeled water through three spouts: a comic theater mask of a bearded man, a dolphin, and a dog.[161] Gutters or water spouts elsewhere in the city might be decorated: a lion-headed gargoyle was found in the courtyard of the main temple.[162] The fountain could have played any one, or more than one, of a number of roles: provision of drinking water for the neighborhood (the fountain is fed by groundwater, not directly from a drainage channel); channeling of water away from the foundations of the fortification walls, to prevent damage; a decorative water feature along a promenade by the river; or washing water for athletes at the gymnasium. Since the fortifications by the Oxus were so badly damaged, it was impossible to identify the location of any passage in the wall that would link the foundation to the street by the gymnasium.[163]

The existence of baths near what would later become the open-air pool may suggest that it carried on their function but, as already discussed, it is difficult to be certain of this enclosure's relationship to adjacent structures. In Phase I, the last phase of the gymnasium, a person might walk from the southern court of the gymnasium proper to the pool by exiting through the door to the south, into the

---

157. Francfort 1984b, 68 and pl. XXXI.

158. Bernard 1971, 400, highlights the Greek aspects of the baths at Ai Khanoum and compares them to other facilities in Greek world.

159. Bernard 1978, 423, 428–29; Veuve 1987, 51–56.

160. Bernard 1978, 425, 429.

161. Leriche and Thoraval 1979.

162. Francfort 1984b, 90–91.

163. Leriche 1986, 40.

street or open space by the wall, then entering the pool enclosure through its western door. Although indirect, the two spaces were therefore in communication. Their precise relationship remains problematic, however, because little is known about the relationship of this enclosure to points to the south and east, including the palace and street below the propylaea. The pool is square, with sides of forty-one meters, two meters deep, and is lined with a double lining of pebbles. The water supply and draining for it were not recovered, and the enclosure seems to be otherwise empty of buildings.[164] Other interpretations than bathing facilities for the gymnasium are possible. It has been suggested, as already noted, that it may have served to water animals.[165] Another possibility is that it is to be related to the palace and should be considered in the context of gardens with pool complexes in Hellenistic-period palaces in the Near East and the Levant.[166]

Did the Oxus have any role in the religious life of Ai Khanoum? There is plenty of evidence from sites elsewhere in Bactria, and from later periods, that the deified Oxus was important in Bactrian religion.[167] Downstream, at the settlement site of Takht-i Sangin,[168] there was a temple facing onto the river at which the deified river Oxus was worshipped, alongside other forms of religious activity, including a possible fire cult.[169] Some of the votives from the temple bear images of gods or other supernatural creatures from the Greek and non-Greek world associated with water.[170] The temple acquired its modern name, the Temple of the Oxus, from a small votive altar carrying a statue of a satyr, with a Greek inscription in which a man with the Iranian name Atrosokes dedicates to the Oxus.[171] The name Ōxos also appears in Greek letters on a more recently discovered fragmentary stone piece.[172]

There is no direct evidence for a cult of the Oxus at any of the religious installations at Ai Khanoum, although we are of course inhibited by the lack of epigraphic evidence and by the severe disturbance of votives and religious paraphernalia from the main temple sanctuary by its later reoccupants. Marine imagery does occur in the occasional piece from the site, such as ivory fish and representations of dolphins on jewelry (although the archaeological context of these finds is not known).[173] There is no reason why the Oxus could not have been one of the

164. Bernard 1978, 425; Veuve 1987, 40–41.

165. Rapin 1992, 9–10.

166. Bedal 2001, 38–39.

167. Boyce and Grenet 1991, 179–81.

168. Litvinskii and Pichikiyan 1981; for full bibliography, see ibid. and Mairs 2011b, 25.

169. Bernard 1994.

170. Litvinskii and Pichikiyan 1995; Bernard 1987a.

171. Litvinskii and Pichikiyan 1981, 153–54; Litvinskii, Vinogradov, and Pichikiyan 1985.

172. Drujinina 2001, 263.

173. Bopearachchi 2005, 105–6.

deities worshipped at the main temple, but there is also no evidence that it was. The open canal across the sanctuary may or may not have had any connection to cult practice or ablutions.[174] Where we are on firmer ground about the importance of the deified Oxus at Ai Khanoum is in the appearance of theophoric "Oxus" names among the personnel in the Greek economic texts from the treasury, and of course in Aramaic and Bactrian texts from Bactria of earlier and later periods (chapter 1).[175] The Oxus was important to Ai Khanoum and to eastern Bactria: it made agriculture, communication, and urban settlement possible, even if not to the extent to which the Nile did in Egypt.

AI KHANOUM AND THE GRAECO-BACTRIAN *KOINĒ*

I have suggested throughout the preceding discussion that there is some merit to considering the architecture and material culture of Ai Khanoum as forming part of a distinctive Hellenistic-Bactrian *koinē*. While the culture of Bactria bears clear influence from neighboring regions, especially those with which it was politically integrated, there are certain idiosyncratic features that make the culture of Bactria Bactrian.[176] The notion of a Bactrian *koinē* may also be useful in assessing continuities in material culture in Bactria in the periods before and after the Graeco-Bactrian kingdom. In concluding, I would like to recap some of the places where I have suggested we may see these and to draw attention to some more.

Hybridity

However we choose to analyze it, the combination of stylistic influences from across the Mediterranean, Near Eastern, Central Asian, and Indian worlds comes together in Hellenistic Bactria in a distinctively Hellenistic-Bactrian way. Hybridity is a quintessential feature of the Hellenistic-Bactrian material assemblage.[177] The analysis of Bernard and others that the architecture of Ai Khanoum is a mixture of Greek and oriental stands, despite the differences in theoretical and terminological nuance we may bring to this assessment.[178] What I suggest is needed is a greater focus on the mechanisms and policies by which this influence came to impact on the material culture and built environment of Hellenistic Bactria. The incorporation of Bactria into two major empires undoubtedly created the circum-

---

174. Bernard 1970a, 337, and 1974b, 298.

175. See also Mairs 2013b.

176. See also ibid.

177. Elsewhere I note my reservations regarding direct application of the postcolonial construction of hybridity to the Hellenistic world: Mairs 2011c.

178. E.g., Bernard 1973, 113 "une architecture grecque acclimatée en pays d'Orient"; 118 "l'architecture gréco-bactrienne me paraît à la jonction de deux courants, le grec et l'oriental."

stances under which institutions, styles, and practices were introduced. I have suggested that some of the apparently Near Eastern features of the landscape of Ai
Khanoum—the palace, the main temple—derive in fact more locally from the official architecture of Achaemenid Bactria. The very Greek elements—such as the
theater and gymnasium—are a product of the colonization of the region by Greeks
and of what ongoing intercourse there was with the wider Hellenistic world. The
culture of Ai Khanoum and of Hellenistic Bactria, however, is more than the sum
of its diverse influences, and more work remains to be done on the novel and complex ways in which outside influences on the material culture of Bactria were combined into a distinctively local *koinē*. Below in the conclusion to this volume, I will
return to consider how postcolonial theories about the nature and products of
cultural interaction—"hybridity" in a slightly different, more technical sense—
may or may not offer interesting approaches to evidence from the Hellenistic Far
East.

Construction Materials and Techniques

In comparison with other materials, little stone was used in the architecture and
sculpture of Hellenistic Bactria. Instead, mud brick, rammed earth, and clay are
the predominant materials. (Bactrian clay sculpture is discussed further in subsec-
tion 4, below.) These were raw materials that were more readily available locally to
Bactrian builders and artisans, and so even where Greek (or other) artistic styles
were adopted, they were also adapted to new media and new techniques of workmanship.[179]

The architecture of Ai Khanoum has a number of idiosyncratic features, some
of which may be observed in other sites of the region. In the absence of excavated
contemporary urban sites of comparable size and importance, it is difficult to say
whether the monumental size of the city's institutions is a feature of Hellenistic-
Bactrian urbanism or simply a feature of Ai Khanoum's architectural program of
the early second century B.C.E. The "isolating" or "circulation" corridors of the
palace and domestic spaces of the city can, however, be identified at other sites,
such as Saksanokhur and, later, Dil'berdzhin. These reflect, in Bernard's view, "an
obsessive concern with using corridors to mark out axes of circulation in material
form, and thereby channelling routes along pathways determined in advance,
which bypassed rooms or groups of rooms, or even entire buildings, without
crossing them."[180] It is at present difficult to say much more about the rationale
behind the adoption of such plans and the forms of behavior and circulation that
they were designed to channel and constrain.

179. Francfort 1984b, 117.
180. Bernard 1976a, 297.

Responses to the Bactrian Environment

The local, continental climate offers further possible reasons for choices in Bactrian architectural design. The iwans of the palace and residences faced away from the prevailing winds. A number of structures—such as the antechambers of the palace's inner "meeting rooms"—contained fireplaces. Long corridors, such as that surrounding the northern courtyard of the gymnasium, could have allowed those engaging in activities usually conducted out of doors in the Mediterranean Greek world—such as promenading and philosophizing—to be protected from extremities of heat and cold, and from precipitation. It may further be suggested that the practice of surrounding buildings with corridors immediately inside the outer walls provided insulation from the elements.

Local Traditions of Craft Production

As well as techniques of manufacture, specific types of artifacts or craft products are typical of Bactria before, after, and during the period of the Graeco-Bactrian kingdom. These include items known in the literature by the Greek term *pyxides*, small (ca. 10–12 cm in diameter), hemispherical, lidded containers used for a variety of purposes.[181] They are made of schist or steatite, locally available in the mountains of the region, bear incised or inlaid decoration on their lids, and contain two or more small compartments. Many of these vessels were found at Ai Khanoum; others are known from nearby Bactrian sites such as Takht-i Sangin.[182] These idiosyncratic items of local Hellenistic-Bactrian craft production started out, it appears, as containers for jewelry, cosmetics, or other such items. Containers in these forms continued to be used and produced in the region, however, and in Gandhāra of the early centuries C.E. were used as reliquaries for Buddhist relics.[183] These *pyxides* are a good example of ways in which changes in purpose and meaning could be couched within the same local Bactrian material idiom.

What is most striking, however: local techniques of clay sculpture, upon wooden armatures and sometimes containing elements in stone, are typical of the region during the Hellenistic period (for example, in the temple and palace of Ai Khanoum) and in later periods. Khalchayan, in the Surkhan-darya Valley, was the site of a settlement of the Hellenistic period. In the first century B.C.E., the immediate successors of the Greek kings of Bactria, forerunners of the Kushans, built a palace adorned with wall paintings and painted clay sculptures.[184] In both their

181. Hiebert and Cambon 2008, 117; Francfort 2013.

182. Bernard 1972, 614–18; Francfort 1984b, 23–24; Guillaume and Rougeulle 1987, 9–12, pl. 6. Similar examples from Takht-i Sangin: Drujinina 2004.

183. Francfort 1976.

184. Pugachenkova 1965, 1971, Nehru 1999–2000.

style and their technique of workmanship, they are visibly an evolution from the existing sculptural tradition of the region.

. . .

In proposing a material *koinē* that gave Hellenistic Bactria its own distinctive identity, I would also like to emphasize that Ai Khanoum itself must be understood first and foremost upon its own terms. Although its architecture and material culture display what to modern analysis are very obviously diverse influences, and although it supported a diverse population, separating people and institutions out in terms of their ultimate origins may not offer the best approach to understanding Ai Khanoum as a city and as a community. These are themes to which I will return in my conclusion.

3

Self-Representation in the Inscriptions of Sōphytos (Arachosia) and Heliodoros (India)

And after all, don't forget that now and then
sophists come to us from Syria,
and versifiers, and other devotees of puffery.
So we are not, I think, un-Greek.

—C. P. CAVAFY, "PHILHELLENE" (1912), TRANS. ADAPTED FROM
MENDELSOHN 2012, 28

IDENTITIES

In the archaeological and textual evidence that I have discussed in the preceding chapters, it is difficult to pick out individual histories. Although we know the names of a small number of the inhabitants of Ai Khanoum, we know little about their personal, social identities. At a community level, I have argued that categories of Greek and non-Greek are not necessarily helpful. A building's architectural form and the motifs with which it is decorated may visibly derive from the traditions of a particular culture or geographical region, but we can presuppose from this nothing of the personal, self-ascribed identities of those who frequented it, nor of the cultural and political capital with which they invested any particular institution and the activities that took place within it.

To ask whether any one inhabitant of Ai Khanoum was a Greek is an even thornier matter than may at first appear. The question, "Was this person a Greek?" or "How Greek were they?" is increasingly less likely to be asked of material from further west in the Hellenistic world—or at least is no longer phrased in quite that way. More interesting and productive discussions emerge from such questions as what strategies of ethnic identification individuals employed, whether categories of Greek or not Greek had any social meaning, or what kinds of behavior and forms of material culture people associated with particular identities. No one really *is* anything objectively. Identities are constructed, defended, and ascribed, and the frameworks and vocabulary of anthropology and postcolonial studies have brought terms such as "hybridity" and "creolization" into common currency in Greek and Roman archaeology.[1] Ethnicity, of course, has become a familiar theoretical trope in dealing with both archaeological and textual data from the ancient Mediterranean world, as was discussed in the introduction to this work.[2] Barth's definition of ethnicity as a constructed identity in which the defense of a boundary around a notional set of common cultural traits is often more important than objective differentiation in language or material culture still presents a useful model for many classical and Hellenistic case studies.[3]

In this chapter, I consider two individuals from the Hellenistic Far East for whom we can reconstruct something of a personal history. Both left inscriptions in territories beyond the Hindu Kush: Sōphytos at Kandahar, in Arachosia, and Heliodoros at Besnagar, in Central India. Heliodoros is the only individual from the easternmost Greek states who is actually given an ethnic descriptor in our sources—he is referred to as a Greek—but it is typical of the material from the region that in the one case where we do have an ethnic this does not make analysis of the person's identity any more straightforward. My purpose in what follows is to investigate the constructed ethnic identities of Sōphytos and Heliodoros: the linguistic registers of their inscriptions, their cultural points of reference, the identities that they attempt to project, and the conscious and unconscious signals that they give their audiences about their backgrounds and identities. I will also set them within a wider geographical context, as the products of multicultural and multiethnic societies similar to those of other regions of the Hellenistic world.

THE INSCRIPTIONS

The newly discovered Greek acrostic inscription of Sōphytos presents us, at first glance, with precisely the degree of peculiarity that we have come to expect from the Hellenistic Far East.[4] It is unprovenanced—although the editors' sources claimed that it came from Kandahar, and it would be at home in an epigraphic context there—and, despite its masterly (some may say excessive) display of Greek erudition, was composed or commissioned by a man whose name is not Greek. One of the most striking aspects of the Sōphytos epitaph, however, is the fact

---

1. See, among numerous possible examples, Webster 2001; van Dommelen 2005; Pitts 2007.
2. E.g., Goudriaan 1988; Jones 1998; Malkin 2001; Jonathan Hall 2002.
3. Barth 1969b.
4. "Newly discovered" in the sense of newly emerged onto the antiquities market, within the last ten years; editio princeps: Bernard, Pinault, and Rougemont 2004.

that it presents us with a kind of mirror image of another inscription, composed or commissioned by a Greek ambassador named Heliodoros in Central India, almost fifteen hundred kilometers away, as the crow flies, but from a broadly similar period in the second century B.C.E. Yet another piece of Hellenistic Far East exotica, this text describes Heliodoros, in the local Prākrit, as both a Greek (*yona*) and a devotee of an Indian god. Both inscriptions raise similar questions about culture, ethnic identity, and self-representation in the region. A few Greek and Latin inscriptions from another frontier zone of the classical world, Lower Nubia, will also enter into my discussion, most notable among them an acrostic verse inscription in Greek by a Nubian Roman soldier named Paccius Maximus. My intention is to contextualize the inscriptions of Sōphytos and Heliodoros in two senses: geographically, with reference to what we know of their archaeological and sociohistorical contexts, and thematically, with reference to the techniques of self-representation that they share with each other and with the Nubian inscriptions.

The inscriptions of Sōphytos and Heliodoros appeal to certain key Greek and Indian cultural tropes, in particular religious and literary culture. Their authors very actively seek to present themselves and their social and cultural backgrounds in particular ways, in the face of what modern scholarship may view as more ambiguous signals about their ethnicity, education, social status, and even native language. These inscriptions all share a consciousness of being looked at and read, and of their authors (or commissioners) being judged by the reader. They were produced, of course, in very different geopolitical contexts, and their authors—aside from their self-consciousness in the epigraphic act and attachments, of varying degree, to Greek identity—probably had little in common. The question who these individuals actually were is only one that we should ask of their inscriptions. Equally important are the questions who they thought they were, what they hoped their inscriptions to achieve, and the common themes and strategies that they employed in their inscriptions' composition.

There are three main points that I would like to make in this chapter. First and most fundamental, that these inscriptions can be used, and that their place is not just as a scholarly aside on the strange things Greeks did in the East. Second, and I assume uncontroversial, that the ethnic strategies employed in public display are considerably more complex and subtle than any polarity of Greeks versus non-Greeks. Such complexity is something that I have tried to illustrate in my discussion of the urban landscape of Ai Khanoum in chapter 2 and that I have also noted above. My third point is that ethnic expression or self-designation is mediated through a written medium in which an individual may be able to exercise only limited freedom of choice. In addition to issues familiar from the epigraphy of other regions of the ancient world (use of formulae, questions of authorship, and so forth), one problem that is particularly acute in the Hellenistic Far East is that choice of epigraphic language, into which we may be tempted to read overt cultural cues (speaking of "an Indian writing in Greek," for example, or "a Greek writing in Prākrit"), may have more to do with the written medium available than anything else. As we have seen with the Aramaic and Greek documentary texts discussed in chapter 1, the use of a particular language as an administrative register may tell us little about the ethnolinguistic identities of the people who used and produced such documents or of their superiors in official hierarchies. In such circumstances, what if any cultural autonomy does an individual have?

Although none of these inscriptions—the Arachosian, the Indian, or even the Nubian comparanda—will be especially familiar to a scholarly audience of classicists, this is not the place for a detailed philological or historical commentary: comprehensive references will be given to the original publications in order that readers may follow up further points of interest for themselves. The inscription of Sōphytos is my starting point. As has already been noted, this remarkable inscription is not particularly user-friendly, because it lacks any archaeological or epigraphic context. There is, at present, little that can be done to remedy this: the future prospects of large-scale archaeological work in Arachosia are not good, although more unprovenanced material is certain to emerge onto the international antiquities market.[5] As for the Prākrit inscription from Besnagar in Central India left by Heliodoros, the ambassador of an Indo-Greek king, not only does it offer the most interesting and valuable regional comparison for the inscription of Sōphytos, but its own various points of interest also merit bringing it, once again, before an audience of classicists and presenting it in a manner that allows it to be critically assessed and used. My commentary on the inscription of Heliodoros is therefore a little lengthier than that on the other inscriptions discussed here. As well as a regional context for the inscription of Sōphytos, what it also provides is a point of comparison for the literary techniques and ethnocultural strategies employed. It has been argued, for example, that Sōphytos adopts a Homeric style and that Heliodoros makes reference to the Indian epic the *Mahābhārata:* What did they thereby seek to demonstrate about their own educations, and did they envisage audiences for their inscriptions who would be alert to such references?

The ethnic ambiguity of Sōphytos and Heliodoros—and whether the perception of such ambiguity is a matter of modern sensibilities rather than ancient ones—will naturally occupy much of my discussion. Such apparent ambiguity is by no means unique to the Hellenistic Far East. There are many potential epigraphic comparisons from elsewhere in the Hellenistic and Roman world, but one of the most fruitful may be the small group of Greek and Latin acrostic inscriptions left by Roman military and administrative personnel on the walls of the

---

5. Much useful information on this trade may still be found on the website of the now-defunct Illicit Antiquities Research Centre at the University of Cambridge (http://www.mcdonald.cam.ac.uk/projects/iarc/home.htm).

temples of Kalabsha and Philae, in Lower Nubia.[6] The author of two of these inscriptions, one Paccius Maximus, has often been viewed as a Nubian who makes an overt but inelegant protestation of his Greek education and cultural affinities. Maximus's identification as Nubian is not, as I will discuss, so secure as some have assumed. But his inscriptions come from a region of the ancient world as culturally and ethnically complex as the Hellenistic Far East, a complexity that seems to have provoked in its literate inhabitants a similar desire to control the presentation of their identities and, perhaps, a similar insecurity in these identities. The authors of the acrostic inscriptions from Lower Nubia know that they are clever—just as Sōphytos, who repeats his acrostic in a separate column to the left of his epitaph, knows that he is clever and wants others to know it. Both Maximus and Sōphytos also make very explicit plays on Greek high culture at cultural and political boundaries, entirely expected places for cultural and perhaps ethnic boundaries to be actively patrolled.

There is no direct connection between these regions (Arachosia and India, and Nubia), but it is no coincidence that we find similar forms of cultural expression and similar levels of ethnic ambiguity in such zones of interaction at the edges of the Hellenistic or the Roman empire.[7] In some way, I view the inscriptions of Heliodoros and Paccius Maximus as responses to that of Sōphytos. They may enable us to enlarge on some issues provoked by the inscription of Sōphytos without drifting too far into speculation or being impeded too much by its lack of any archaeological context.

THE STELE OF SŌPHYTOS
(OLD KANDAHAR, ARACHOSIA)

THE STELE OF SŌPHYTOS

(Acrostic: Through Sōphytos the son of Naratos)

The irresistible force of the trio of Fates destroyed the house of my forefathers, which had flourished greatly for many years. But I, Sōphytos son of Naratos, pitiably bereft when quite small of my ancestral livelihood, after I had acquired the virtue of the Archer [i.e., Apollo] and the Muses, mixed with noble prudence, then did consider how I might raise up again my family house. Obtaining interest-bearing money from another source, I left home, keen not to return before I possessed wealth, the supreme good. Thus, by traveling to many cities for commerce, I acquired ample riches without reproach. Becoming celebrated, I returned to my homeland after countless years and showed myself, bringing pleasure to well-wishers. Straightaway I built afresh my

---

6. Mairs 2011b. Mairs 2012 presents a full discussion of these, alongside some Latin acrostic verse inscriptions from the Roman fort at Bu Njem in Libya (Adams 1999).

7. A direct comparison between these two "resource frontiers" in the Hellenistic period is made by Burstein 1993 and Holt 1993.

paternal home, which was riddled with rot, making it better than before, and also, since the tomb had collapsed to the ground, I constructed another one and during my lifetime set upon it by the roadside this loquacious plaque. Thus may the sons and grandsons of myself, who completed this enviable work, possess my house.

The Stele of Sōphytos[8]—the title he himself gives to his inscription—does not come from an excavated context and is not at present generally accessible to scholars. It is in a private collection,[9] the identity of which is not a matter of public knowledge, and it appears to have been acquired from the antiquities market without passing through any official regulatory channels. The editors propose that it was found at Kandahar or in its immediate vicinity. Very little information has thus far been published on the circumstances of its discovery or acquisition. The editors' informants appear to have known the provenance, and that of the other Greek Central Asian inscription published in the same article, but chose to remain reticent on the subject.[10] The case for a provenance in Kandahar is nevertheless a good one. The literary quality of the piece suggests that it can only have been produced in a center where Greek speakers had settled and brought with them their cultural traditions and system of education. Although the Hellenistic-period city at Old Kandahar has not been fully excavated (see further below), it has yielded a small number of Greek inscriptions from the third century B.C.E.: a votive thank offering[11] and two longer translations of edicts of the Indian emperor Aśoka, under whose political control Kandahar lay at this period.[12] One of these edicts is on a stone of remarkably similar size, material, and workmanship to the stele of Sōphytos,[13] which is on a square block of white limestone (62.0 × 62.0 cm, 12.5 cm deep). Both stones are roughly worked on the back, and were evidently designed to be set into the walls of buildings. The Aśokan inscription contains only a partial text, indicating that it was one of several such inscribed stones placed into the same wall. Likewise, Sōphytos's stele may have been only one of several such epitaphs for individual members of a family, mounted on the walls of their communal tomb. As will be discussed below, the possible Indian affinities of Sōphytos and his father, Naratos, mean that an Arachosian origin also makes sense.

The question of the inscription's authenticity cannot be avoided. At present, little can be verified about its point of origin or emergence onto and trajectory

8. Text: Bernard, Pinault, and Rougemont 2004; *SEG* 54 (2004), 1568. Trans. after Hollis 2011. The reader may wish to compare two other English translations, by Nagle and Burstein 2006 (285) and by Lougovaya 2009, for the choices that they make in giving literal or nonliteral renderings of sometimes obscure words, and for their choices of sense: e.g., l. 11, "on merchant ships" vs. "as a merchant."

9. Bernard, Pinault, and Rougemont 2004, 227.

10. Ibid. 338.

11. Fraser 1979.

12. Schlumberger et al. 1958; Schlumberger 1964; Benveniste 1964.

13. Schlumberger 1964.

FIGURE 7. Inscription of Sōphytos. For transcription and translation, see the appendix. (Bernard, Pinault, and Rougemont 2004, Figure 1; © Académie des Inscriptions et Belles-Lettres.)

through the antiquities market. The only faults in the text are two spelling aberrations and a metrical error,[14] but the greatest point of suspicion is whether the inscription is too good to be true. The Greek is refined and literary, the quality of the carving good, and—either generic or ambiguous though they are—the references within the text itself give the historian of the Hellenistic Far East more mate-

14. Rougemont (Bernard, Pinault, and Rougemont 2004, 231) corrects as follows: l. 5, ἤσ(κ)ηκα; l. 6, (τ)ῆμος. I have retained the spelling as it appears on the stone.

rial to work with than almost anything that has come out of the region south of the Oxus since the cessation of the excavations at Ai Khanoum. The points in favor of the inscription's authenticity are, according to the editors, as follows: the fine lime-stone of the stele is identical to that bearing the Aśokan edicts discussed above; metrical errors may be found in poetic inscriptions whose authenticity is not in doubt; and, if the inscription was made by a faker, it was made by one of unparalleled skill—extremely well-versed in literary Greek, familiar with the obscure names Sōphytos and Naratos and the equally obscure history of the Hellenistic Far East, and able to carve an inscription indistinguishable from a Hellenistic original.[15] Another point in favor of the inscription's authenticity is, to my mind, the fact that it is not the strangest Greek inscription to have come out of Hellenistic Kandahar: here, the edicts of Aśoka, with their exposition of a Buddhist ethical code and Indian *bramenai* (brahmans) and *sramenai* (Buddhist mendicants) transliterated into Greek, still take the prize. There is always the risk that the inscription is a fake—as there is, to whatever degree, with any inscription that has not come from an excavated context—but unless that conclusion should be demonstrated, it would be a great pity not to take advantage of it.

The letter forms and vocabulary of the inscription enable it to be dated only very broadly; Georges Rougemont finds an exact palaeographical parallel in the recently published funerary inscriptions from Ai Khanoum, a city whose Greek period came to an end around the middle of the second century B.C.E.[16] Bernard, on the basis of his interpretations of Sōphytos's cultural and familial background (see further below), gives a lower limit of around 100 B.C.E. (Bernard, Pinault, and Rougemont 2004, 318–19). So a date somewhere in the second century B.C.E., perhaps even a little earlier, seems not unreasonable. The editio princeps includes a lengthy, detailed philological and historical commentary,[17] and it is to this that the reader is referred for a full discussion of such matters as palaeography, literary style, and the possible connections of this Sōphytos to a Sōphytes or Sōphytos known from the numismatic record in the Hellenistic Far East.[18]

The Greek text below in the appendix follows that of Rougemont,[19] with the exception of two places where his reading corrects letters clearly visible on the excellent color photograph of the stone itself:[20] *ēskhēka* in line 5 and *thēmos* in line 6. In each case the expected voiceless stop (*ēskēka, tēmos*) is replaced by the corresponding aspirate before eta. Although this rule does not apply elsewhere in the

15. Ibid. 134 n. 5.

16. Ibid. 2004, 234–36, fig. 4; these inscriptions were published as Rougemont 2012, nos. 136–37.

17. The inscription was the subject of a preliminary note in Bernard and Rougemont 2003 and full publication in Bernard, Pinault, and Rougemont 2004; see also Rougemont 2005 and Pinault 2005.

18. On whom see also Bopearachchi 1996.

19. Bernard, Pinault, and Rougemont 2004.

20. Ibid. 230, fig. 1.

inscription (e.g., *aretēn* in l. 5) or in the other Greek texts from Kandahar, the appearance of the same phonological deviation twice in as many lines is suggestive of some distinctive feature of the spoken language rather than a simple spelling error.[21] Perhaps aspiration was a feature of the Arachosian Greek accent.

The inscription is in elegiac couplets, with an irregularity in the meter in line 18. This line should be a dactylic pentameter, but has two syllables too many: a curious slip in an otherwise elegant text. Two corrections have been suggested to resolve this difficulty,[22] but the text on the stone is clear. Did the author perhaps intend to change meter (note the variation in meter in the Lower Nubian inscriptions discussed below) and then think better of it? One solution is to view the mistake as that not of the poet but of the stonemason, who for some reason altered the wording of the line.[23] The first letter of each line of the poem is repeated in the large margin to the left, to make the acrostic more visible. Overtly literary acrostic verse inscriptions of this sort, as will be discussed further below, frequently signpost their acrostics for the reader, whether by laying out the inscription in a certain way or by making direct reference to the acrostic form.

HELLENISTIC KANDAHAR

As signaled in Bernard's historical commentary, the inscription of Sōphytos most urgently demands to be considered alongside the archaeological evidence for funerary practice at Kandahar itself.[24] It would be especially helpful to be able to relate the stele to an archaeological context, since it makes explicit reference to a roadside family tomb upon which, given the stone's form, it appears to have been mounted. Parallels may be suggested with the excavated mausoleum from the cemetery at Ai Khanoum,[25] but potentially useful and evocative as these are, they must remain hypothetical. Old Kandahar, a ruin field outside the modern city, is a site of great archaeological promise, but most of this potential remains unrealized.[26] A small number of excavation seasons were carried out by a British team in the 1970s,[27] and these revealed a small amount of material from the Hellenistic period. The evidence for funerary practice more specifically is sparse and, for the most part, of uncertain date. Two wreathed amphorae containing the remains of

---

21. As Rougemont (ibid. 232–33) notes, following Chamoux.

22. Ibid. 233–34.

23. Hollis 2011.

24. The most recent discussions of the archaeology of Hellenistic Kandahar, and Arachosia as a whole, are those of Bernard 2005 and Mairs 2011c; on funerary practice in the Hellenistic Far East, see Grenet 1984 (a multiperiod study) and Mairs 2007.

25. Bernard, Pinault, and Rougemont 2004, 322–23; Bernard 1972, 608–25.

26. Helms 1982, 8–9.

27. McNicoll 1978; Whitehouse 1978; Helms 1979, 1997; McNicoll and Ball 1996.

calcinated bones in the museum at Kandahar, studied by Umberto Scerrato, are divorced from any knowledge of their archaeological context or the ethnic or social affiliation of their owners. Scerrato dates one tentatively to the Sasanian period.[28] A pre-Islamic cemetery lay under a later Muslim cemetery at Pir-i Sabz, by the side of the road toward Girishk and Herat, but this was the subject of only a brief exploration in 1958, which revealed a number of *pithoi* and bronze bathtub-shaped basins. On the basis of ceramic evidence, Scerrato (again, very tentatively) dates these between the second and fourth centuries C.E.[29] Archaeologically, the funerary architecture of Hellenistic Kandahar therefore remains completely unknown. On the literary-historical side, references in later Zoroastrian texts to unorthodox funerary practices in Arachosia are ambiguous and not useful for our purposes.[30]

Politically, Arachosia changed hands several times between the fourth and first centuries B.C.E. Although the region played a part in wider power struggles in this period, in particular between the Seleucid and Maurya empires, it is difficult to escape the conclusion that it was for most of this time effectively autonomous, or at least only loosely integrated into the administrative structures of the external states that claimed to control it, perhaps by some of the same strategies of effective governance by administrative continuity proposed for Bactria above in chapter 1.[31] Certainly, the theme that emerges most strongly from the archaeological record of Old Kandahar is the predominance of local forms—for example, in ceramics—alongside the more spectacular evidence of cultural and economic contacts with adjacent, and also distant, territories. Arachosia, famously, was sold by Seleukos I to the Maurya emperor Chandragupta for five hundred elephants in a peace treaty of 303 B.C.E. that also included a marriage agreement, the terms of which have provoked some debate.[32] Seleukos, it is generally agreed, got rather a good deal. Politically and militarily, one of the main reasons for a Near Eastern ruler to attempt to assert control over this region—which lacked the agricultural potential of Bactria, to the north—was to secure the route to India and his supply of war elephants. With regard to the *epigamia* (marriage clause) of the treaty, the two main possibilities that have been considered are: first, that either Seleukos or Chandragupta supplied a daughter to be married into the family of the other (if this was the case, then there is no subsequent trace of this princess in the historical record); or second, that the *epigamia* refers to an interstate agreement on rights of intermarriage, such

28. Scerrato 1980, esp. 638–39; cf. Bernard, Pinault, and Rougemont 2004, 325; but note that Bernard had not been able to take account of Scerrato's work.

29. Scerrato 1980, 641, 645, 647.

30. See, e.g., Benveniste 1962, 42.

31. See Fussman 1982 on the Maurya empire.

32. Bernard 1985, 85–95; Karttunen 1997, 261–63; Foucher and Bazin-Foucher 1942–47, 313–14; Mairs 2011c, 181–82. Historical sources: Strabo 15.2.9; Appian 9.55; Plutarch, *Alexander* 62.4.

as those instituted between some Greek states to guarantee the citizenship of the children of mixed marriages.[33] This *epigamia* may therefore have been designed to guarantee the civic rights and official Greekness of the population of Arachosia now that they were passing under Indian rule.[34] Although this theory cannot be proved, raising questions of official identities, civic status, and the position of individuals within local social hierarchies and heterarchies is potentially a useful way of approaching all these inscriptions. In Indian terms, the institution of caste makes such questions still more relevant. The position of Heliodoros and other Greeks with regard to contemporary Indian caste-style systems of social organization will be discussed in the next section. Chandragupta's grandson Aśoka, as has already been noted, continued his empirewide practice of setting up edicts proclaiming his new Buddhist ethical code at Kandahar. Although the edicts from the Indian subcontinent display little linguistic deviation from the standard northern Indian, Middle Indo-Aryan Prākrit of the Maurya court and administration, it is notable that in Arachosia and the Indo-Iranian borderlands in general both Aramaic and Greek were used.[35] Aramaic, it seems probable—as I have suggested in chapter 1—was not simply a fossilized remnant of Achaemenid control of the region but continued to have some currency as a language of administration and literate communication. The Achaemenid Aramaic documents from Bactria provide new evidence for the extensive and linguistically creative use of Aramaic as a written lingua franca by Iranian speakers in the Upper Satrapies. Arachosia, therefore, was part of Aśoka's empire but a region in which, unusually, he sought to appeal to local populations in their own languages and on their own terms.

As well as the sociopolitical changes that were potentially wrought on Arachosia by the transition from Seleucid to Maurya rule in 303 B.C.E., another important transition was that from Maurya to Graeco-Bactrian control in the early second century B.C.E., as Graeco-Bactrian kings began their military expansion south of the Hindu Kush into Arachosia and India. The second Greek inscription published by Bernard, Pinault, and Rougemont in their article (2004) on the Sōphytos inscription honors the Graeco-Bactrian king Euthydemos and his son Demetrios, whose was primarily responsible for the Graeco-Bactrian "Drang nach Süden." It therefore seems likely that Sōphytos lived at least part of his life in a Kandahar that was part of a wider Greek-ruled state. This state still produced coinage with Greek legends and Greek portraiture and religious imagery, although bilingual Greek-Prākrit legends and syncretic religious imagery were becoming more com-

33. See, e.g., Lysias 34.3 on fifth-century-B.C.E. Athens and Euboia.
34. Bernard 1985, 92–93.
35. Aramaic: Schlumberger, et al. 1958; Benveniste and Dupont-Sommer 1966; Dupont-Sommer 1969.

mon.[36] Bernard suggests that this sudden reacquaintance and political subjection of the Greek population of Kandahar to their fellow descendants of Alexander's army from Bactria may have provoked a desire to reinforce and reassert Greek culture and identity.[37] It may even have been politically expedient. Such arguments about the sociocultural implications of regime change are, however, difficult to support with any firm evidence one way or the other. They may also color our assumptions about Sōphytos's supposed cultural insecurity, a supposition based on the notion that his display of Greek erudition, from a man with a non-Greek name, is assertive to the point of being defensive.

SŌPHYTOS AND HIS INSCRIPTION

Sōphytos's inscription fits within the tradition of Greek funerary epigrams, displayed with an implicit or explicit appeal to the passerby to stop, read the inscription, and think about the accomplishments or misfortunes of the person commemorated.[38] The *proskunēmata* of Paccius Maximus and others on the temples of Lower Nubia, discussed below, sometimes offer the reader an additional reward— that they, too, will benefit from the author's prayer to the god—but Sōphytos's references to Greek gods are as patrons of the arts, and the achievements of Sōphytos and his family are the major theme.

The names of Sōphytos and his father, Naratos (or Narates: the name appears only as the patronymic *Naratiadēs*), are not Greek. Pinault makes a strong case for their being Indian, from original forms Subhūti and Nārada, both well-attested Indian names.[39] There were no absolute rules for the transcription of Indo-Aryan languages into Greek (as there were none for the transcription of Greek into Middle Indo-Aryan Prākrits: see further below), but there seems to have been some attempt to adapt the phonology to something more usual in a Greek name, even if the result is semantic nonsense. The composer of the inscription clearly has no problem adapting and integrating these names into a Greek text, freely forming a Greek patronymic from the foreign name Naratos.

---

36. For a case study involving Agathokles (fl. ca. 190–180 B.C.E.), one of the first kings to be a Greek *basileus* and an Indian *rāja* on the same coin, see Holt 1988, 1–7.

37. Bernard, Pinault, and Rougemont 2004, 318.

38. Ibid. 2004, 237.

39. Ibid. 2004, 249–59; Pinault 2005. Given our lack of knowledge of the indigenous Iranian languages of the Hellenistic Far East at this period, it is as well not to rule out alternative origins. The Iranianized Aramaic of the region under Achaemenid rule suggests one or more local languages that lacked any written form (Kandahar: Schlumberger, et al. 1958; Benveniste and Dupont-Sommer 1966. Bactria: Shaked 2004; Naveh and Shaked 2012. See also an ostrakon in Aramaic script from Ai Khanoum: Rapin 1992, 105).

Although Naratos is not otherwise known in this Greek form, the name Sōphytos appears on a series of Greek coins of various denominations from the Hellenistic Far East from sometime around the turn of the fourth-to-third century B.C.E.[40] On one side is a Greek-style portrait with an Attic helmet, on the other a cockerel and the legend *Sōphutou*, without any title. Since his name appears only in the genitive, he may be a Sōphytos or a Sōphytes. Bernard treats the question of this earlier Sōphytos and his relationship to the Sōphytos of our inscription at some length.[41] He argues that "Sōphytos A" was a Mauryan satrap of Arachosia, of Indian origin, and that "Sōphytos B" was a descendant. Other than the coincidence of the names, we have the circumstantial evidence of Sōphytos B's reference to his family's wealth and lineage and the fact that both, despite their common non-Greek name, presented themselves *à la grecque*. This family tradition of philhellenism, Bernard suggests, can only have been reinforced when Arachosia reentered the *oikoumenē* of Hellenistic Central Asia at the beginning of the second century B.C.E.

This is a seductive hypothesis, not least because we have nothing else to go on. It is worth bearing in mind, however, that the issues of Sōphytos A have more usually been considered to come from a mint north of the Hindu Kush, in Bactria, a case that Osmund Bopearachchi restates in response to Bernard,[42] making Sōphytos A an independent dynast of Bactria about 315–305 B.C.E. At the present state of our knowledge, we are not in any position to base any argument about Sōphytos B's background and lineage on our deductions about Sōphytos A. It would be nice if Bernard's argument for a prominent Kandaharan family of Indian origin could be confirmed, but there remains the possibility that the origins of both Sōphytoi are to be looked for in a more local context, in the power struggles of local dignitaries in Bactria and Arachosia of the late fourth century B.C.E.

Sōphytos—if he is the author of his verse—is extremely well educated, not just well educated for an Arachosian. (Questions of authorship will be discussed in my remarks concluding this chapter.) In both Sōphytos's inscription and Heliodoros's, commentators have noted some affinity with Greek or Indian literary culture. Whether or not these impressions are correct—and I will argue below that we should be a little more cautious in tracing direct quotation or literary inspiration—such affinities raise the question of the relationship between individuals' ethnic identities (and the ethnic milieux within which they can comfortably and convinc-

---

40. Bopearachchi 1996. Pinault (Bernard, Pinault, and Rougemont 2004, 262) considers the minor king Sopeithes encountered by Alexander in northeastern India (see, e.g., Curtius 9.1.24, Diodorus Siculus 17.91.4, Strabo 15.1.30–31) to be another Greek transcription of the same name, Subhūti, but here it is still more difficult to argue any direct connection.

41. Bernard, Pinault, and Rougemont 2004, 282–317.

42. Bopearachchi and Flandrin 2005, 195–201.

ingly operate) and the cultural means of induction by which we suppose people to have acquired the ability to operate in more than one such sphere, this "functional ethnicity," and its underlying *habitus*.[43] Although ethnic identity is and has always been an important topic in Hellenistic studies,[44] the approach to it is relatively static: the questions examined relate to ethnicity and its functioning within a particular community or contact situation (as in my discussion of Ai Khanoum in chapter 2) or in a particular individual's life. One area that has not received so much attention is the question how individuals acquire any notion of their own ethnic identities in the first place, in childhood, or how they integrate the new cultural stimuli to which they are exposed later in life, and the new skills, practices, or languages that they may acquire, into evolving notions of their own identities.[45] Sōphytos, as it happens, does make explicit reference to his education and early exposure to Greek culture in his cultivation of the virtue (*aretē*) of Apollo and the Muses, even after being deprived while still young of his family's wealth and reputation (ll. 5–6). It is a combination of this culture and sense of family honor—along with hard cash—that enables him to establish himself and to provide for his children and grandchildren later in life.

Compared with Heliodoros's, Sōphytos's verse is the more overtly intellectual of the two inscriptions, self-conscious in its own erudition. He clearly has his audience in mind and is concerned to project a particular image of himself: he is successful and cultured, a man who has restored the fortune and reputation of himself and his family. Even the layout of the inscription is an opportunity to show off. The acrostic DIA SŌPHYTOU TOU NARATOU is repeated in a column to the left of the inscription, making immediately obvious to the reader just how clever and skillful he has been in constructing it and also, probably, to indicate that he composed the text personally. An example from Roman Egypt, the Stele of Moschion, may serve as illustration of the studied playfulness typically involved in such an exercise.[46] Moschion's stele contains eleven preserved inscriptions, in Greek and Demotic Egyptian, including word squares and acrostics bearing his own name. The subject matter of several of the inscriptions is the very fact that they have been composed in such a way, and they include guides to the reader as to how to approach deciphering them. Just as Sōphytos does, Moschion repeats his Greek and Demotic acrostics in a column alongside the text to make them more immediately obvious. Moschion has reason to be proud of his epigraphic sophistry. Constructing an acrostic in a language, such as Greek or English, that uses a purely alphabetic script is clever enough. But in Demotic, written in a script that combines alphabetic

---

43. Bourdieu 1977 and 1998, 8.
44. See, e.g., Goudriaan 1988.
45. See Casella and Fowler 2004 for some archaeological case studies.
46. Brunsch 1979; Bresciani 1980; Vleeming 2001, 199–209 (text 205); Mairs forthcoming (1).

signs and semantic determinatives, as well as fossilized conventional writings of words that defy straightforward alphabetic reading, it is another matter entirely.[47] The inscriptions' intended audience—other than the dedicatee, Osiris—is stated in the Greek inscription: *Hellēsi kai endapioisin*, "Greeks and natives." Sōphytos, however, is clearly appealing to an audience that identifies itself strongly with Greek culture. Although he never calls himself a Greek—or anything else—his inscription is linguistically and culturally monolingual.

Sōphytos's emphasis on his learning is so insistent that it is tempting to read some insecurity into it. His learning is the very Greek learning of Apollo and the Muses, and of recherché literary vocabulary. The verse is composed in elegiac couplets, with a number of the words being rarities otherwise found only in occasional poems,[48] or antiquated terms ordinarily found only in Homeric verse.[49] A direct Homeric homage appears in line 11, where Sōphytos apparently echoes the opening lines of the *Odyssey* (Sōphytos l. 11, *iōn eis astea polla*; cf. *Odyssey* 1.3, *pollōn d' anthrōpōn iden astea kai noon egnō*). This kind of Homeric touch was not unusual in the literary tradition of Greek epitaphs within which the inscription of Sōphytos is cast, and reference to this particular line was especially popular: a nice way of summing up a well-traveled man's life and achievements, within a familiar Homeric framework.[50] So Sōphytos's reference, although oblique, is probably not accidental. Sōphytos's sense of honor and reputation emerges in his frequent references to family fortune, praise, the restoration of highly visible symbols of wealth such as the family tomb, and the joy that his new wealth and status bring to those who wish him well. But Sōphytos is a practical man as well as a poet, and he stresses that he has rebuilt his family's wealth and reputation by himself—with the help of "start-up capital" (*teknophoron argurion*).[51]

In the absence of any explicitly stated claim to Greek identity by Sōphytos, the interplay between ideas of ethnicity, culture, social status, and prestige on the stele invites us to reconsider our assumptions about the relationship between intellectual culture, language use, and ethnic identity. It is clear that Sōphytos is using the Greek language to express his claims to high status, filial piety, and intellectual and cultural refinement; but what significance, in this context, did his use of Greek have? Was there an alternative language or cultural convention within which he could have chosen to make these statements? There is evidence of the use of Aramaic and Prākrit at Kandahar, in the Aśokan edicts, but this is not sufficient to give

---

47. For a hieroglyphic example see Zandee 1966.

48. E.g., l. 1, *kokuōn*, "ancestors": Callimachos, *Hecale* fr. 137, inter alia. L. 3, *tunnos*, "so small": Callimachus fr. 420, Theocritus 24.139.

49. E.g., l. 4, *eunis*, "deprived"; discussed in Bernard, Pinault, and Rougemont 2004, 242–44, with other examples, and by Hollis 2011.

50. Bernard, Pinault, and Rougemont 2004, 240–41.

51. The translation is that of Lougovaya 2009.

us a detailed picture of the domains within which each language was used. On the Stele of Sōphytos, it is interesting to note how notions of high socioeconomic status, Greek culture, and perhaps even Greek burial go together, but we should hesitate to prioritize these facets of the inscription's overall presentation of Sōphytos's identity. Whether Sōphytos's acquisition and projection of a Greek education made him Greek—or whether he ever considered that it did—remains a matter for debate. The example of post-Renaissance Europe shows that Greek (and Latin) learning might be something that individuals could perceive strongly as the basis of their intellectual culture, and that they might use to display their social status, without ever choosing to use it as a statement of their ethnic identity.[52] At no point in his inscription does Sōphytos ever attach an ethnic to himself, and we should be similarly hesitant to do so, concentrating instead on the questions raised about the interplay between culture, language, status, and ethnicity at Hellenistic Kandahar.

Alongside the great heuristic potential of cautious and comparative analysis of the inscription of Sōphytos, a few other, more positive conclusions to this discussion may be made. The Stele of Sōphytos provides us with a window onto the crossing and restating of cultural and ethnic boundaries in Hellenistic Kandahar. An Indian name in a Greek inscription, however open-minded we should remain about the individual's ethnic identity and status, is still a remarkable occurrence, one that allows us an insight into a process of ethnic and linguistic change and variation in Hellenistic Arachosia of which we might otherwise remain ignorant. That this evolved alongside a more formal system of ethnic categorization may perhaps be deduced from the *epigamia* of 303 B.C.E., if its terms remained in force, or from the possible repercussions of the Graeco-Bactrian takeover of the early second century. Finally, Sōphytos's statement of his restoration of his family's fortunes is explicitly couched in terms of his restoration of their house and of their tomb. A tomb is a visible symbol in the landscape, one that could be used to project an individual's or a community's sense of his or its own identity and relationship to the local environment. Sōphytos's family tomb was bound up with his ideas of personal and familial prestige, and it was one of the key vehicles through which he chose to make a statement of his own status and identity.

THE INSCRIPTION OF HELIODOROS
AT BESNAGAR (CENTRAL INDIA)

Our second inscription, although very roughly contemporary with that of Sōphytos, presents a number of contrasts. It has been known for over a century: it

---

52. See, e.g., Shanks 1996, 80, on nineteenth-century Romantic nationalism: "A nationalism focused upon monuments, history and other cultural phenomena was combined with an international concern for the Classical Greek past stemming not from ethnic interest but from ideas of cultural descent."

remains in situ and may still be visited today; and it appears to present a Greek in Indian clothing rather than the converse. The desirability of making this inscription more accessible to classicists means that my discussion here, especially as regards the archaeological context and Indian cultural and religious milieu of the inscription, will be rather longer and more heavily referenced. Even more so than the Stele of Sōphytos, the dedication of Heliodoros is an orphan inscription, in that classics and South Asian Studies both seem to think that it properly belongs to the other discipline.[53] In devoting space to a longer commentary, it is my intention is that those without an Indological background may thereby gain more confidence in using and working with it. For these purposes, Richard Salomon's handbook of Indian epigraphy is highly recommended.[54]

The inscription appears on a pillar of pinkish brown sandstone with a bell-shaped capital, a little over seven meters in height, the first report of which was published by Sir Alexander Cunningham, founder of the Archaeological Survey of India, in 1880.[55] The inscription initially went unnoticed, since at the time of Cunningham's inspection the pillar was still very much an object of cult and pilgrimage—as it continues to be.[56] The column shaft had been smeared by pilgrims with a thick coating of vermilion paint. Cunningham was therefore unable to examine it further and reluctantly restricted himself to recording the report of local people that it was uninscribed. John Marshall, in 1909, was the first to record the presence of an inscription, which was given an initial transcription and translation by Jules Bloch in the same publication.[57]

The inscribed area of the main inscription (A) is approximately fifty-six centimeters wide by fifty-two centimeters high. A briefer inscription (B) appears on the opposite side of the pillar. The script is Brāhmī of the Śuṅga period, and the language is central-to-western epigraphic Prākrit, with some Sanskritic spellings. Inscription B may be in verse.[58] The relationship between the two inscriptions is nowhere fully discussed, although their similarity in script and position on opposite sides of the same pillar would suggest that they were engraved on the same occasion, for or by the same person.[59]

---

53. Note, however, Burstein 1985 (72 no. 53) and 2003, 234.

54. Salomon 1998.

55. Cunningham 1880, 41–42.

56. Bhandarkar 1917, 187–88; Khare 1975–76, 177–78; Theuns-de Boer 1999.

57. Marshall 1909. The first full publications or commentaries are those of Fleet (1909, 1910), Barnett (1909), Venis (1910), and Vogel (1912). The best published illustration of the inscription remains the rubbing in Marshall (1909), which is reproduced by Narain (1957) and Salomon (1998). Illustrations and photographs of the pillar: Bhandarkar 1917 and Vassiliades 2000. There are inaccuracies in the drawings in Cunningham 1880: Irwin 1975–76, 166. Diagrams of the pillar's structure and plans of the various excavations carried out at Besnagar: Irwin 1975–76.

58. Salomon 1998, 265.

59. Raychaudhuri 1922; Audouin and Bernard 1974, 16 n. 1; Narain 1957.

A date of 110 B.C.E. has become commonly accepted and reproduced in the scholarly literature, but as will be discussed below, internal references in the inscription
itself really enable us only to place it somewhere in the late second century B.C.E.[60]

The most up-to-date edition with translation of the inscription of Heliodoros is
that of Salomon, which I reproduce here.[61] (I have not included a full *apparatus
criticus*.)[62] Variations in readings—due to the worn surface of the pillar and the
poorly known historical context—are mostly minor. Names repeated in square
brackets below are the Greek or Sanskrit forms of the Prākrit versions used in the
inscription.

INSCRIPTION A

[de]vadevasa v[ā][sude]vasa garuḍadhvaje ayaṃ
kārit[e] i[a?] heliodoreṇa bhāga-
vatena diyasa putreṇa ta[khkha]silākena
yonadūtena āgatena mahārājasa
aṃtalikitasa upa[ṃ]tā sakāsaṃ raño 5
kāsīput[r]asa bhāgabhadrasa trātārasa
vasena ca[tu]dasena rājena vadhamānasa.

This Garuḍa pillar of Vāsudeva, the god of gods,
was constructed here by Heliodora [Hēliodōros], the Bhāgavata,
son of Diya [Diōn], of Takhkhasilā [Taxila],
the Greek ambassador who came from the Great King
Aṃtalikita [Antialkidas] to King   5
Kāsīputra [Kāśīputra] Bhāgabhadra, the Savior,
prospering in (his) fourteenth regnal year.

INSCRIPTION B

trini amutapād[ā]ni [i][me?] [su]anuṭhitāni
neyaṃti sva[gaṃ] dam[e] cāga apramāda.   2

(These?) three steps to immortality, when correctly followed,
lead to heaven: control, generosity, and attention.   2

HELIODOROS, TAXILA, AND ANTIALKIDAS

Heliodoros's inscription provides us, at first sight, with precisely the kind of specific
information that Sōphytos's lacks. We have a man with an identifiably Greek
name and patronymic (Hēliodōros son of Diōn)—albeit with Prākrit case

60. Salomon 1998, 265–66.
61. Ibid.
62. Previous readings may be consulted in Narain 1957, caption to pl. VI, and Sircar 1965b, 88–89.

endings[63]—an ethnic (*yona*, "Greek"), occupation or political role (ambassador), his king (Antialkidas) and point of origin (Taxila). The problem with many of these specifics is that our knowledge of the historical context is severely compromised. How we should refer to Heliodoros is a question that provokes varying degrees of scholarly angst. Most often, he is a "Greek," with disquisitions on his cultural and religious identity reserved for a longer discussion. He has also been represented as a "foreign convert [to Vaiṣṇavism]"[64] and a "half-Indianized Greek."[65] The more doubts an author has about his ethnic and cultural identity, the greater the number of brackets and subordinate clauses that are introduced. The definitive Hellenistic-style designation of Heliodoros is that of Klaus Karttunen, who refers to him as "a Greek (or at least someone using a Greek name even in an Indian inscription)":[66] this is precisely the level of doubt over the ethnic implications of nomenclature that the study of the evidence from other areas of the Hellenistic world should condition in us. What we make of the ethnic identity and self-presentation of Heliodoros is of critical importance for what we judge to have been the range of identities experienced and openly articulated by his epigraphically unattested compatriots.

Heliodoros came from the easternmost of the states of the Hellenistic Far East. Under Demetrios I in the early second century B.C.E.,[67] as has already been mentioned, the Greek-ruled kingdom of Bactria began to expand south of the Hindu Kush, into the territories that had been ceded by Seleukos I to the Maurya empire in 303 B.C.E.[68] Although briefer incursions may have taken place into Central India and along the Ganges Valley, the power base of the various Indo-Greek kings was always in the northwest, around modern northern Pakistan and the Panjāb. Taxila (Sanskrit Takṣaśilā; Prākrit Takhkhasilā), Heliodoros's home city, was in this

63. For other examples of Greek names in Indian inscriptions, besides those of Indo-Greek kings on coin legends, see Karttunen 1994 and 1997, 296–97, 308–9; Seldeslachts 2004, passim. Some of those previously identified are, as Karttunen and Seldeslachts both note, more probably not to be considered Greek at all. The identification of the name of the Indo-Greek king Menander in an inscription from Reh, in the central-to-eastern Ganges Valley (Sharma 1980), is a case in point: Fussman1993a, 117–20.

64. Khare 1966, 24.

65. Harmatta 1994, 406.

66. Karttunen 1997, 296.

67. Demetrios—to whom I shall return in chapter 4—is historically and epigraphically the best attested of the Graeco-Bactrian and Indo-Greek kings: there are brief mentions by Polybios (11.34) and Strabo (1.11.1), and he appears, alongside his father, Euthydemos, in a dedicatory altar inscription, probably from northern Bactria (Kuliab, Tajikistan: Bernard, Pinault, and Rougemont 2004, 333–56). His only potential rival is Menander I, in the mid-second century B.C.E., who appears in the same passage of Strabo and inspired a later Pāli Buddhist text, the *Milindapañha* or *Questions of King Milinda*, in which he debates with a Buddhist sage (Rhys-Davids 1890). A regnal year of Menander appears on a reliquary from Shinkot (Bajaur, Pakistan: Fussman1993a, 95–111), but a supposed appearance in an inscription at Reh now seems unlikely. (See the previous note.)

68. Strabo 15.2.1; Bernard 1985, 85–95; Karttunen 1997, 261–63; Foucher and Bazin-Foucher 1942–47, 313–14.

region. The city lay to the west of modern Islamabad, in Pakistan, and had a long history of habitation on several separate sites in the same vicinity.[69] The second major city at Taxila, Sirkap, a substantial site built on a grid plan, was founded by the Indo-Greeks in the first part of the second century B.C.E.[70]

Heliodoros's king, Antialkidas I (reigned ca. 115–95 B.C.E.),[71] like the vast majority of the Indo-Greek kings, is otherwise known only from numismatic evidence;[72] the uncertainty of the identification and date of Bhāgabhadra (see further below) does not permit us to use the inscription of Heliodoros to furnish more precise information on the dates of his reign. At the time of Heliodoros's mission, Taxila evidently belonged to his kingdom, the territorial extent of which seems to have varied. The inscription of Heliodoros provides an extremely rare case, in which we can tie a numismatically attested Indo-Greek king to other forms of evidence. It also gives us some information on Antialkidas's political alliances and his relations with rulers of regions of India to the south and east.

The coins of Antialkidas share monograms (in this case used to denote mints) with those of a number of other Indo-Greek kings, placing them in roughly the same geographical area: Gandhāra and the Panjāb—as the mention of Taxila in the inscription of Heliodoros confirms.[73] An especially close relationship may be posited with Lysias; the coinage of the two kings displays the same monograms, and some examples exist of "mules," intentionally or unintentionally struck with opposite dies of each king. Whether or not Antialkidas and Lysias reigned simultaneously, they were certainly using the same mints.[74]

69. The principal publication of the archaeological material is Marshall (1951), with a briefer guide in Marshall (1960).

70. Ghosh 1948; Coningham and Edwards 1997–98.

71. According to the chronology proposed by Bopearachchi 1992. For earlier discussions of Antialkidas's date, territory, and relations with other Indo-Greek kings, see (e.g.) Tarn 1951, 313; Narain 1957, 156.

72. For a blunt but somewhat pessimistic assessment of the use of numismatic evidence to furnish information on the Indo-Greek kings, see Seldeslachts 2004, 249–50, following on from Guillaume 1990 and 1991. A concise and well-referenced introduction to Graeco-Bactrian and Indo-Greek numismatics may be found in Karttunen 1997, 299–306, as well as Holt's study on the Diodotids and their coinage (1999b). Guillaume 1990 provides an in-depth critique of the processes of scholarly reasoning and categorization involved in the study of these coins. The corpora of Graeco-Bactrian and Indo-Greek coins that I have principally consulted are Bopearachchi's catalogues of the collections of the Cabinet des Médailles, Paris (Bopearachchi 1991), and of the Smithsonian Institution, Washington, D.C. (Bopearachchi 1993), and the online databases of the *Sylloge Nummorum Graecorum* (http://www-cm.fitzmuseum.cam.ac.uk/coins/sng/sng_search.html) and the American Numismatic Society (http://www.amnumsoc.org/search/).

73. See Bopearachchi 1993, 41, for the use of monograms and overstrikes to establish the succession of Strato I, Lysias, Heliokles II, and Antialkidas, although interpretations of the chronology and sequence of this period vary; see also Senior and MacDonald 1998.

74. Bopearachchi 1991, 280, and 1993, 43.

Antialkidas minted monolingual Greek drachmas and tetradrachms, as well as square coins on the Indian standard, displaying bilingual legends: *basileōs nikēphorou Antialkidou* in Greek and *maharajasa jayadharasa aṁtialikidasa* in Prākrit.[75] This was common practice among the Indo-Greek kings of the region. *Jayadharasa* (bearing victory) is a literal translation of *nikēphorou* and appears as the equivalent term on the coins of other Indo-Greek kings. The *aṁtialikidasa* of the coin legends differs from the *aṁtalikitasa* of the inscription of Heliodoros. (Both are in the genitive case.) Evidently there was no standardized transcription of the king's name current in an Indian script; note, however, that this inconsistency in transcription may not have been restricted to foreign names at Besnagar.[76]

Heliodoros himself is described as a *yonadūta* (Greek ambassador). Comment on this occurrence of *yona-*, "Greek" (to be discussed further below), has tended to overshadow the interest of the second part of the compound, *-dūta*, "ambassador," "envoy," "negotiator." Greek ambassadors to Indian courts are known in the persons of Megasthenes, Daimachos (or Deimachos), and Dionysios, but these are early Hellenistic envoys from Western kings.[77] Heliodoros is a representative of a closer, more immediate form of diplomacy, between an Indo-Greek king and an Indian neighbor. The Indo-Greek kings' political relations, as we might have assumed even without the evidence of the inscription of Heliodoros, extended beyond the orbit of their (evidently complicated) interactions with one another. What this diplomacy consisted of is in this particular case unknown. A. K. Narain suggests that the context of the embassy of Heliodoros may be Antialkidas's loss of a considerable portion of his kingdom to another Indo-Greek king, Apollodotos: Antialkidas would have been in need of an ally. "But again," Narain concedes, "we are left guessing as to what happened as the result of this alliance, if it had any political significance."[78] John Marshall proposes that "Antialcidas was seeking to make common cause with the Śuṅga king [Bhāgabhadra] against their mutual rival Strato I, whose dominions in the Eastern Panjāb lay wedged in between their own."[79] The uncertainties of Indo-Greek chronology and geography, much debated and founded almost entirely on numismatic evidence, are such that the precise details of the political situation must remain elusive.

Heliodoros's representation (or self-representation?) has further implications in the context of such an embassy. The duration of his mission to the court of Bhāgabhadra is unknown, but we may argue that his dedication at a local cult site

75. See, e.g., Bopearachchi 1991, 273–79, and 1993, 81–82, pls. 10 and 11, nos. 147–57.

76. For other Indian transcriptions of Greek names on coin legends, see Karttunen 1997, 306–7; on the often highly dubious identifications of Greek names in Indian texts, see Seldeslachts 2004. On Greek and Indian religious imagery on the coins of Indo-Greek kings, see Karttunen 1997, 309–15.

77. See ibid. 69–94, mostly on Megasthenes.

78. Narain 1957, 157.

79. Marshall 1960, 21–22.

suggests long-term residence, or at least some ostentatious demonstration of local commitment. His inscription contains, as will be discussed in my concluding remarks, a possible although uncertain reference to the Indian epic the *Mahābhārata,* which invites us to consider some of the same questions of education as a vehicle of high culture as the inscription of Sōphytos. This reference may also suggest that Heliodoros had been exposed to Indian literary culture either as a child or through long-term residence. Here, however, the issue of authorship clouds matters. Whatever his role as an ambassador—short-term negotiator of relations between the two kings or longer-term representative of Antialkidas's interests at the court of Bhāgabhadra—his personal attributes and capabilities would have been key, and his behavior and its reception would have had wider political implications of which he can only have been very aware.

BESNAGAR (VIDIŚĀ) AND BHĀGABHADRA

Besnagar, in the present-day Indian state of Madhya Pradesh, is the site of the ancient city of Vidiśā, which is mentioned in a number of ancient Indian textual sources and by the fourth century B.C.E. was a flourishing town on the trade route to southern India.[80] The first description of the pillar's immediate surroundings was given by Cunningham, who believed that it stood in the ruins of a monastery.[81] The discovery of the inscription of Heliodoros, and subsequent interest in this, led to the first excavations in the vicinity of the pillar, carried out by Bhandarkar in 1914 and 1915.[82] M. D. Khare, during excavations between 1963 and 1965, revealed traces of an elliptical temple-building, dated to the fourth century B.C.E.; nothing remained of the superstructure of the building.[83] A Viṣṇu temple on a similar elliptical plan is known from fourth- or third-century-B.C.E. Nagari.[84] This early Besnagar temple was destroyed at some point and rebuilt on a raised platform, the rubble retaining walls of which are preserved. The dates of the various phases of the site are not securely known.[85]

The pillar of Heliodoros was not the only one at the site, although it is the only one that currently remains standing. Three capitals—erroneously used by Cunningham in his proposed reconstruction of the pillar of Heliodoros—were found

80. On the archaeology of Besnagar (Vidiśā) see (concisely) Khare 1989; Chakrabarti 1995, 221–22; and (full study of the wider region) Tripathi 2002. Summaries of the excavation history of the site surrounding the pillar of Heliodoros: Khare 1966, 21; Irwin 1975–76, 168–70.

81. Cunningham 1880, 41.

82. Bhandarkar 1917; earlier explorations at the site, under Lake in 1910, revealed nothing substantial.

83. For a proposed reconstruction, see Khare 1966, 26, fig. 1.

84. Ibid. 25; see further below on the pillar inscription's Vaiṣṇavite affinities.

85. Ibid. 23–24.

in the vicinity, and traces of several pits occur at uniform distances on a north-to-south alignment outside the temple's rubble retaining wall.[86] As in the archaeo-logical remains of the temple and sanctuary, this permits us to reconstruct some-thing of the wider cult practice at the site, of which the pillar of Heliodoros formed only a part. The question of the divinity worshipped and its relation to the cult of Viṣṇu will be considered further below.

The inscription of Heliodoros provides only tantalizing evidence regarding the political status of contemporary Besnagar. "King Kāsīputra Bhāgabhadra, the Sav-ior," appears in no other source under this name. In the absence of any firmer chronological anchor, the regnal date given (Year 14) cannot be used even to date the inscription, although it does at least give us a minimum length for his reign. His identity and status are a matter of debate: he may be a local ruler or a member of the Śuṅga dynasty, which controlled much of northern and northeastern India between about 185 and 73 B.C.E.[87] This possible appearance of a Śuṅga king in the inscription of Heliodoros is often used as supporting evidence for the extent of Śuṅga rule in the Vidiśā region in the period around 110 B.C.E., but the fact of the matter is that our evidence is thin on the ground and open to varying interpreta-tions. Leaving aside the debate over Śuṅga control in the region, a case can be made for Bhāgabhadra's being a local ruler, whether or not he answered to any higher imperial authority.[88] A second pillar from Besnagar bears an inscription dated in the twelfth year of one "King Bhāgavata," possibly an alternative spelling of the name of the same king rather than simply the word for "devotee" (as in ll. 2–3 of the inscription of Heliodoros: see further below).[89]

Bhāgabhadra's additional titles provide us with little in the way of further clues as to his identity. Kāsīputra [i.e., Sanskrit Kāśīputra] is most probably a metro-nymic, meaning "son of the lady from Kāśī" (modern Benares; Sanskrit Vārāṇasī).[90] We do not know the name or status of Bhāgabhadra's mother, but she—or her con-nections with Vārāṇasī—were evidently important enough to be mentioned as part of her son's royal title. The occurrence of the title t
rātāra (Sanskrit trātṛ), "savior," is curious. It is used to translate the Hellenistic title sōtēr on the coin legends of sev-

86. Ibid. 23.

87. Possible candidates are the ninth king of the Śuṅga dynasty, Bhāga (Bhāgavata), or the fifth, Odraka (Andhraka, Bhadraka). For a full discussion, with references, see Narain 1957, 157; Narain ac-cepts the identification with the ninth Śuṅga king. Note that Fleet 1909, corrected by Venis 1910, identi-fies an additional Indian ruler based on a misreading of the inscription.

88. On the basis of Härtel's then-unpublished excavations at Sonkh, Irwin 1975–76, 168, argues that Śuṅga rule did not extend beyond 120 B.C.E. at Vidiśā, although the case appears to me to be not above criticism; see now Härtel 1993, 86.

89. Bhandarkar 1917, 190; Narain 1957, 157.

90. Fleet 1910, 127, 142; Venis 1910, 814; Narain 1957, 171 n. 148.

eral Indo-Greek kings.[91] Narain notes that "this is an unusual epithet to be adopted by an Indian king, and must have been given to him by Heliodorus, in the inscription which was engraved at his instance. But we do not know why he chose the epithet Trātāra, which means 'the Savior,' for Bhāgabhadra, especially when this title was not adopted either by Antialcidas or his immediate predecessors."[92] Dinesh Chandra Sircar attributes the use of the title to a similar origin: "This word which is a translation of Greek *Soteros* and found on the coins of the Indo-Greek kings shows that a Greek (possibly Heliodorus himself) was responsible for the draft of the record."[93] *Pace* Narain and Sircar, we need not assume that the title was given to Bhāgabhadra by Heliodoros: the king may, for whatever reasons, have adopted it himself. Either alternative raises some interesting questions. Does the use of the epithet *trātāra,* for example, suggest some fondness on the part of an Indian king for Hellenistic-style royal titles, or even philhellenism? Was it simply a name to him, or an honor to be earned or bestowed, as was the case at least in the early Hellenistic West? Was it the habit of Indo-Greek kings to bestow such titles on their allies, and what prestige, if any, would an Indian king have accorded it? The use of the title by some of the Indo-Scythian and Kushan kings who succeeded the Indo-Greeks in northwestern India suggests that in this later period it had become something of a fossilized royal title, to be repeated in much the same way as they adhered to aspects of the form and style of their predecessors' coinage, including the use of the Greek language on legends. In the period of the Besnagar inscription of Heliodoros, in a region outside the sphere of Indo-Greek rule, the political and cultural implications of the use of the title are best left open.[94]

THE INDIAN RELIGIOUS CONTEXT

We are told that the inscription of Heliodoros is on a "Garuḍa pillar of Vāsudeva, the god of gods" (ll. 1–2), and Heliodoros himself is described as a "Bhāgavata." The use of freestanding stone pillars for inscriptions has an established Indian context: they were used for the Maurya emperor Aśoka's Pillar Edicts, and might also be erected in commemoration of a king's victories or in dedication to a deity.[95] The

91. For a list of the titles used on coin legends by Indo-Greeks kings, and their Prākrit translations, see Karttunen 1997, 304–5.

92. Narain 1957, 158.

93. Sircar 1965a, 89 n. 2. Sircar 1966, 343, gives *trātāra* as a "royal title of foreign origin."

94. See Sircar 1965a, 331, on the use of titles of foreign origin such as *trātāra*; 330–51 on Indian royal titles and epithets in general, and on *rāja* vs. *mahārāja*, the use of the latter on coin legends being an innovation of the Indo-Greeks.

95. Salomon 1998, 111, 126–28. The Pillar Edicts were part of Aśoka's (reigned ca. 272—232 B.C.E.) wider program of inscriptions promoting his new Buddhist ethical creed, which included the rock inscriptions in Greek and Aramaic at Kandahar already noted (Thapar 1997, with texts in appendices).

term *dhvaja,* in literary texts, more commonly applies to portable standards. Its occurrence on the pillar of Heliodoros represents the first historical instance of its use to describe a monumental stone column.[96] The inscription on a second pillar from Besnagar also identifies it as a *garuḍadhvaja* dedicated by a *bhāgavata.*[97] It has been suggested that both pillars were originally surmounted by images of the mythical bird Garuḍa,[98] in later tradition the emblem and mount of the god Viṣṇu.[99]

The religious references in the inscription all point to a connection with Vaiṣṇavism, a spectrum of religious practice incorporating the cults of the numerous manifestations of the supreme god Nārāyaṇa-Viṣṇu, of which Vāsudeva-Kṛṣṇa is one.[100] The term *bhāgavata* refers to the devotee of a Vaiṣṇavite cult.[101] A point that must be emphasized is that the inscription of Heliodoros is itself the earliest epigraphic reference to the cult of any Vaiṣṇavite divinity. Pre-Gupta-period (fourth-to-sixth-century-C.E.) inscriptions of Vaiṣṇavite affinity are few, mostly of a votive nature or simply containing an opening invocation to a Vaiṣṇavite deity.[102] Our understanding of cult practice and devotion at a popular level must, of necessity, be rather limited. Within early Vaiṣṇavism, we should at any rate posit some fluidity of doctrine and practices.[103] The precise implications of the various names and associations in the inscription are therefore open to debate, and we should remain cautious about tracing later associations back to the second century B.C.E.[104] The briefer second inscription on the pillar of Heliodoros is on the side facing the platform that at the time of the pillar's erection bore the cult temple. The tone of the inscription is ethical rather than political, facing inward toward the sanctuary rather than outward for more public or political display.[105]

Heliodoros's dedication of a pillar at a local cult site fits well with the idea that this Greek ambassador was aiming to present himself within a firm local Indian

96. Irwin 1975–76, 170; cf. Sircar 1965b, 283–85, for an example from the fifth century C.E.

97. Bhandarkar 1917, 190; Chanda 1920, 152.

98. Fleet 1910, 127–28; Chanda 1920, 154.

99. *Mahābhārata* 1.33.16–17; Chanda 1920, 152; Jaiswal 1967, 72–73.

100. On early Vaiṣṇavism and its development, see Jaiswal 1967—still a valuable collation of sources and discussion of the religion's early development. Epigraphic sources: Salomon 1998, 239–40. The coins of Agathokles from a hoard at Ai Khanoum (Audouin and Bernard 1974) are also an important early source. Chanda 1920 still contains stimulating comments on the *Vaiṣṇava* aspect of the Besnagar inscriptions. *Vaiṣṇava* is an adjective form from the name of the god Viṣṇu, meaning "pertaining to Viṣṇu" or "follower of Viṣṇu." Vāsudeva is Kṛṣṇa's patronymic, "son of Vasudeva."

101. Jaiswal 1967, 32, 37–40.

102. Ibid. 13, 28, 31.

103. Audouin and Bernard 1974, 17.

104. Jaiswal 1967, 71–72, 170–75; Irwin 1975–76, 168, 172, 175.

105. Audouin and Bernard 1974, 16 n. 1.

FIGURE 8. Bronze coin of Agathokles with bilingual legend. (© Trustees of the British Museum.)

context of cultural attributes and associations. The implications of this aim for Heliodoros's own cultural identity will be considered further below, alongside similar questions arising from the inscription of Sōphytos. It is worth noting, however, that Vaiṣṇavism and its associated cults were not forms of religious practice unknown to Greeks, even at the time of Heliodoros. A hoard of Indian and Indo-Greek coins from Ai Khanoum contains a coin type of the Indo-Greek king Agathokles. These coins are square and on the Indian standard, with bilingual legends, like the Indian issues of many subsequent Indo-Greek kings, including Antialkidas. Two figures appear on the coins, one on the obverse and one on the reverse, whose attributes may be interpreted as those of the Vaiṣṇavite deities Vāsudeva and Saṅkarṣaṇa. The place of issue, by comparison with another series of Agathokles, is Taxila, the home city, several decades later, of Heliodoros.[106] This suggests that Vaiṣṇavite cults were known in second-century Taxila—whether patronized by Indo-Greeks or merely given prominence on their coins for reasons of ethnic politics—and that Heliodoros may therefore have been familiar with the cult of Vāsudeva, even a devotee of it, before his arrival at the court of Bhāgabhadra. Important though it is to consider the Indian religious context of the inscription of Heliodoros, it is also important, therefore, to bear in mind that much of the situation in which he found himself at Besnagar must have been more familiar to him than it would to an individual of Greek descent from the Hellenistic states of the eastern Mediterranean.

106. Ibid. 10–14, 23–25, 30–31, figs. 1 and 5.

How may Heliodoros have regarded Vāsudeva and his own attachment to his cult? The Greeks with Alexander, and later Megasthenes, identified some Indian cults with those of Herakles and Dionysos,[107] and it has been argued that Megasthenes' "Indian Herakles" was in fact Vāsudeva-Kṛṣṇa.[108] Syncretism, both theoretical and practical, was a common phenomenon in Hellenistic cult, a way of making sense of coexisting pantheons of Greek and non-Greek gods or of driving home a political message. If "Heliodora" had made a Greek dedication as Heliodoros, might he have referred to his chosen deity by a Greek name, or transcribed the god's Indian name into Greek letters? I suggest, rather, that this would simply not have been an occasion on which to make a Greek inscription at all. Earlier Greek commentators made equations between Greek and Indian gods, but there is no need to assume that those of Greek descent living in India in the second century B.C.E. did the same. The issue is that of familiarity. Just as the *bramenai* and *sramenai* of the Aśokan edicts required no Greek cultural translation for the Greeks of third-century Kandahar, Heliodoros and his community, for whom the Indian cultural sphere evidently bore some relationship to their own identity, may well have felt no need to rationalize a local god into the framework of Greek religion.[109] If this was the case, then the official status of Indian cults (not just appearing on coins for the benefit of a native Indian constituency but patronized also by Greeks) may suggest a contrast with the case in third-century-B.C.E. Bactria, where the existence of a complicated religious reality (as, for example, in the temples of Ai Khanoum) contrasts with an official, civic identity, on coins and in public inscriptions, which is entirely Greek.

GREEKS AND THEIR STATUS IN SECOND-CENTURY-B.C.E. INDIA

Heliodoros is described as a *yona* (Sanskrit *yavana*). The term, especially in later periods, came to be a generic term for foreigners from the West,[110] but its original derivation is from the word *Iōn*, "Ionian," like the word for "Greek" in many Indo-Aryan and Afro-Asiatic languages.[111] In the inscription of Heliodoros, we may confidently translate it "Greek."

---

107. Karttunen 1989, 210, and 1997, 89–90.

108. Audouin and Bernard 1974, 18–19.

109. See also Rapin 1995, 277–80, on Indian objects at Takht-i Sangin and Ai Khanoum that may provide evidence that the Greeks of Bactria were in contact with Indian cults, even specifically Vaiṣṇavite ones.

110. In nineteenth-century India it might even occasionally be used to refer to the British: Killingley 1997, 127–28.

111. Persian *yaunā* (Sancisi-Weerderburg 2001), Hebrew *yavan*, Demotic Egyptian *wynn*, Sanskrit *yavana* and Pali or Prakrit *yona* or *yonaka*.

What would it have meant to a contemporary Indian reader for Heliodoros to be a *yona?* First and foremost, a *yona* was a foreigner (Sanskrit *mleccha,* Prākrit *milakkha*) and a speaker of a foreign language. In contemporary and later Indian textual sources, Greeks are regularly listed alongside other peoples of the Northwest, such as Kambojas (probably an Iranian people) and Scythians.[112] In a neat reversal of the usual classical perspective, they are a group on the geographical fringes of the civilized Indian world: the *mleccha,* the outsider who does not subscribe to the established norms of Indian society, is not simply strange, but barbarous.[113] Furthermore, Greeks were noted for their nonadherence to the Indian caste system, at least in any standard form. In the *Majjhima Nikāya* (discourses attributed to the Buddha and his chief disciples, but probably for the most part of later composition), the Buddha asks: "Have you heard that in Yona and Kamboja and other adjacent districts there are only two castes, the master and the slave?"[114]

This difference in social structures not only provoked comment from contemporary observers, Greek and Indian, but has been the focus of much modern debate on the position of Greeks as outsiders in the more regimented Indian caste system. Greek writers such as Megasthenes recognized that India had a rigidly stratified social system in which endogamous groups occupied a particular economic niche. Inevitably, this has provoked comparisons with the caste system of

112. See, e.g., Manu 10.44. Many of the texts cited here are of uncertain date or products of long revision, even when they purport to relate to events of the last few centuries B.C.E. For an introduction to the relevant Sanskrit and Pāli texts, see Parasher 1991, appendix I. Two of the principal sources are the *Mānavadharmaśāstra* or *Manusmṛti* (*Laws of Manu*), trans. Doniger 1991 and Olivelle 2004, and Kauṭilya's *Arthaśāstra,* trans. Rangarajan 1987. Each can be dated only broadly and is likely to represent the product of more than one authorial or editorial hand. Manu: "sometime about the beginning of the Common Era or slightly earlier" (Doniger 1991, xvii); Kauṭilya: broadly 300 B.C.E.–150 C.E. (Rangarajan 1987, 20).

113. Parasher 1991, 222–23; on the naming of outsiders and social exclusion see also Parasher-Sen 2006. "Barbarous" is an apposite term in more ways than one and is illustrative of the paradox of Graeco-Indian relations: two societies that were both, by the other's criteria, to some extent strange and uncivilized. That the Sanskrit *barbara* (barbarian, stammering, fool) is cognate with the Greek *barbaros* seems beyond doubt, not only because of its phonological similarity but also because of its range of meanings, which take in notions both of barbarity and of incorrect or uncouth speech. Whether it is a loanword or reflects some common Indo-European inheritance, it draws another striking parallel between Greek and Indian attitudes toward outsiders who did not speak their language. Thapar 1971, 420, suggests that "although Megasthenes does not describe the Indians as barbarians, the Indians undoubtedly regarded him as a *mleccha.*" They may even have regarded him—or, indeed, Heliodoros—as a *barbara.* An interesting analogy occurs in several places in 2 Maccabees, where the Jewish author refers to Greeks (in Greek) as *barbaroi:* Gruen 2001, 348–49. The term may also occur in Central Asia with reference to Greek settlements. See Bernard, "Aï Khanoum 'la barbare,'" in Bernard and Francfort 1978, 22: "Did they take this derogatory term from the Greeks in order to turn it back against them? This exchange of bad conduct is a little too neat to be true. I think, rather, that autochthonous people found in their own language the word which they needed."

114. Trans. Horner 1954–59, 341; text: Chalmers 1898, 149.

more recent times, and attempts to map Megasthenes' seven castes onto some historical reality.[115] It is not my intention to commit the hubris of tackling the Indian caste system in any depth here: its complexities are legion,[116] and it is uncertain how much may be established about its operation in historical periods.[117] The term "caste" covers two interrelated systems, *varṇa* and *jāti*. Varṇa refers to the four hierarchical categories of *brāhmaṇa* (priest), *kṣatriya* (warrior or king), *vaiśya* (merchant), and *śūdra* (artisan or agriculturalist).[118] The *jāti* system operates on a smaller-scale, practical, and often more local level. People's *jāti* serves to identify their social and ritual status very precisely and the relationships that they may have with members of other *jātis*.[119] It is only to be expected that such a system should have particular attitudes toward foreigners.

The theory is reasonably clear: the foreigner was set outside the pale of brahmanical society.[120] Contact with *mlecchas*, or even travel among them, was considered tainting not just by *brāhmaṇa*s but even by nonbrahmanical sects such as the Jains. Given the emphasis placed by *brāhmaṇa*s on the accurate oral transmission of sacred texts and their correct use in rituals, the non-Sanskritic speech of *mlecchas* was a particular problem.[121] The very term *mleccha* first occurs in the *Śatapathabrāhmaṇa* defined by speech,[122] and the *Vasiṣṭha Dharmasūtra* (6.41) warns against learning a *mleccha* language. In Buddhist texts, too, *mlecchas* are noted for their incorrect speech and deviation from the standard (in this case, Māgadhī Prākrit). The *Sammohavinodanī* of Buddhaghosa (fl. fifth century C.E.) states, "the rest of the eighteen tongues beginning with the Oṭṭa, the Kirāta, the Andhaka, the Greek [*yonaka*], and the Tamil, change; only this Māgadha tongue correctly called the perfect usage, the noble usage, does not change."[123] Buddhaghosa's *Manorathapūranī* also includes the Greek language alongside *mleccha* languages.[124]

Such prohibitions against travel and speaking foreign languages, as ever, indicate that people were acting to the contrary. Not only was India not closed off from

---

115. Karttunen 1997, 69–94; Falk 1991.

116. See Bayly 1999, 1–24, for an introduction to the problems of dealing with caste and its academic literature.

117. Fussman 1996, 243 n. 1: "[The] scanty data [are] enough to show that around the Common Era, Indian society was still far from functioning like the ideal Hindu society depicted in the probably much later *dharmaśāstras*";cf. Bayly 1999, 25, on change and development in the caste system. On the archaeological visibility of caste, see Coningham and Young 2007.

118. *Ṛg Veda* 10.90.12.

119. Bayly 1999, 9.

120. Manu 2.23–24; Parasher 1991, 102–3; on *yonas* (or *yavanas*) specifically, see Ray 1988.

121. Parasher 1991, 14–15, 44–49.

122. *Śatapathabrāhmaṇa* 3.2.1.23–24: ca. first half of the first millennium B.C.E.; Parasher 1991, 42–43, 116.

123. Trans. Ñānamoli 1991, 128; text: Buddhadatta Thero 1923, 388.

124. Walleser and Kropp 1967, vol. 2, 289.

the outside world, but foreign groups, especially from the Northwest, had an inconvenient habit of invading or migrating into the subcontinent and achieving political dominance. High-status foreign immigrants or invaders had to be accommodated in some way within the norms of *varṇa* and *jāti,* and active strategies of rationalization might be employed to do so.[125]

For this reason, more pragmatic works such as the *Laws of Manu* and the *Arthaśāstra* display a certain flexibility behind their theoretical prescriptions on *varṇa* and *jāti,* especially in implementing strategies for coping with incoming groups within the existing system.[126] This implicitly gives us some information on the social reality with which the system was confronted: "Pre-colonial kings and their subjects did not treat caste norms as one-dimensional absolutes, but as reference points to be negotiated, challenged or reshaped to fit changing circumstances."[127]

Political expediency was one of the key factors in determining the cultural acceptance or rejection of *mleccha* groups. *Mleccha*s could be useful as military or political allies, and brahmanical pronouncements on their low ritual status and the inadvisability of contact with them were not going to stop this:[128]

> The *brāhmaṇas* were clearly aware of the rule of foreign dynasties but chose to ignore them and sometimes their *mleccha* origins as it suited them. Political expediency may have been one of the reasons for this, as court *brāhmaṇas* could not have maintained their position without royal support. But when the foreign rulers adopted brahmanic ways the question of dubbing them as *mlecchas* could not arise as then their behaviour could not be considered 'uncivilized'.

In the early centuries C.E. there is still a great deal of literary emphasis on the threat of *mleccha*s and their way of life to the maintenance of the social order. The *Yuga Purāṇa* (ca. first or second century C.E.) dwells at some length on the chaos arising from *yavana* and Saka invasions and the consequent mixture of castes.[129] In addition to concern about those groups who were still on the fringes of the Indian world, there remained some unease about those who had made the transition from *mleccha*s to integrated members of Indian society. The memory of their non-Indian, non-*varṇa* origins persisted, and stories arose—or were constructed—to account for their current status.[130] One popular option was to designate an ambiguous group a "mixed caste," or a group of higher status that had been degraded by

125. Parasher 1991, viii–ix.

126. Doniger 1991, xxviii, xxxix–xl, liii; Rangarajan 1987, 34.

127. Bayly 1999, 30.

128. Parasher 1991, 243.

129. Ibid. 114, 119, 125–26, 140, 240–41.

130. On this process, see Thapar 1974, who (usefully) treats the rationalization of dynasties of low origin and those of foreign origin as essentially the same phenomenon. Mythical origins for the *yavana*s are given in: *Mahābhārata* 1.165.30–38, 1.80.23–24; *Rāmāyaṇa* 1.55.15–20; *Mātsya Purāṇa* 34.29–30.

its negligence of ritual or by intermarriage with other *varṇas*. This became a favored way of rationalizing any number of groups, with increasingly complicated morganatic permutations. The *yavanas*, as a militarily powerful ruling group, were usually considered *kṣatriyas*.[131] The *yavanas* were, however, "*kṣatriyas* with complications," degraded *kṣatriyas*, because of their known foreign origin. Manu includes them in his list of castes that had sunk from *kṣatriya* to *śūdra* status "by failing to perform the rituals or to seek audiences with priests."[132] Medhātithi's *Bhāṣya* has a slightly different reason for this decline in ritual status:[133] it has happened because they inhabited border regions, in which there was no clear *varṇa* division—a fitting point at which to recall the *Majjhima Nikāya*'s statement that the Greeks have only two *varṇas*. Similar theories occur elsewhere, including the idea that the Greeks were the product of the intermarriage of *kṣatriyas* with lower groups.[134]

For the most part, therefore, foreign groups whose political power demanded their social acceptance—or at least acknowledgment—had to be enrolled in a *varṇa* "by some legal fiction."[135] Although this analysis is useful for assessing the rationalization of high-status groups of foreign origin in the textual evidence, it contributes little to elucidating the actual processes of their assimilation into *varṇa* society.[136] It is unlikely that any single formalized strategy was adopted for encouraging or enforcing this assimilation. On the contrary, the silence of the texts on this issue presupposes that affairs were conducted on a more informal, individual-case basis. Literary texts are of limited use in attempting to examine these processes, for the very good reason that they did not have to acknowledge that they existed, whatever the compulsion for them to accept the end result: "The ancient literary traditions do not provide us with a clear-cut model or pattern for *mleccha* outsiders to transform themselves as members of the acknowledged *varṇa-jāti* schema of social organization."[137] It is tempting to bring the *epigamia* between Seleukos and Chandragupta of 303 B.C.E. into the discussion, as a possible mechanism whereby the offspring of Greek-Indian intermarriage might be integrated into Greek or Indian social structures (or both). But hard evidence is lacking.

Heliodoros, perhaps, provides us with our best chance of accessing the acceptance of a foreigner on an individual level. We do not know how much previous

---

131. The common sense of treating politically powerful groups as *kṣatriyas*: Gombrich 1988, 50. Medieval dynasties of low social origin being accorded *kṣatriya* status after seizing power: Mandelbaum 1970, 435. The legendary non-*kṣatriya* origin of the Nanda dynasty: ibid. 454.

132. 10.43.

133. 10.44, a commentary on Manu.

134. *Harivaṃśa* 10.41–45; *Gautama Dharmasūtra* 4.21.

135. Gombrich 1988, 39.

136. Parasher 1991, 264, for example, states that her concern is the flexibility of the image of the *mleccha* rather than the social practice of incorporation.

137. Parasher 1991, 2.

contact Besnagar and its rulers had had with foreign groups, so it is impossible to tell whether Heliodoros was aided by a precedent set for behavior toward eminent foreigners. His inscription does not attempt to disguise the fact that he is a *yona*, a foreigner, with a foreign name and origin: probably this would have been neither possible nor desirable. His position as intermediary with a foreign king is clearly stated. But at the same time, his description as devotee of an Indian cult and his dedication of a pillar and votive inscription makes no attempt to exclude him from local cultural practices and religious activities. What reticence (if any) Heliodoros experienced on a ritual or social level from the local population because of his *yona* status we do not know; but his pillar dedication and personal involvement with a local cult—heartfelt or politically motivated—demonstrate just one of the individual, personal inroads individuals of foreign origin might readily make into a theoretically closed social structure.

PACCIUS MAXIMUS (LOWER NUBIA)

My discussion of the final inscriptions considered in this chapter—the Greek acrostic verses of Paccius Maximus from Lower Nubia—will be comparatively brief. I intend to use them, for the most part, to highlight strategies and structural elements that they have in common with the inscriptions of Sōphytos and Helio-doros, and to illustrate that such aspects of these inscriptions are by no means confined to the Far East of the Graeco-Roman world.[138]

The temple of the gods Mandoulis and Isis at Kalabsha (Roman Talmis) was constructed—in the form in which it is presently preserved, relocated above the water level of Lake Nasser—in the period between Augustus and Vespasian.[139] Kalabsha was a military garrison, and many of the graffiti and inscriptions on the walls of the temple were left by Roman soldiers. The vast majority are in Greek. The Roman decurion Paccius Maximus was responsible for three texts at Kalabsha and one at Maharraqa.[140] He belonged to Legio III Cyrenaica, which was stationed at Kalabsha in the first century C.E.

Paccius Maximus is of particular interest in our discussion of the inscriptions of Sōphytos and of Heliodoros because he was stationed at one of the fringes of the Graeco-Roman world, because he makes reference to Greek religious and cultural themes in his verses, because he composes two of his inscriptions in acrostic form and makes use of other forms of wordplay, and because he has, inevitably, been accused of being a Nubian protesting his Greek culture and erudition. With

---

138. A full discussion of these inscriptions, alongside other Greek and Latin acrostic verses from Lower Nubia and Libya, is found in Mairs 2012.

139. Gauthier 1911–14; Curto et al. 1965.

140. *I.Metr.* 168, 169 (E. Bernand 1969); *SB* 4597; *CIG* 5119; Wagner 1993; Burstein 1998, 1999–2000.

Maximus, however, the modern prejudices that have influenced his perception as Greek or Nubian have been directly addressed.[141] The two inscriptions that I quote here are the acrostic ones. It should be borne in mind that not only did Paccius Maximus leave his mark elsewhere, but his verses form part of a small but significant corpus of acrostic inscriptions in Greek and Latin concentrated around the region of the First Cataract.[142] Some of these are of a very high literary quality.[143]

> (Acrostic: [I,] Maximus, a decurion, wrote [it])
> When I had come to gaze on this blessed place of peace,
> And to let wander free in the air the inspiration desired by my soul,
> a way of life strange to me stirred my mind from all sides.
> As I could not convict myself of any evil,
> my nature urged me to cultivate mystic toil.
> In my wisdom I then composed a complex song,
> having received from the gods a holy and expressive idea.
> When it was clear that the Muse had accomplished something pleasing to the gods,
> I shook out my festival song, like the flower of a green shoot on Helicon.
> Then a cave enticed me to enter and sleep,
> although I was a little afraid to yield to a dream of fantasy.
> Sleep picked me up and swiftly bore me away to a dear land.
> I seemed to be gently washing my body in the flowing streams of a river
> with the bountiful waters of the sweet Nile.
> I imagined that Calliope, a holy member of the Muses,
> sang together with all the nymphs a sacred song.
> Thinking there still remained a bit of Greece,
> I set down in written form the idea that my wise soul had inspired in me.
> Just as one moving his body in time to music beaten by a staff,
> I summoned rhythm as a partner for the inscription of my song,
> leaving those of a critical bent little reason for blame.
> The leader urged me to speak my clever poem.
> Then great Mandoulis, glorious, came down from Olympus.
> He charmed away the barbaric speech of the Aithiopians
> and urged me to sing in sweet Greek verse.
> He came with brilliant cheeks on the right hand of Isis,
> exulting in his greatness and the glory of the Romans,
> and uttering Pythian oracles like an Olympian god.
> You declared how because of you men can look forward to a livelihood,
> how day and night and all the seasons revere you
> and call you Breith and Mandoulis, fraternal gods,

141. Ibid. 48.

142. Catilius: *IG Philae* 143 (A. Bernand and E. Bernand 1969). Faustinus: *CIL* III 77 = *CLE* 271 = Courtney 1995, no. 26; Mairs 2011b.

143. *I.Metr.* 168 (E. Bernand 1969; trans. after Burstein 1997, 66–68) and 169.

stars who rise as a sign of the gods in heaven.
And you yourself told me to inscribe these clever words,
in order that they be viewed by all without flattery.

. . . trusting in the first twenty-two letters.

(Acrostic: Paccius)
At all times I celebrate you, son of Leto, Pythian Apollo,
Guide of the immortals and Paean of the golden lyre.
For I have come before your gates. Give me,
Lord, great successes in the army.
For if you give me them, I will give you libations,
Such as those due to a great god and to Isis the queen.
I will always make libations to both for these successes.
To find out the name of the one who wrote this,
Count two times two hundred and twenty-one.
Act of dedication for the one who wrote it
And for the one who recognizes the sign
For the god Mandoulis.

I have quoted these inscriptions in full for ease of reference, but once again I do not intend to provide a full commentary.[144] In addition to the acrostics, the second inscription above contains as isopsephic puzzle that allows the reader to find the name "Maximos" as well: "Count two times two hundred and twenty-one [i.e., 421]" is the sum of the numerical value of the letters in his name.

Maximus, like Sōphytos, is clever and wants to make sure that everyone knows it. Unlike Sōphytos, he makes direct reference to the word and number puzzles hidden in his inscriptions rather than trusting solely in the visual trick of reproducing the acrostic in a separate column. His Greek is good and of a reasonable literary quality. Previous criticisms of his stylistic technique not only are patronizing but fail to give him credit for producing perfectly acceptable literary Greek—without the inaccuracies and spelling aberrations common and acceptable in contemporary papyrological Greek—even if he is not, perhaps, the world's greatest poet. Maximus is a literary show-off, but it is unfair to sneer.[145] He also makes frequent reference to Greek gods and cultural tropes, and to Apollo as a poetic patron and source of inspiration. Apollo is the Greek name commonly given to the local Nubian god Mandoulis, which introduces an interesting note of ambiguity. Where does Maximus mean Mandoulis, and where does he mean Apollo; or are the two completely conflated in his mind? Is this religious lip service or more genuine devotion to the god of the place (a question that also arises for Heliodoros)?

144. This may be found in Bernand 1969.
145. As does, for example, Weill in Sayce 1894, 289.

The question of whether Maximus is a Nubian—a key point in most discussions of his inscriptions—turns on the lines "Mandoulis . . . charmed away the barbaric speech of the Aithiopians."[146] At no point does Maximus state that this barbaric speech is his own, and in my view the question of his ethnic background and what languages he may have spoken is utterly open. Paccius and Maximus are fairly generic Roman names—not that that counts for much. If his person is intrusive in a Greek inscription—as it has been claimed that Sōphytos the Indian and Heliodoros the Yona are ethnically intrusive in theirs—then his being intrusive as a Roman is equally as likely as his being intrusive as a Nubian.

INTELLECTUAL AND LITERARY CULTURE

Discussions of all these inscriptions have focused to some extent on what the overt display of Greek (or Indian) literary culture in an inscription in a zone of cultural interaction ought to mean. The notion that the author is in some way culturally insecure is often raised, or it lies implicit beneath discussions of the durability or extent of Greek culture at such frontiers. Sōphytos, Heliodoros, and Paccius Maximus, I suggest, are not simply insecure, social-climbing *nouveaux grecs* or autodidacts with chips on their shoulders. We may assume cultural conservatism as a reaction among the Greeks of Arachosia, for example, to their position as mixed-blood colonists of a city outside the political control of a Greek state; but this assumption, along with that of an insecurity accompanying this conservatism, is an imposition from outside, from our own greater familiarity with the Greek states of the Mediterranean littoral, not a picture that emerges directly from the local evidence. The local societies in which Sōphytos, Heliodoros, and Paccius Maximus lived, and local forms of identity ascription and self-ascription, were much more complex and structured than this. The constraints imposed on the authors of these inscriptions by local social structures and forms of acceptable public behavior will be discussed in the next section. The question remains, however, of what an overt display of the literary intellectual culture (such as Homer or metrical verse in general) associated with a specific cultural group (such as Greeks) means in terms of the educational background and claimed cultural identity of the one who makes such a display.

Sōphytos's Homericisms and his reworking of the first lines of the *Odyssey* to reflect his own journey through foreign lands are the clearest example of the influence of a particular Greek author on the literary style of these inscriptions, although Maximus's verses are also self-consciously literary, and he too namedrops Apollo and the Muses. Sōphytos had certainly read his Homer, and, as can be seen from the dominance of Homer as a school text in contemporary Egypt,[147]

146. *I.Metr.* 169, ll. 23–24.
147. Cribiore 1996, 46–49.

this familiarity with the Homeric epics is something that came as part and parcel of a Greek education. This is the education that Sōphytos himself tells us he has had. There are other indications, some of which are of a rather later date, that the populations of the Hellenistic Far East knew their Homer. The motif of the Trojan Horse appears in Gandhāran art.[148] The overall proportion of heroic to ordinary Greek names (or non-Greek names such as Sōphytos) in Central Asia—although it should be remembered that our onomastic corpus is small—is a little more elevated than may be expected. Does this reflect a desire to connect to their Greek heritage?[149] Our literary references are more enigmatic. Plutarch asserts that Alexander taught the Gedrosians the tragedies of Sophocles and Euripides[150]—but this tells us more about his ideas on literary culture as a vehicle of civilization and the impact of the Greek conquest on "uncivilized" Gedrosia than it does about the reading habits of any actual Gedrosians. Dio Chrysostom mentions Indians reading Homer in translation.[151] This notice may refer to the Indo-Greeks rather than native Indians,[152] but it has generally—whether correctly or not—been taken to refer to the great Sanskrit epics such as the *Mahābhārata*.

Heliodoros may have known his Homer (or he may not have), but the phrasing of Besnagar Inscription B has suggested to some that he was also familiar with the *Mahābhārata*.[153] There is no direct quotation, and the similarities to several passages in the *Mahābhārata* are still more remote than those of Sōphytos's inscription to the *Odyssey*. Similar expressions have also been cited from the *Dhammapada*.[154] Opinions vary as to the implications of Heliodoros's (possible) reference to the *Mahābhārata*. H. C. Raychaudhuri contends that "It is not unreasonable to think that Heliodoros of Taxila actually heard and utilized the teaching of the Great Epic. Evidently the *Mahābhārata* played an important part in the Hinduisation of the foreign settlers of the Indian border-lands."[155] Tarn, on the other hand, notes that, even if Besnagar B does represent an indirect quotation from the *Mahābhārata,* this is not conclusive evidence for Heliodoros's personal acquaintance with the epic, as the inscription may well have been composed by a local Indian scribe rather than the *yonadūta* himself.[156] The question of authorship is key, and this is a topic to which I shall return in the next section.

148. Allan 1946, Khan 1990.

149. Bopearachchi and Bernard 2002, 261–62; Mairs 2014a.

150. *De Alexandri Magni Fortuna aut Virtute* 1, 328C–329D.

151. 53.6; cf. Aelian 12.48.

152. Karttunen 1997, 285.

153. Venis 1910, 1093; Raychaudhuri 1922; Bhattacharya 1932, with no transliteration or translation of the original Sanskrit and little commentary.

154. Salomon 1998, 267, for references.

155. Raychaudhuri 1922, 271.

156. Tarn 1951, 351.

To view the matter more negatively, what the literary style of the inscriptions of Sōphytos, Heliodoros, and Maximus have in common is a lack of direct quotation. Any literary references are rather evocative allusions, part of a wider network of cultural and literary associations. I suggest that the value of these references lies to a great extent in their content and familiarity, their source, if known, being secondary. We may draw a contrast with the inscription from the sanctuary of Kineas at Ai Khanoum, where the Greek text places considerable emphasis on the source and process of transmission of the text of the Delphic maxims, noting that Klearchos personally copied the precepts *epiphradeōs*, "conscientiously."[157] Any *Mahābhārata* reference in Besnagar B does not, I argue, belong to a specifically textual tradition or scheme of reference and quotation. Similar expressions, as noted above, occur elsewhere. What this phrase does in fact remind us of is the role of oral tradition in the reinforcement and transmission of culture. This tradition may include the oral transmission and performance of epic verse—a tradition in both Greece and India—but it also occurs on a less formal level, in the phrases and proverbial expressions that people repeat in everyday speech as familiar reference points and reinforcers of shared background or cultural values.[158] A certain degree of misquotation or flexibility is inherent in such activity and is generally irrelevant to the value of the exercise, which is to repeat something familiar to both speaker and listener, perhaps considered to state some deep cultural or social truth. In religious terms—and the position of Besnagar B on a pillar dedicated at a cult site means that we must consider it in these terms—much the same interrelation of textual and oral culture may occur. There is text; there is conscious, direct quotation; and then there is the more flexible, socially reinforcing repetition of shared religious values.

The theme of allusion to the *Mahābhārata* and the *Odyssey*, however, even if we may challenge the directness of the references, introduces other aspects of cultural transmission, education, and ethnicity that the inscriptions invite us to consider. In particular, the recognition of passages from the *Mahābhārata* and the *Odyssey* in the inscriptions of Heliodoros and Sōphytos, respectively, is interesting from the point of view of how modern scholarship works—someone who has had to read, translate, and comment upon long passages from an epic for an examination

---

157. Robert 1968, 455–56, considers this Delphic inscription, too, as to some extent a statement of the local community's Greek identity and attachment to Greek education and values: "L'inscription des maximes delphiques, gravée sur l'initiative du philosophe au sanctuaire du fondateur, atteste la primauté du 'moral,' des règles de vie et de pensée helléniques, de la παιδεία grecque. C'est, dans ce pays étranger, une affirmation et une pénétration morale, comme il y a une pénétration technique et didactique. Cette affirmation de soi—ou plutôt du groupe—est fréquente chez les pionniers, comme sont ces colons, amateurs de 'philosophes.'"

158. A similar process is proposed by Adams 1999 as the source for poetic allusion in verses from Bu Njem.

will be attuned to notice quotation from or reference to it elsewhere—and of how scholars imagine culture was transmitted. The image of Greeks poring over their *Mahābhārata* or Indians over their Homer, as a means of education or cultural induction, has a certain modern resonance. The idea of culture's being carried in literature, often in particular "set texts," may also demonstrate the process of prioritization in the transmission of the cultural indicia that go to make up an individual's ethnic identity. Dio Chrysostom relates how on a visit to Olbia he met a young Greek man who dressed like a Scythian but knew his Homer but not more recent Greek authors such as Plato.[159] Cultural transmission, and with this the construction of an ethnic identity, is a process of selection, and the attributes retained are often telling.

NAMES, ASCRIPTIONS, AND AUTHORSHIP

Heliodoros is the only figure in these inscriptions who describes himself (or is described: see further below) with an ethnic indicator. He is a *yona,* a term, as noted above, with a spectrum of implications in Indo-Aryan languages, but that may be translated "Greek" here. Heliodoros may therefore be considered to have explicitly marked himself as an outsider (or to have been so marked), whereas Sōphytos and Maximus, despite their apparent foreignness in a Greek context, do not mark themselves as outsiders—or indeed as anything at all.

This political edge to Heliodoros's representation must be borne in mind when we consider his private cultural and ethnic identity: it could have been diplomatic—in more senses than one—for him to make a public demonstration of his devotion to a local cult,[160] even if his otherness as a *yonadūta* is stated along with this. If Heliodoros had a mixed ethnic background or the ability to function in more than one cultural sphere, this may have been helpful in his role as an ambassador. Functional bilingualism at the very least should be assumed, quite apart from the question of whether the inscription is of his own composition;[161] Helio-

---

159. Dio Chrysostom 36.11; Skydsgaard 1993, 124–25.

160. Domestic politics in the kingdom of Antialkidas may also have had an impact in this decision, as argued by Marshall 1960, 22: "No doubt it was part of the political propaganda of Antialcidas for his ambassador to proclaim himself a follower of Vishṇu (Bhāgavata) and set up a pillar in honour of that deity; and indeed it is quite possible that in the Panjāb itself Antialcidas was playing up to the Brāhmanical faction and making such use of it as he could to undermine the power of the Euthydemids east of the Jhelum."

161. Harmatta 1994, 407, insisting on Heliodoros's "good knowledge of Brāhmī script and Prakrit language," appears to me to conflate two separate issues: the evidence of the inscription (which we may hardly suppose Heliodoros to have also carved himself, even if he did compose it) and the supposition that, in his role as ambassador, he would have needed some ability in the local Middle Indo-Aryan language. The latter is a reasonably safe assumption but is not to be deduced from the former.

doros's own king, Antialkidas, minted coins with bilingual legends. The religious content of Heliodoros's inscription and his dedication of the pillar at a cult site— whether this was personal piety, shrewd politics, or a combination of the two[162]— similarly presuppose a degree of ease in operating in an Indian cultural sphere. The fluency of this cultural bilingualism may, of course, be questioned. As was the case with the inscription of Sōphytos from Kandahar, we may suspect cultural insecurity or wonder how local people would have perceived his language and actions.

The source of Heliodoros's ability to function in two cultural spheres, Indian and Greek, is most probably to be sought in his own background. If anything, it is the Greek side of his identity that should be questioned: he has a Greek name, but all the cultural reference points in his inscription are Indian. His designation as a *yona*, however, shows that, in local perception at least, he was considered Greek, although we do not know whether he ever spoke the Greek language or displayed anything that modern (or perhaps even contemporary) observation would consider attributes of Greek culture. We may recall Cavafy's philhellenic Parthian dynast, who protests that his acquaintance with Greek ways and culture makes him as "not un-Greek" as anyone else in the East. By the late second century B.C.E., the vast majority of Bactrian and Arachosian Greeks, I argue—including those who invaded and established states in India—must have been of mixed descent: the fact that the Greek settlement of the Hellenistic Far East was a predominantly male, military one all but guarantees this.[163] Such mixed descent will have given them the potential to cross or redefine ethnic boundaries, although many issues will have impacted on whether or not they chose to do so in practice. The position of Heliodoros gives us an example of a situation in which cultural bilingualism could have carried a practical advantage—if indeed his presentation in his pillar inscription represents any deviation at all from his normal behavior.[164]

On the Greek (or Indo-Greek) side, Heliodoros cannot have been an ambassador in the mold of Megasthenes, an outsider observing and commenting upon an alien cultural and political environment, perhaps unable to make critical judgment on the reports of his informants. Heliodoros must have had much closer points of cultural access to the environment in which he found himself at Vidiśā: this appears to have been his own sphere of cultural operation, or something close to it.

162. Audouin and Bernard 1974, 37 n. 4.

163. Holt 1988. On intermarriage with the early Greek settlers in the East, see Burstein 2012.

164. Foucher and Bazin-Foucher 1942–47, 314, highlight the potential of individuals of mixed descent, familiar with Indian languages and customs, to act as intermediaries between Greeks and Indians. Foucher's contrast with "Yavanas de race pure" is, however, a somewhat artificial one: the example of Menander is given, but this king is known as Milinda, a patron of Buddhism, in a Pāli Buddhist text, the *Milindapanha*: Rhys-Davids 1890.

Sōphytos, tellingly, does not give himself an ethnic. This, to my mind, suggests a number of things that are not necessarily mutually compatible: that he felt secure in his identity, that the local community felt secure in their judgment of his identity, or that a funerary inscription was not the time or the place to make overt statements of ethnic belonging, especially ones that might be contradicted—or all these possibilities. It is quite possible that Greek ethnic identity in this context was not salient—or, to use a linguistic analogy, "marked"—and that the forms of identity Sōphytos does stress (family background, culture and education, wealth and good reputation) were. Paccius Maximus, likewise, refers to himself only as a decurion, because his rank in the Roman army was the form of identity (professional) most appropriate to display in this context, an imperially patronized temple in a Roman garrison town.

Whatever has been stated on the basis of the Indian roots of the names of Sōphytos and his father, Naratos,[165] the question of Sōphytos's ethnic identity is in no way resolved. The Stele of Sōphytos in fact presents just the kind of (apparent) ethnic ambiguity or duplicity that we are familiar with from elsewhere in the Hellenistic world: an Indian name in a Greek composition. It is worth pausing, however, to consider what we do not know about Sōphytos. We do not know whether his family were immigrants from India and, if they were, how recently they had arrived in Kandahar. We do not know whether his family had intermarried with Greeks or Iranians and to what extent. We do not know what language he spoke at home and in public, and whether he was competent in more than one language—none of these inscriptions has any real indication of what we call linguistic interference. We know nothing of what kind of house he lived in, what he wore, what he ate and—perhaps most important—how other residents of Kandahar perceived him and his ethnic identity. By comparison with the picture from Hellenistic Egypt, we may suggest a few things that we do know about him, at least from negative evidence. His retention of the purportedly Indian name Sōphytos in a Greek public inscription suggests that this was the only name he used—unlike the situation in Egypt, where some individuals displayed dual naming or would present themselves with a Greek name in a Greek context and an Egyptian one in an Egyptian context. On the other hand, etymologically-speaking Sōphytos may be Subhūti, but was he ever called by the Indian form of his name? And if so, in what contexts? Sōphytos was a name that had a previous history of being presented in a thoroughly Greek official context, on the coins of the Sōphytos who was a local ruler in Arachosia or Bactria at some point during the third century. By the time of the Sōphytos of the inscription, how would it have been perceived? Was it a name with sufficient cachet in Kandahar for any ethnic implications it

165. Bernard, Pinault, and Rougemont 2004, 261: "l'appartenance ethnique du personnage ... est heureusement certain."

may have borne to have become subordinated to its familiarity and (perhaps) pedigree?

Although Heliodoros unlike Sōphytos is given an explicitly ethnic description, the fact that he is a *yona* in no way resolves any ethnic ambiguities about either him or the cultural cues in his inscription. Questions of authorship, sociopolitical context, and linguistic register may go some way toward clarifying the possibilities and uncertainties in ascribing identities to Sōphytos and to Heliodoros. First, authorship, an issue that I have signposted in a number of places above but that I have deliberately reserved for discussion in these concluding remarks. Sōphytos's very personal inscription, with its acrostic, at least claims to be personally authored by him. Personal authorship would also fit with the co-occurrence of a claim to a good education and the production of verse that could only be the product of such an education. Likewise, Paccius Maximus's verses, which are similar in theme and in content to each other, are either the genuine, proud display of a Roman soldier's skill in poetry and wordplay or a deliberate attempt to mislead the reader. The inscription of Heliodoros, in contrast, lacks the more personal tone and indications of personal authorship of the inscriptions of Sōphytos and Maximus. In judging whether he composed it himself, however, I am conscious of an ingrained cultural and linguistic prejudice: that an Indian or a Nubian might aspire to Greek education and succeed merely in coming across as insecure, but that a Greek must have remained detached from a foreign culture and commissioned another to make a Prākrit dedication to an Indian god, as lip service to local customs in his role as ambassador. Certainly, Heliodoros claims to have made (and probably therefore paid for) the dedication—his is the dedicator's name, which appears in the instrumental case—and it is possible that he personally composed his inscription; but we do not know.

Second, sociopolitical context and linguistic or epigraphic register. There is no doubt that each of these dedicators was constrained to a great extent by the local society and political circumstances in which he operated and by the written register in which he chose to (or had to) produce an inscription. Any claim to an identity had to have been made within these frameworks. As I have suggested above, social structure—which we may approach through a knowledge of the historical operation of the Indian caste system or the Roman army, or through theoretical models such as ethnicity—imposed rules on how individuals might perceive and publicly define themselves. In some of these contexts there may have been very definite rules about who could be what: a *yona*, for example, was a *mleccha*; Sōphytos may or may not have been Greek in the sense that he could be a member of the gymnasium (if there was one at Kandahar); Paccius Maximus could call himself a decurion only because he had been promoted to this rank.[166] (One earlier

---

166. Wagner 1993.

inscription dates from before his promotion.) Heliodoros was professionally Greek, a Greek ambassador resident at an Indian court, a dual identity meaning that he cannot very well have called himself anything else. If he was not the composer of his inscription, then the influence of local social structures may have been still more acute: he may have been designated a foreign *yona* because this is how he was perceived, despite his possible efforts at rapprochement and integration in his dedication to an Indian god in an Indian language.

The epigraphic and linguistic register must also have imposed constraints on any choice of self-designation or theme. In terms of language, we may ask what other choice any of these inscribers had. The languages used for these inscriptions are the dominant epigraphic languages in use at Kandahar, Besnagar, and Kalabsha. The picture at Kandahar is incomplete, but Greek for now dominates. At Besnagar, to my knowledge, only Prākrit inscriptions are known. At Kalabsha, by far the majority of inscriptions and graffiti are in Greek, with only very few in Latin or Demotic Egyptian. In terms of epigraphic convention, Heliodoros and Paccius Maximus both set up religious votives at major sanctuaries that were objects of official patronage. Reference and appeal to the relevant gods were therefore de rigueur, alongside self-conscious reference to the act of dedication itself. These inscriptions, too, are set within a local epigraphic context where others set up inscriptions for similar reasons and with similar themes. We lack an epigraphic context for Sōphytos's epitaph, but it seems likely that it was only one of several such commemoratory inscriptions on a family tomb. The use of written language, inscribed in stone, automatically adds a degree of formality, and when people present their identities in a public context they will, for all sorts of social or political reasons, be careful in selecting where they set the boundaries of that identity, and which elements of their cultural background they wish to present. A Prākrit dedication to Vāsudeva would have been neither the time nor the place for Heliodoros to go off on a personal epigraphic tangent about how his father was Greek and his mother Sogdian, but his nurse spoke to him in Gāndhārī[167]—or any of the (I suspect more subtle and complicated) alternative permutations his Greek cultural background may have undergone in order for him to arrive at his present identity. There may well have been no appropriate time or place for such introspection or conscious self-examination within the framework of either Greek or Indian modes of public presentation. Whether the dedicator of the Besnagar pillar-inscription thought of himself as a *yona* or a *Hellēn,* as Heliodora or Hēliodōros are ultimately questions that we cannot answer. Either *yona* or *Hellēn* would have been a rationalization, a simplification of his doubtless more complex personal identity into one that allowed him to be a member of a distinct ethnic group, recognizable by other members of that group and by outsiders.

167. Fussman 1989.

CONCLUSIONS

The four inscriptions (by three authors) discussed here, despite their differences in language, region, date, and purpose, have certain points in common that make them worth discussing together. The inscriptions of Heliodoros and Paccius Maximus come from excavated religious centers, whereas that of Sōphytos is without any verifiable archaeological context. Sōphytos and Maximus are compulsive Greek cultural name-droppers and seem at pains to display their education and erudition. Heliodoros, Sōphytos, and Maximus leave us to speculate about their identities and self-definitions—although Maximus claims a professional identity as a Roman decurion, whereas Heliodoros assumes the double title, both ethnic and professional, of Greek ambassador.

The problem with recognizing ethnic identity and ethnic behavior in the archaeological record, as has frequently been pointed out, is that it is usually very difficult to identify which forms and styles of material culture were held to have significance as indicia of group identity and which were not.[168] This is a problem that I touched upon in the introduction and confronted directly in chapter 2, on the urban landscape of Ai Khanoum. When is a Corinthian column in the Hellenistic Far East a sign of Greek identity,[169] and when is it simply something that supports a roof? Similarly, in the epigraphic record from the Hellenistic Far East, it is difficult to tell which descriptors, references, language choices, and literary styles should be read as ethnic cues and which should not. In the preceding discussion, I have tried to demonstrate that such apparent cues, even when they come in such beguilingly straightforward forms as the description of a man with a Greek name as a Greek ambassador, are open to more than one interpretation. In particular, the impression we come away with may be influenced by our own background. To a classicist, Heliodoros will always look as though he has gone native,[170] and Sōphytos will look at first glance like a try-hard *nouveau grec*. To an Indologist, however, both are equally foreign.

There is little that is in itself problematic in either Sōphytos's or Heliodoros's statement of his cultural reference points or identity. Ethnic ambiguity is, crucially, something that individual public display may go to great lengths to avoid, however keen we may be to recognize it in the exotic archaeological and epigraphic material from the Hellenistic Far East. Analysis of the conflicts between claimed ethnicity and other factors such as descent or language use is a key modern research question, but one that the ancient sources—for the reasons already stated—may have deliberately sought to obscure. The ethnic loading of terminology and the

168. Smith 2003 provides a refreshingly practical approach to the question, using the kind of detailed archaeological case studies lacking in Jones 1998.

169. Bernard 1968a.

170. Green 1990, 320, has this impression of the Indo-Greeks in general.

contemporary resonance of inscriptions to which modern analysis gives a particular ethnic weight are research questions and methodological issues that the Hellenistic Far East has in common with other regions of the Hellenistic world.

Another point that the communities of the Hellenistic Far East have in common with their Greek neighbors to the west is that the supposedly rigid Greek-barbarian divide is in practice permeable—in contrast to what might be protested in public display and rhetoric. Just as in the south individuals such as Sōphytos and Heliodoros lived in a dynamic zone of interaction between Greek and Indian cultures, in the north communities and polities displayed shifting political and cultural allegiances to the settled Greek civilization of Bactria and the nomadic world of the Central Asian steppe.

Waiting for the Barbarians

The Fall of Greek Bactria

And now what's to become of us without barbarians?
Those people were a solution of a sort.

—C. P. CAVAFY, "WAITING FOR THE BARBARIANS" (1904), TRANS.
MENDELSOHN 2012, 192–93

MOBILITY

The Graeco-Bactrian expansion into northwestern India was followed within a few decades by the loss of the kingdom's Bactrian heartland. The world of Helio-doros and his king was that of the Indian subcontinent, and whatever diplomatic, commercial, or cultural contacts the Greeks of Bactria had maintained with the other Hellenistic states were now effectively impeded by the intervening Parthian empire and various nomad confederacies. In the first century C.E., the author of the *Periplus of the Erythraean Sea*, a practical manual to the ports and trade routes of the Red Sea and Indian Ocean, noted that "to the present day ancient drachms [from Bactria] are current in Barygaza [on the northwestern coast of India] . . . bearing inscriptions in Greek letters and the devices of those who reigned after Alexander, Apollodotus, and Menander."[1] But by this period the Indo-Greek states too had ceased to be politically independent and culturally distinct entities.

The sudden decline and fall of the Graeco-Bactrian state was precipitated by forces both within and without the kingdom.[2] The Indian conquests had evidently offered opportunities for ambitious men to advance themselves. Eukratides was, according to Justin's *Epitome* of Pompeius Trogus, murdered by his own son, but we also find "new men," such as the great Menander,[3] whose connection to

---

1. *Periplus* 47: Casson 1989.
2. See Posch 1995 for a study of Bactria between the fall of the Graeco-Bactrian kingdom and the rise of the Kushans.
3. Coloru 2009, 241–44; Widemann 2009, 156–59, 170–74.

previous royal families is not obvious. The general picture is one of heterarchy, not hierarchy: political fragmentation among several Greek-named kings ruling concurrently in different regions of the conquered Indian territories.

The most destructive forces at work in the period of instability in the 140s and 130s B.C.E., however, came from the lands to the north and west of Bactria. There was war with Parthia, but the principal agents of the fall of the Graeco-Bactrian kingdom have long been considered to have been the nomadic groups who moved into the region of the upper Oxus at this period. Ever since Chinese historical sources became available to Western scholars, the potential of Chinese and classical Greek and Roman sources to corroborate each other on this point has been recognized.[4]

My purpose is not to fundamentally challenge or alter this narrative of the fall of the Graeco-Bactrian kingdom under the pressure of invasions from the north but to give new shades of emphasis to how it is told. In earlier scholarship, the nomad invasions of Bactria were inevitably romanticized as the fall of the barbarian wolf upon the civilized Greek fold. The rhetoric with which they were described might make either direct or indirect reference to wider scholarly narratives that pitted the forces of Greek civilization against the barbarian desert, mountains, or steppe.[5]

More recently, two phenomena central to this narrative of the settled Greek civilization of Bactria overrun by steppe tribes—nomadism and migration—have come to be recognized as more problematic concepts.[6] A number of related phenomena at work in mid-second-century-B.C.E. Bactria—nomadism, migration, pastoralism, seasonal transhumance, even the social mobility of Greek kings and generals—may be grouped under the broader rubric of "mobility," an approach that has the potential to improve our understanding of the wider socioeconomic processes at work in the nomad conquests. In addition to the historical sources (Graeco-Roman and Chinese), the data available to consider these questions includes the information garnered from several archaeological field-survey projects in Bactria and neighboring regions and material from excavations at settlement sites, especially those that experienced alternating periods of Graeco-Bactrian and steppe-nomad control. In addition to the value in examining relations between settled and nonsettled populations, and patterns of land usage in and of themselves, I also use this archaeological data to address the problem of the nomad

---

4. de Guignes 1759; Coloru 2009, 37.

5. In Dalton's view, for example, in his work *The Treasure of the Oxus* (1964, 18): "The condition of declining Hellenism in Bactria and in the colonies of South Russia offers many points of analogy. Both became isolated from the Greek world and succumbed at last before the barbaric vigour of Scythian tribes."

6. See, for example, the studies in Barnard and Wendrich 2008.

conquest of Bactria. If the divide—geographical and socioeconomic—between settled society and nomadic or pastoral ways of life has been shown to be shifting and indistinct, then this has implications for the picture so vividly painted in the historical sources (and even some modern studies) of barbarian nomadic hordes sweeping down upon the settled civilization of Bactria. The complex symbiotic relationship between settled and mobile populations in Bactria and Sogdiana is in fact one of the constants in the history of the region, and attempts to break these ties, as with Alexander on the Jaxartes (chapter 1), might incite revolt.

THE SIEGE OF BACTRA IN 206 B.C.E. AND THE NOMAD THREAT

For Euthydemos was himself a Magnesian and, defending himself to Teleas, alleged that it was unjust for Antiochos to demand his removal from power, since he himself had not rebelled against the king. Rather, when others had revolted, he had destroyed their descendents and thus gained possession of the Bactrian throne. After further discussing this matter along these same lines, he begged Teleas to mediate peace in a kindly manner, exhorting Antiochos not to begrudge him his royal name and state. For if Antiochos did not make these concessions, neither of them would be safe: not far away were great numbers of nomads who not only posed a danger to them both but also threatened to barbarize the whole area if they attacked [plēthē gar ouk oliga pareinai tōn Nomadōn, di' hōn kinduneuein men amphoterous, ekbarbarōthēsesthai de tēn khōra homologoumenōs, ean ekeinous prosdekhōntai]. After saying these things, Euthydemos sent Teleas to Antiochos. The king had long been looking for a way out of the situation, so hearing these things from Teleas he readily accepted peace for the aforementioned reasons.

Polybios's account of the siege of Bactra by Antiochos III in 206 B.C.E. is one of the very few episodes in the history of the Greek kingdom of Bactria to be recounted in a narrative historical source.[7] It is also one of the only such indications of Graeco-Bactrian relations with and attitudes toward the peoples of more northerly regions of Central Asia, and in particular those living a nomadic way of life. Polybios presents the incident as an encounter between two Hellenistic kings, who find a common language in their fear of the "hordes of nomads" (*plēthē tōn Nomadōn*). Euthydemos makes a shrewd political appeal to the classic opposition of Greeks and barbarians, although Antiochos is also glad to be offered a chance to withdraw and save face. How real was the nomad menace appealed to by Euthydemos during the siege of Bactra? Can this be connected to the destruction and abandonment of Ai Khanoum some sixty years later, and to Greek and Chinese historical sources that relate how the Greek kingdom of Bactria was overrun by nomads from the

---

7. Polybios 11.34, 6–14; trans. after Holt 1999b, 181–82.

north? In some ways, Euthydemos's intimation of a nomad threat may indeed be seen as an augur of things to come, but contextualizing Polybios's account with other historical and documentary sources reveals that this is not the sudden arrival on the scene of a new external enemy, the threat of what might be described as an invasion. There was no clear territorial or socioeconomic divide between a settled, urban Graeco-Bactrian civilization and mounted steppe nomads to the north. Euthydemos, as someone in command of Bactria's military and economic affairs, cannot have been unaware of just how indistinct this boundary was, even if Polybios may have been less well informed on such matters. Euthydemos may, however, have found it to his advantage to simplify or even misrepresent it.

Euthydemos's appeal to the Greek-barbarian polarity appears all the more cynical when it is considered that the Graeco-Bactrian kings were very likely using nomad mercenaries. As often with the economy and society of Hellenistic Bactria, there was an Achaemenid precedent.[8] Bactria and its neighboring satrapies were not only themselves sources of manpower and natural resources to the Achaemenid state, but they also served as channels through which manpower and resources from regions under looser Achaemenid control were brought into the empire (chapter 1). Different groups of Scythians, including those "from beyond Sogdiana," appear among the subject peoples and the bearers of tribute in the inscriptions and reliefs at Persepolis.[9] In his description of the preparations for the battle of Gaugamela, Arrian notes the presence on Darius's side of Indians and Sogdians under the command of Bessos the satrap of Bactria, as well as Saka mounted archers who were "not subject to Bessos but in alliance with Darius."[10] He considers the Saka to be a subtribe of the Asian Scythians. Other Central Asian horsemen served under the satraps of Arachosia and Aria, and were perhaps therefore more securely integrated into the Achaemenid empire. The Bactrian Aramaic documents make no specific reference to Scythian mercenaries or allied troops, but an order by Akhvamazda to Bagavant that he should build a wall and ditch around the town of Nikhshapaya may indicate a fear of military attack from precisely this quarter.[11] Nikhshapaya has been identified with the medieval city of Nakhshab, modern Qarshi in southern Uzbekistan, which lies around two hundred fifty kilometers to the northwest of Bactra as the crow flies, on the far side of the Oxus.[12]

Qarshi is also, significantly, beyond the Surkhan-darya and Sherabad-darya archaeological survey areas, and is the site of the Iron Gates at Derbent. The

---

8. On the close relations between the Achaemenid empire, the satrapy of Bactria, and Saka and Scythian peoples of Central Asia, see Briant 1982, 203–26, and 2002, 747.

9. Schmidt 1953.

10. *Anabasis* 3.8.3–4.

11. Naveh and Shaked 2012, A4 (Khalili IA 1).

12. Shaked 2003, 1529.

material from these sites, as I will discuss below, reveals them to have formed an important liminal zone in the Hellenistic period, both politically and socioeconomically speaking, between settled Bactria and the nomadic north. Just as they were to the Achaemenid authorities, Scythians were both a resource and a threat to the Graeco-Bactrian state. Euthydemos appealed to a mutual nomadic threat, but he may have been literally as well as figuratively employing the barbarians to scare off Antiochos. One of the Greek administrative documents from Bactria contains an intriguing reference to Scythians,[13] in a context that suggests that these are not barbarian hordes sweeping down from the steppe but a group with whom the persons mentioned in the text have close dealings.

> In the reign of Antimachos in year 30 [month + day]
> in Amphipolis near Ḳarelote has introduced [NN of the]
> mercenaries[(?) to NN] of the for[ty - - -]
> Scythians, of one hundred drachmas of coined silver [- - - -],
> [.] of [the above-mentioned(?)] sum of money [
> [*traces*]

Although some readings in this transcription are uncertain, the word *Skuthoi*, "Scythians," at the beginning of line four is clear. The word *xenoi*, "foreigners," which may be used of mercenaries, of line three is also quite clear. The nature of the document, Clarysse and Thompson propose, is the record of a transaction between two military commanders of groups of foreign mercenary troops. The date is from the reign of a king named Antimachos in the late third or early second century B.C.E., and so not very distant in time from the siege of Bactra and Euthydemos's appeal to the barbarian menace. This is not to deny the existence of a military threat to the security of the Graeco-Bactrian state from mobile populations to the north but to balance this with an appreciation of the role played by Scythian troops within Bactria's own forces.

GREEK AND CHINESE HISTORIES OF THE NOMAD MOVEMENTS OF THE MID-SECOND CENTURY B.C.E.

Graeco-Bactrian relations with the state's nomadic hinterland were evidently complex and not exclusively antagonistic. The events of the 140s and 130s B.C.E., however, represent something closer to the traditional view of a clear-cut bilateral conflict in which the Graeco-Bactrian state was faced with a large-scale invasion by mounted nomads from the north. Viewed from Bactria, this is an invasion, but the Chinese historical sources, in particular, enable us to see something of the wider picture. The mid-second-century incursions into Graeco-Bactrian territory were

---

13. Clarysse and Thompson 2007; these documents were discussed in greater depth in chapter 1.

the product of a southward population movement that took place on a large scale across Central Asia at this period. The process is documented, at least in our surviving sources, from a distance and from both ends of a long chain of population movement. But the sources also document the chronological beginning and end of this process as it affected Bactria. Strabo and Justin (summarizing the lost work of Pompeius Trogus) deal rather briefly with the events and with the nomad groups involved. Chinese sources record the same process from the other end of the conveyor belt. Many of the details of what happened in between are obscure. In *The Greeks in Bactria and India,* Tarn stated: "In 141 the curtain falls on Greek Bactria, to rise again in 128 upon new peoples and new names; somewhere between these two dates lies the end of the Greek kingdom."[14]

Neither set of sources on its own offers us the historical or ethnographic precision that Tarn and other scholars have attempted to extract from them—a date for the "end of the Greek kingdom" or precise identities of the groups who brought this about. Nor, equally important, can the peoples named and events narrated in the Graeco-Roman and Chinese sources be made to match up with one another, or at least not as neatly as one may hope. Attempts to make them do so offer an illusion that a particular author has reconstructed a history of the fall of the Graeco-Bactrian kingdom, in which the two sets of sources corroborate each other in the small-scale and specific in addition to in the large-scale, *longue-durée,* and general. But this is unfortunately not the case, as I shall discuss. The most productive approach to the written sources comes in refraining from trying to discern single events in the narrative—or in matching the details in one to those in the other—but in accepting that these sources simply are what they are. In giving us a picture of a conveyor belt of population movements over a period of some decades, they in fact complement the data from archaeological field survey and excavations that I shall discuss in the sections that will follow. My interest here is not in establishing the movements of specific exonymous groups but in looking at the general domino effect, if such it was: its causes and its results in Bactria, in both the shorter term (the end of Graeco-Bactrian kingdom) and the longer term (the rise of Kushan empire).

The Graeco-Bactrian state's troubles of the mid-second century B.C.E. were not confined to the nomads. That population, however, is the element in the kingdom's collapse that has received the most attention, since it is the one best-documented in the historical sources and because the group known in the Chinese sources as the Yuezhi were those who subsequently occupied and achieved hegemony over what had once been the Graeco-Bactrian heartland around and to the south of the river Oxus. Justin's account of the events of the reign of Eukratides balances the nomad threat with that from Parthia, from various peoples to the south of the

14. Tarn 1951, 274.

Hindu Kush, and within the Bactrian royal house (or perhaps more than one) itself:[15]

> At about the same time that Mithridates was beginning his rule in Parthia, Eucratides was beginning his in Bactria, both of them great men. But the fortunes of the Parthians prevailed, carrying them to the zenith of their power under this king. The Bactrians, for their part, were buffeted in various conflicts and lost not just their empire but their liberty as well. Worn down by wars with the Sogdians, Arachosians, Drancae, Arei and Indians, they finally fell, virtually in a state of exhaustion, under the power of the Parthians, a weaker people than themselves. Eucratides nevertheless conducted many wars with great valour. Weakened by these, he found himself facing a siege by Demetrius, king of the Indians, but by making repeated sorties he was able to defeat 60,000 of the enemy with 300 men. Delivered from the siege after four months, he then brought India under his sway. During the return journey from India, he was murdered by his son, whom he had made partner in his royal power. The son did not conceal his parricide and, as though he had killed an enemy rather than his father, drove his chariot through his blood, ordering the corpse to be cast aside unburied.

In Justin's—or perhaps rather Pompeius Trogus's—analysis, multiple factors contributed to the decline and fall of the Greek state of Bactria. The kingdom was weakened by territorial loss and military attack from several quarters. Given this fatal conjunction of circumstances, a mass nomadic invasion such as scholars both ancient and modern have envisaged does not necessarily have to have been the case: populations and military forces were able to move into a power vacuum.

Strabo's account shifts the focus more clearly to the nomads, and he names and blames a number of individual groups—thus supplying an apparent but illusory level of ethnographic precision that for the modern historian has probably caused more trouble than it is worth. His reference to Bactria in the first passage quoted here is in fact in the context of a discussion of Central Asian nomads, not vice versa:[16]

> On the left and opposite these peoples are situated the Scythian or nomadic tribes, which cover the whole of the northern side. Now the greater part of the Scythians, beginning at the Caspian Sea, are called Däae, but those who are situated more to the east than these are named Massagetae and Sacae, whereas all the rest are given the general name of Scythians, though each people is given a separate name of its own. They are all for the most part nomads. But the best known of the nomads are those who took away Bactriana from the Greeks, I mean the Asii, Pasiani, Tochari, and

---

15. Justin, *Epitome* 41.6.1–5, trans. Yardley and Develin 1994. In an aside, Justin here supplies us with one of the few (roughly) fixed points in Graeco-Bactrian history: correlation with the reign of Mithridates I of Parthia allows us to position the beginning of Eukratides' reign around 171 B.C.E.

16. Strabo 11.8.2; Loeb translation.

Sacarauli, who originally came from the country on the other side of the Iaxartes River that adjoins that of the Sacae and the Sogdiani and was occupied by the Sacae. And as for the Däae, some of them are called Aparni, some Xanthii, and some Pissuri. Now of these the Aparni are situated closest to Hyrcania and the part of the sea that borders on it, but the remainder extend even as far as the country that stretches parallel to Aria.

[The Greeks of Bactria] also held Sogdiana, situated above Bactriana towards the east between the Oxus River, which forms the boundary between the Bactrians and the Sogdians, and the Iaxartes River. And the Iaxartes forms also the boundary between the Sogdians and the nomads.

The priorities of the Chinese sources on the mid-second century-B.C.E. Central Asian population movements are naturally rather different than those of Trogus and Strabo, but they share the perspective of a settled civilization that perceives a clear dividing line between itself and a barbaric, threatening nomadic hinterland. This claimed self-other, civilized-barbarian polarity is a matter of rhetoric as much as socioeconomic and political reality, as I will discuss in following sections.

Chinese historical sources are principally concerned with the movements of two major nomad confederacies—the Xiongnu and the Yuezhi—in the mid-second century B.C.E., inasmuch as these are immediate threats to the security of the Chinese empire. There have been a number of important recent studies on the archaeology of the Xiongnu confederacy and the Xiongnu-Chinese frontier regions,[17] and the problem of viewing the material culture of the Xiongnu through an historical lens—or simply of identifying a Xiongnu archaeological culture—is as acute as it is for the Greek sources and for the archaeology of Bactria and neighboring regions. Sima Qian's *Shiji* (*Records of the Grand Historian*) draws extensively on the account of Zhang Qian, who undertook a diplomatic mission to the West around 138–125 B.C.E., spending considerable periods of time among the Xiongnu and Yuezhi. Zhang Qian visited Bactria in 126 B.C.E., in the very immediate aftermath of the fall of Bactria to the Yuezhi. *Shiji* 123 gives an account of Zhang Qian's difficult mission and the political and military circumstances that led to it.[18] That chapter deals at length with Dayuan (the Ferghana Valley) and the affairs of the Xiongnu and Yuezhi, including their antagonistic relationship with each other. Sima Qian's quotation of Zhang Qian's report contains the following passages of relevance to Bactria and the mid-second-century population movements:[19]

---

17. Ibid. 11.11.2. In connection with the second quoted paragraph, see especially Brosseder and Miller 2011.

18. An excursus on this section of the *Shiji* is included in Posch 1995.

19. *Shiji* 123, trans. Watson 1993. A later history, the *Han shu* (trans. Dubs 1938–55), covers the period from around 206 B.C.E. to 25 C.E. and contains accounts of the Yuezhi after the conquest of Bactria, and of the Kushan empire. For earlier periods, it draws extensively on the *Shiji* as a source.

The Great Yuezhi live some 2,000 or 3,000 *li* west of Dayuan, north of the Gui (Oxus) River. They are bordered on the south by Daxia, on the west by Anxi (Parthia), and on the north by Kangju. They are a nation of nomads, moving from place to place with their herds, and their customs are like those of the Xiongnu. They have some 100,000 or 200,000 archer warriors. Formerly they were very powerful and despised the Xiongnu, but later, when Maodun became leader of the Xiongnu nation, he attacked and defeated the Yuezhi. Some time afterwards his son, the Old *Shanyu*, killed the king of the Yuezhi and made his skull into a drinking cup.

The Yuezhi originally lived in the area between the Qilian or Heavenly Mountains and Dunhuang, but after they were defeated by the Xiongnu they moved far away to the west, beyond Dayuan, where they attacked and conquered the people of Daxia and set up the court of their king on the northern bank of the Gui River. A small number of their people who were unable to make the journey west sought refuge among the Qiang barbarians in the Southern Mountains, where they are known as the Lesser Yuezhi. . . . [There follow brief accounts of Anxi (Parthia) and Tiaozhi (perhaps Mesopotamia).]

Daxia (Bactria) is located over 2,000 *li* southwest of Dayuan, south of the Gui River. Its people cultivate the land and have cities and houses. Their customs are like those of Dayuan. It has no great ruler but only a number of petty chiefs ruling the various cities. The people are poor in the use of arms and afraid of battle, but they are clever at commerce. After the Great Yuezhi moved west and attacked Daxia, the entire country came under their sway. The population of the country is large, numbering some 1,000,000 or more persons. The capital is called the city of Lanshi (Bactra) and has a market where all sorts of goods are bought and sold.

Chinese ethnographic and historical information is qualitatively and quantitatively different from Greek sources on Central Asian nomads in regions to north of Bactria.[20] The material in the *Shiji* also represents a real departure in Chinese writings on Central Asia, away from fantastical descriptions of mythical creatures (not unlike some Greek accounts) and toward something resembling ethnography—including, for example, details of the Xiongnu pastoral economy.[21] The Chinese historical sources are written from a position of intensive interaction and diplomatic relations with a steppe-nomad confederacy, involving named historical figures. Sima Qian's source on the Yuezhi and Bactria, the well-traveled diplomat Zhang Qian, who actually lived for several years as a captive among the Xiongnu, provided him with a much better account of Central Asian affairs in the mid-second century B.C.E. than anything available to Strabo or Justin. Sima Qian is thus able to recount the long migration of the Yuezhi in some detail. Zhang Qian's visit to Bactria in the aftermath of the Yuezhi conquest allowed him to see for himself that this conquest was not one of outright destruction. Bactria was still a wealthy,

20. See, in general, Di Cosmo 2002, 255–93.
21. Ibid. 272–73, 290.

productive, and densely populated country. Militarily, the Bactrians were no longer a formidable force, and political power had been decentralized, but under the Yuezhi the city of Bactra continued to flourish. Settled, urbanized civilization in Bactria had not been destroyed, and under its new (formerly) nomad rulers it still continued to function. The Chinese historical accounts lack anything more in the way of socioeconomic or political nuance, but what is remarkable is how extensively their complex picture of Central Asian population movements and their complex effects fits with the archaeological evidence.

If Sima Qian or another Chinese historian had been able to provide an account of the actual Yuezhi invasion of Bactria rather than simply its aftermath, comparison with the Greek and Roman sources might have some purpose and chance of success. But the possibility of having and comparing good-quality Greek and Chinese sources on the invasions of Bactria is something we should not torment ourselves with. Where the information of the *Shiji* has been much used and abused is in trying to marry Zhang Qian's account with the information presented in Strabo's and Justin's works. I have no intention of playing the game of trying to identify the Yuezhi of the Chinese sources with any of the myriad Scythian groups of the Graeco-Roman sources; such an approach is methodologically unsound for any number of reasons. The various historical accounts draw on different sources of information, some closer to primary, firsthand testimony than others. Sima Qian, Strabo, and Justin all share the perspective of outsiders, although Zhang Qian lived among the Central Asian nomads and was in a position to observe their ways and actions at first hand. We have no information on what the various exonymous groups of the historical sources called themselves and how they thought of themselves. The account of the movements of the Yuezhi, Xiongnu, and other nomad groups show how political and military alliances might be made and broken, and large confederacies split into smaller groups: the tribes named in the historical sources were not static, bounded entities. For all these reasons, and others, the equation of the Yuezhi with the Tocharoi, Sakas, or generic Scythians simply does not work. Even if it did, it is doubtful what further light it would shed on the affairs of Central Asia in the mid-second century B.C.E. beyond tidying up the evidence and imposing a false neatness that some may find comforting. Where the historical sources do complement one another is in illuminating some broad trends of nomadic population movement, the perception of such movement as threatening by the settled civilizations of China and the Graeco-Roman world, and the impact of this movement locally upon Bactria. This impact was certainly dramatic and brought a new political order (or new political orders) to the region, but Zhang Qian's account of a prosperous Bactria under the Yuezhi provides evidence for the same kind of administrative continuity through regime change as experienced in earlier periods (chapter 1).

Tarn falls into the same unproductive trap of trying to pair up the nomad groups named in the classical sources with those in the Chinese and of trying to trace their movements, but other points in his analysis and commentary on the historical sources are worth revisiting.[22] His frustration at the ubiquity of Sakas is evident—"I may perhaps venture the remark that Asia is getting very full of Sacas."[23] (I may equally venture that Asia is getting very full of Tocharoi.) But I wish to conclude by restating his view that "Bactria bled to death"—a statement that he attributes to Justin,[24] although Justin does not put it in quite these terms.[25] Tarn puts the fatal exsanguination sometime after the bloody murder of Eukratides by his son, since Bactrian Greeks were still making territorial advances in India. But by this point the affairs of the Greeks in Bactria and Greeks in India are already two separate histories. The decline of the Mauryan empire and Seleucid disinclination or inability to turn their attentions to the East created a power vacuum in northwestern India that the Greeks of Bactria could move into. India, as we have seen, offered opportunities for ambitious commanders to carve out their kingdoms and to turn their attentions back against Bactria. India, distant from both Parthians and steppe peoples, could be held when Bactria could not. The Greek kingdoms of India continued to be healthy even as and after Bactria finally bled out.

THE ARCHAEOLOGY OF POPULATION MOVEMENT IN CENTRAL ASIA

If writing a history of the Central Asian population movements of the mid-second century B.C.E. is problematic in both essence and execution, then tracing them archaeologically is equally fraught with problems of source criticism and methodology. In the Graeco-Roman and Chinese historical sources, we are confronted with the perennial failure of settled populations to understand nomads and their way of life. This failure leads to confusion, terminological imprecision, and a tendency to fall back on the same ethnonyms and rhetorical topoi (barbaric nomad horsemen, the self-other civilized-barbarian divide). A lack of reliable, up-to-date information on Central Asian populations, their movements and current locations, and their political and socioeconomic affairs also means that ancient historians (with the notable exception of Sima Qian) simply did not have the opportunity to be good anthropologists or ethnographers, even if such an enterprise had had a place in their worldviews.

I turn now toward the archaeological record from Bactria and regions immediately to the north of around the third century B.C.E. to the second century C.E. This

22. Tarn 1951, 270–311.
23. Ibid. 287.
24. *Epitome* 41.6.3.
25. Tarn 1951, 270.

period extends considerably before and after the specific population movements of the mid-second century B.C.E. that affected the Greek kingdom of Bactria, but such is the nature of the archaeological record—and, in fact, just such a *longue-durée* view is desirable. I begin with a general discussion of mobility (migration, nomadism, pastoral transhumance) and its visibility in the archaeological record before proceeding to a Central Asian case study—that of Xiongnu-Chinese inter-action—that has useful lessons for the study of population mobility and mixed subsistence strategies in Bactria and neighboring territories. Finally, I review the archaeological evidence—from the excavation of settlements and burials, and from field surveys—from these territories themselves.

The topic of migration has undergone a—not atypical—theoretical cycle of simplistic, unnuanced application (further compromised by political and racial overtones from which subsequent scholars have sought to distance themselves), enthusiastic debunking, and a limited reclamation and redefinition. Archaeologi-cal cultures do not equate to peoples—or at least not in the senses intended by earlier generations of prehistorians such as Gustaf Kossinna, V. Gordon Childe, or Sir William Flinders Petrie—and the spread of cultural traits or assemblages does not have to be explained in terms of the movement of peoples.[26] The processual emphasis on internal processes of social, cultural, and economic change, on the other hand, does not deal particularly well with the observable fact that people indeed do move, often in large groups and over great distances.

In the Hellenistic world, and more specifically in Hellenistic Bactria, we are directly confronted with this fact, not just because of well-documented population movements associated with Graeco-Macedonian military expansion and coloniza-tion but because the Greek and Chinese historical sources just discussed attest the movement of peoples in Central Asia. These peoples—I use the term precisely because it is vague—are described in the historical sources as groups with particular names, with their own cultural traits and customs, and acting under the political authority of single leaders. Such descriptions inevitably tell us more about outside— Chinese or Greek—attempts to understand and categorize such groups than they ever can about their internal affairs and organization, and conception of themselves, but they also indicate very clearly that population movements were going on. Can we identify or corroborate archaeologically these waves of population movement without lapsing into the kinds of cultural-historical approaches that first discredited the whole project of going looking for migration in the archaeological record?

David Anthony's seminal rehabilitation of the concept of migration in archae-ology reviews a few points of particular relevance to the material from Central Asia in the late first millennium B.C.E.[27] The first step is to gain an idea of how

26. See, for example, the discussions in Graves-Brown, Jones, and Gamble 1996.
27. Anthony 1990.

migration typically works—the kinds of activity and social process involved—from the documentation and analysis of historical and contemporary migrations by scholars of other disciplines, before deciding what kind of archaeological signature we may reasonably expect such migration to have. In the classical and Chinese historical sources on the population movements of the second century B.C.E., I propose that we have a better treatment of the social and political functioning of migration than may at first appear, an argument that I will return to in summing up. More recent discussions of migration in archaeology develop further useful points.[28] The movement of an archaeological package is more indicative of the movement of the people who originally created and used that assemblage than is any single material item or trait, and there are a few places in the Central Asian archaeological record where we may identify the movement of such packages. Perhaps of greatest salience for my discussion here are the notions that mobility should be regarded as a spectrum and that seasonal transhumance, and migration in the colloquially understood sense of long-distance, permanent mass population movement, lie at different points on this spectrum. The inclusion of pastoral transhumance as an intermediate point permits us to break down the false dichotomy between nomadism and settlement in Central Asia, in the same way that Graeco-Bactrian use of Scythian mercenaries (inter alia) may enable us to blur the sharp Greek-barbarian divide of Euthydemos's rhetoric at Bactra.

Much of the recent literature on pastoral nomadism and the archaeological record concerns the Near Eastern Bronze Age and makes extensive critical use of ethnographic comparanda,[29] but Bronze Age and Iron Age Central Asia has increasingly emerged as a source of case studies and an area of inquiry for such questions.[30] In the regions I shall go on to consider, nomadic groups are characterized by their social and economic symbiosis with settled populations: they occupy the same territories, and an individual's or group's participation in activities such as arable farming or herding may not be stable but may vary over time. This symbiosis, however, tends not to be archaeologically visible readily as such, because the remains of settled agriculture—farmsteads, settlements, irrigation channels—are far more prominent in the landscape than the ephemeral remains of seasonal or temporary tented encampments and forms of subsistence—herding—that make extensive rather than intensive use of the landscape. Nor does the notional category of nomadism necessarily have a distinctive material culture, but

28. See, e.g., Kristiansen 2005, Hakenbeck 2008, and for a case study Stevenson 2007.

29. Saidel and Steen 2007, Szuchman 2009, Porter 2011.

30. Davis-Kimball, Bashilov, and Yablonsky 1995; Kohl 2002, 2007; Frachetti 2008. I provide a few references and highlight some especially pertinent themes here, but this is not the place for a full critical review of the scholarship. I have drawn in particular upon the discussions in Roger Cribb 1991, Barnard and Wendrich 2008, Szuchman 2009.

rather it may offer one incorporating elements from the settled groups with whom the nomads come into contact.[31]

In the case-study sites and regions I discuss below, my emphasis is on precisely this kind of symbiosis, but the second century B.C.E. is also a period when large-scale, long-distance mobility of populations within Central Asia makes specific, intrusive groups of nomads archaeologically visible through the appearance of new ceramic styles and distinctive structures such as kurgan burials in territories in which a mixed economy already operated. In some places, incomers also have a visible impact on existing sites and patterns of land use. As will become clear, considerable caution is necessary in assessing this material, and it has often been viewed through the lens of a traditional reading of the Chinese and Graeco-Roman historical sources. The historical accounts make it clear that several main nomad groups were involved in the second-century population movements. Rather than attempt to trace these on the ground, we should instead take from this the lesson that the arrival of multiple new groups should become manifest in the archaeological record in diverse forms.[32] The point is not that one should attempt to use ceramics or any other form of evidence to plot the movements of a single mass migration or invasion but that the very difficulty of identifying a single nomad-invader archaeological signature—for example, a Yuezhi style of ceramics or other material culture—in itself may reflect the long-standing nomad-settled socioeconomic continuum (rather than divide) in Central Asia, the gradual and incremental movement southward of northern groups into the Oxus Basin, and the diversity of the various population groups to which the historical sources assign particular names. Although I speak in general of a "conveyor belt" or "domino effect," within this wide region of Central Asia there were of course local and small-scale population movements by numerous peoples,[33] which at different periods may have gone with or against the general northeast-to-southwest flow.

In my discussion of the Chinese historical sources above, I noted that recent studies of the Xiongnu confederacy, which became the major nomad power in northeastern Central Asia around the turn of the third to the second century B.C.E., and its relations with China offer a picture of nomad-settled relations more

31. Smith 2008, 343.

32. This provides a work-around solution of sorts to the problem posed by Gardin (1990b, 135) in his treatment of the potential ceramic indicators of nomad movements into Bactria in the second century B.C.E.: "Let us suppose that we were to be confronted the ensemble of the preceding finds, from Ai Khanoum to Bukhara, from Bactra to Ksirov, without any hypothesis regarding the nature of the peoples who made or used all these types of pottery. Would we have any grounds to attribute them to the same movement of pastoralist-nomads from the Eurasian steppes, in the process of sedentarising in the cultivated lands of Bactria? The response, honestly, is negative. In other words, ceramics are not, in this case, despite appearances, a sure indicator of such movements."

33. Abdullaev 2007, 73.

finely attuned to the theoretical considerations just reviewed than does the tradi-tional model. Although bipolar antagonism between Xiongnu and Chinese cer-tainly existed and is foregrounded in the historical sources, the relationship was more complex—in all the ways I have just reviewed that nomad-settled relations typically are. This dichotomy has been most successfully challenged and broken down in recent work by Nicola Di Cosmo, upon which I draw for my discussion here.[34] Many of the points Di Cosmo makes with regard to the Xiongnu in the east pertain equally to the Yuezhi in the west: the nomadic pastoralist–agriculturalist divide is not so stark as traditional analyses of the historical sources may make it appear; population movements and military invasions are set into motion by a range of factors, not simply a desire to acquire the products of a settled civilization; and intergroup and intragroup relations among nomads themselves are impor-tant. Methodologically, the point upon which I wish to place greatest emphasis is that time spent unpicking and knitting together the evidence of historical sources and the archaeological record is well spent and need not come down to deciding whether the sources corroborate or contradict one another. In this regard, I speak, to some extent, in defense of the usefulness of the historical record.[35]

BACTRIA AND NEIGHBORING TERRITORIES:
THE ARCHAEOLOGICAL EVIDENCE

Just as with the Yuezhi's arrival in Bactria some decades later, Xiongnu expansion in the first half of the second century B.C.E. into regions already inhabited by sed-entary and semisedentary populations did not result in the destruction of existing agricultural systems and settlements;[36] rather, there was a new power balance within an existing symbiotic relationship. Although I have suggested that the Xiongnu and their relations with China provide a useful comparative case study for the Yuezhi (and their fellow travelers) and their relations with Bactria, the archaeological and historical data on the Xiongnu is altogether more copious.[37]

The deficiencies of the western Central Asian record, for our purposes, are many. For those who do not read Russian or do not have access to libraries with

34. Di Cosmo 1994 and the longer study Di Cosmo 2002.
35. A similar position is taken by Di Cosmo (1994, 1109): "The wisdom of the written sources is seldom questioned by archaeologists and historians that research the Xiongnu and their relations with China. Indeed, passages from the *Hanshu,* the *Shiji,* and other sources are often quoted as ultimate authorities to prove or dismiss a point, provide ancient names for peoples and places, and furnish a basic historical framework in which to enplot the archaeological narrative. While remaining aware of the potential pitfalls of this method, it is also true that such sources—the only historical records in our possession—cannot simply be set aside under the pretense of their being entirely mendacious."
36. Ibid. 1115.
37. For which I refer the reader, again, to Brosseder and Miller 2011.

relevant collections, simply accessing the information in primary publications of Central Asian archaeological sites is difficult.[38] The dating of much archaeological material that I shall go on to discuss is contentious, and even a difference of a hundred years (a level of precision that we do not always have) can be fatal to making any connections with movements at the time of the end of the Graeco-Bactrian state. The archaeological evidence simply does not provide the level of fine detail necessary to trace population movements with any precision—especially across such a vast region. But this deficiency does not mean that there are no productive directions in which to take our analysis of that evidence. Even where their remains are identifiable, tracing an individual nomadic tribe through Central Asia is not simply a matter of joining dots on a map of burials or habitation sites with similar contents and characteristics. Such a method would require that people, objects, and their meanings always travel together—which they do not.[39] It would also require group membership and intergroup relations to remain stable over time, which (as I have already discussed with regard to the historical sources) they also do not. Comparing the composition of assemblages *within* structures of similar type, however, can often be productive.

Several sites that I shall consider below, for example, offer useful test cases wherein we may propose alternative ways of locating nomads in the archaeological record and examine intimate and localized points of contact between mobile and sedentary populations and ways of life. These include the urban sites of Samarkand and Ai Khanoum. Mobile groups carrying their possessions with them and living in shelters made of light, perishable materials do not leave as durable an archaeological signature as groups who build structures in brick, earth, and stone. But when living in close proximity and interaction with people who built and used more permanent architecture, their remains may be visible in negative: suggestive empty spaces within fortification walls with room for tent cities or corralling livestock.[40]

Although I organize my discussion below primarily by region and site, the archaeological evidence I consider here may also be divided into three main cate-

38. Although Abdullaev 2007 and Rapin 2007 provide excellent up-to-date treatments of the material and questions in English; see also Zadneprovskiy 1994.

39. See, e.g., Kopytoff 1986, Gosden and Marshall 1999.

40. Abdullaev 2007, 83–86. As with many matters to do with Achaemenid, Hellenistic, and Kushan Bactria, evidence from the city of Bactra itself would be extremely welcome and add much to our understanding of the political and administrative affairs of the region—but in the present state of archaeological investigation, such evidence simply does not exist. (See Bernard, Besenval, and Marquis 2006, 1176–80, for a history of archaeological work at Bactra; for further references, Mairs 2011b, 29–30.) What is to be hoped for from new projects at Bactra-Balkh is an idea of the evolution of this city over time, of its fortifications and what they had to deal with over the *longue durée,* and of such questions of long-term administration and continuity and change as are considered in chapter 1, not the single catastrophic events looked at here.

gories: field-survey data, fortifications, and burials. Each of these, in its own way, speaks to the relationship between nomadic and settled communities in Central Asia over the *longue durée,* but in some cases we can also see shorter-term processes at work, or even individual events of conquest or abandonment. Fortifications, for example, may tell us something about the kind of military forces they were expected to withstand, indicative of long-term patterns of nomad-settled relations and conflict, but the creation of new fortifications or destruction of existing ones may be placed in a more immediate political context. Below I discuss these questions further. Toward the end of this chapter, I will return to sum up the specific evidence with relation to Ai Khanoum and then look at continuities from the period of invasions through into the Kushan empire.

SYMBIOSIS: THE SURKHAN-DARYA AND SHERABAD-DARYA FIELD SURVEYS

The Alexander historian Quintus Curtius Rufus rightly noted that the land of Bactria "multiplex et varia natura est."[41] It was capable of supporting various forms of subsistence. The region of the Surkhan-darya—a right-bank tributary of the Oxus (Amu-darya) in what is now southern Uzbekistan—is perhaps the place where the nomad-settled divide has been most productively broken down and explored in the archaeological record of the Hellenistic Far East. Recent archaeological projects have been able to build on the foundations of decades of Soviet research into the different landscapes of the region and their potential for human exploitation.[42] The Surkhan-darya region contains a few areas suitable for dry farming and other low-lying areas where irrigated agriculture may be practiced, but far more of the land area is better suited to grazing than to agriculture. Landscape and ethnographic studies have revealed a close symbiosis between pastoral and agricultural economic strategies and populations, indicating that ethnic groups often occupy specific economic niches, but it is inevitably easier to recognize the traces of settled agriculture—villages, irrigation canals—in the landscape than the scantier traces left by nomadic and seminomadic groups and lifestyles.[43] Historically, in the northern half of the Surkhan-darya region in particular, populations relying on irrigated and dry agriculture and herding depended upon the same regional center, came into regular contact, and even shared the same resources. The differ-

---

41. Curtius 7.4.26–31.

42. Stride 2007, 102; on the creation of an archaeological GIS of the region, see Stride 2004; more recent field reports by the Catalano-Uzbek project: Gurt et al. 2007, 2008a, 2008b; Gurt and Pidaev 2009.

43. "The heavy bias of the archaeological evidence in favour of sedentary groups who practiced irrigated agriculture is well known: however the *feeling* that, in *normal conditions,* the Surkhan Darya province *should be* sedentary remains" (Stride 2007, 104).

ent ecological zones and populations of the Surkhan-darya watershed were closely interdependent, and the relationship between agriculture and pastoralism was one of symbiosis.[44]

The benefits of considering adjacent regions suitable for different exploitation strategies together may also be seen in the region of the Sherabad-darya, which was originally a smaller right-bank tributary of the Oxus (Amu-darya) downstream from the Surkhan-darya but no longer reaches the river. On-the-ground prospections and the use of Google Earth have allowed the relationship between a fairly well-investigated irrigated agricultural plain in the south and the less archaeologically known mountains and foothills to the north to be explored in greater depth.[45] The field work has enabled an increasing number of seasonal campsites and burial sites to be identified in marginal zones, even if it is still difficult to date these precisely by ceramics, given a lack of parallels.[46] The case, at any rate, has been made that—as with the Surkhan-darya—arable farming and herding and their practitioners interacted closely. This has been demonstrated particularly in the discovery within the citadel area of the settlement of Jandavlattepa of concentric rows of postholes forming a plan reminiscent of that of a nomadic yurt.[47] Jandavlattepa is a multiperiod site including levels of the Graeco-Bactrian period, although the precise date of the yurt remains to be clarified. The barbarians, it seems, were already within the gates.

FORTIFYING THE NORTHERN MARCHES: THE IRON GATES AND SOGDIANA

Although socioeconomic symbiosis prevailed within the Surkhan-darya and Sherabad-darya valleys, however, the Graeco-Bactrian state monitored and regulated movement on northern routes from the cities of the Oxus Valley, such as Bactra, to Samarkand and Sogdiana in the north. We find defensive structures aimed at protecting these territories and routes even within the Surkhan-darya Valley, at sites such as Kurganzol, a fortress with massive walls and semicircular towers whose period of occupation coincides with the era of Alexander's conquests through to the first half of the second century B.C.E. and the final years of the Graeco-Bactrian kingdom.[48] The remains at Kurganzol display several features that recur in many of the major fortified sites of the regions to the north of the Oxus that I shall go on to discuss. The fortifications are designed to withstand

44. Ibid. 112.
45. Stančo 2009, Tušlová 2011.
46. Danielsová, Stančo, and Shaydullaev 2010.
47. Stančo et al. 2006; cf. on Jandavlattepa, Abdullaev and Stančo 2003, 2004, 2005, 2007.
48. Sverchkov 2008.

particular forms of attack—in the case of Kurganzol, hollow walls with internal chambers and loopholes suggest that this was lighter cavalry or infantry attack rather than siege engines. Occupation at the site was periodic. Although destruction layers do appear, at other periods abandonment seems to have been a strategic decision, because firm control of territory north of the wall made the fortress superfluous.[49]

In the Hellenistic West—as for that matter in the Chinese East—the state's attempt at boundary construction and maintenance may therefore be traced in a very tangible, physical sense: in the remains of walls and other fortifications. These provide evidence of the constriction and expansion of Graeco-Bactrian political control at different periods and of attempts to establish and defend rigid boundaries. In the relevant sections below, I shall discuss material from the sites of Derbent (the Iron Gates), Samarkand-Afrasiab, and Koktepe, all to the north of the Oxus, on the northern marches of the Graeco-Bactrian kingdom, and sometimes beyond its control. The fortifications of Ai Khanoum (chapter 2) and evidence of attacks on them will also be revisited in the concluding parts of this chapter. I have, I hope, established that even where we may identify such a thing in the archaeological record, a single traumatic event—a nomadic attack—tells only part of the story of what happened in Bactria in the mid-second century B.C.E. Fortifications (of urban sites and as independent structures) in their creation, destruction, and renewal may show the impact of the various thrusts and feints under which Bactria bled to death, but they may also reveal longer-term patterns of defensive strategy and boundary maintenance in Central Asia. Furthermore, one may give further consideration to the question of what, precisely, Central Asian fortifications were designed to protect. The format is seldom if ever simply a matter of a walled urban settlement or bounded agricultural territory in the traditional sense. In many cases, Graeco-Bactrian fortifications enclose wide areas empty of permanent construction that could have served to shelter people and livestock from the settlement's pastoral and agricultural hinterland, or to have contained tents or other constructions in light materials—or both. Even in the one place—in fortifications—where the nomad-settled confrontation appears at first sight to manifest itself most strongly and concretely, we can also destabilize it by questioning the urban, settled character of this civilization.

In addition to the existence of fortifications—their creation, destruction, or neglect—it has been argued that the format and character of Central Asian fortifications change depending upon the prevailing—or anticipated—type of assault in the region and period in question. Henri-Paul Francfort's 1979 study *Les fortifications en Asie centrale de l'Age du Bronze à l'époque kouchane* identifies two main types of fortification: hollow ramparts, characterized by thin walls with internal

49. Ibid. 131.

galleries, and semicircular towers with loopholes offering archers lines of sight and trajectory over all angles (as at Kurganzol); and massive ramparts, with thick, solid walls and rectangular towers, where defensive operations were conducted primarily from atop the walls rather than from inside them. Hollow ramparts predominate in periods before and after the era of the Graeco-Bactrian kingdom and continue to be the main model outside the Graeco-Bactrian domain, in Chorasmia. Massive ramparts are typical of towns and fortresses of the Graeco-Bactrian empire. The two main models, Francfort proposes, are responses to two different types of military tactics: attack by mounted archers on the one hand, and on the other siegecraft, using artillery and siege engines (Francfort 1979, 40–43). My arguments in the present instance do not depend upon the chronological aspect of Francfort's theory, or indeed the geographical: my point is simply that different types of warfare and raiding, waged by different military forces, required different types of fortification and that this was something to which Central Asian policy makers were sensitive.

DERBENT: THE IRON GATES

The field-survey data from the Surkhan-darya and Sherabad-darya districts, which can be supplemented by evidence from two sites in the Zeravshan Valley— Samarkand-Afrasiab[50] and Koktepe—and the Iron Gates at Derbent shows how dynamic the vast zone of interaction between settled Bactria and the nomadic steppe was, and that it might be subject to sudden violent disruptions. The mid-second-century-B.C.E. events in Bactria, in terms of the security of the Graeco-Bactrian state, were only the most traumatic of these disruptions. Although the settled-versus-pastoral-nomadic divide was indistinct, and no one group had exclusive use of any one circumscribed territory, this concession does not mean that the situation was static or that the Greeks kings of Bactria did not find this dynamism problematic and try to do something about it. On the contrary, the periodic investment of resources in the construction of major fortifications in the areas to the north and west of the Surkhan-darya indicate an attempt to assert control over the Zeravshan Valley when it was possible to do so and to define and patrol a defensible boundary when it was not.

The archaeological evidence from the sites of the Zeravshan Valley and the material from the site of the Iron Gates at Derbent complement each other in the sense that both reveal the constriction and expansion of Graeco-Bactrian territory

50. As is a recurrent pattern in Central Asia, the Samarkand region has an ancient *tepe* site, and an adjacent, more recent settlement constructed after the Mongol conquests (another nomad invasion) of 1220–21 C.E. Afrasiab is the ancient city, the Marakanda of the classical historians, and neighboring Samarkand is the medieval and modern city.

at the same periods. There was a two-phase Greek occupation of Samarkand, the first commencing under Alexander and the second representing a reconquest or reoccupation under Eukratides in the early or mid-second century B.C.E. Both were of brief duration.

The Iron Gates occupy a natural place of defense on the mountainous road between Termez and the Surkhan-darya Valley and Samarkand and the Zeravshan Valley, near the modern village of Derbent.[51] The ancient defensive system consisted of ditches and a massive wall. The first phases of construction of this wall date to the Graeco-Bactrian period, perhaps even as early as the activities of the Seleucid king Antiochos I in the region,[52] and from this time on "the history of the wall coincides with the history of the states controlling the region, since their frontiers are incessantly redrawn depending upon relations with their nomadic neighbours."[53] The extent to which the Iron Gates ever represented a meaningful cultural boundary remains a matter for debate. As in other regions of Bactria and Sogdiana, local, intraregional variations in material culture suggest rather that political and cultural or socioeconomic boundaries should not be assumed to coincide.[54]

SAMARKAND, KOKTEPE, AND
THE ZERAVSHAN VALLEY

Like the Surkhan-darya and Sherabad-darya valleys in northern Bactria, and despite their mutual inclusion at various periods within the fortified boundaries of the Graeco-Bactrian kingdom, Sogdiana and the Middle Zeravshan Valley fall within the Central Asian mixed zone: "an ecological zone characterized by comparatively small areas suitable for irrigated agriculture, surrounded by much larger resource-rich pastoral areas such as desert, steppe, or mountains (or all these). This variety of landscapes encourages mixed economies (mostly combining agriculture and mobile pastoralism), in which close interaction between pastoralists and agriculturalists is the rule" (Stride, Rondelli, and Mantellini 2009, 80). Sogdiana and its major city, Samarkand, however, lay toward the northernmost edges of the Graeco-Bactrian political and cultural sphere for most of the Hellenistic period, and for considerable spells within this period were in fact outside it. As I have already noted, affairs at Samarkand are intimately connected to those at the Iron Gates: periods of destruction and abandonment at Samarkand reflect the same episodes of the expansion and constriction of Graeco-Bactrian power.

---

51. Historical geography: Rtveladze 1990, Grenet and Rapin 1998a, Rapin 1998 and 2005.
52. Lyonnet 1998, 153–54.
53. Rapin 2007, 47.
54. Lyonnet 1993.

As in the rest of the Zeravshan Valley, the comparatively brief periods of Graeco-Bactrian control are interspersed by others where Samarkand, and indeed the whole region to the north and west of the Iron Gates were abandoned to the control of steppe nomadic groups. Although only small areas of the vast *tell* (mound) site of Afrasiab, the ancient city of Samarkand, have been excavated, it is already clear that there were two separate periods of Graeco-Bactrian occupation. Each concluded with a destruction event and was followed by a period in which new populations moved into the area. The period of occupation under Alexander and the early Seleucids was brief.[55] Between around the second third of the third century B.C.E. and the beginning of the second century, Graeco-Bactrian control retreated back to the Iron Gates. The site of Afrasiab was uninhabited, and archaeological remains from the surrounding plain indicate settlement by mobile populations new to the area, as I shall discuss further below. This was the state of affairs at the time of the siege of Bactra, recounted by Polybios, where the Greek kings of Bactria faced an additional threat from the Seleucid empire and Euthydemos made direct appeal to the common barbarian-nomad threat. Whatever Euthydemos's relationship with them, the archaeological evidence certainly reveals that the steppe-nomad sphere was closer to the Oxus at this period than in earlier and later ones.

Following the second conquest of Samarkand and the Zeravshan Valley by Eukratides in around the 160s B.C.E., the Graeco-Bactrian frontier shifted to the north, and the walls at Derbent, now somewhat superfluous, fell into disrepair. This pattern of conquest is reflected at Afrasiab in a brief but intense program of urbanization and a general reconstruction of the city wall. Not much later, however, the nomad invasion of the 140s brought an abrupt end to construction activities at the walls of Afrasiab and inaugurated a new phase of occupation marked by light constructions.[56] A subsequent destruction period, marked by the interruption of a new building program at the fortifications and other structures and the rapid destruction of the most recently constructed elements of the wall, took place at or around the time of the mid-second-century-B.C.E. nomad conquests.[57] Although confirming the potential destructiveness of the population movements of the mid-second century, however, the disturbances at Samarkand also confirm the extent to which this movement involved diverse groups with different material cultures and not a unified invasion by a unified political or cultural entity.[58] Current and future archaeological work in the area around Samarkand may be

55. Lyonnet 2010, 147–48.

56. Rapin, Isamiddinov, and Khasanov 2001, 75–77.

57. Rapin (2007, 48) dates this to a little after 145 B.C.E., and Lyonnet 1991 proposes that it could be as late as 130 B.C.E., but the point is that there is a destruction of around this time.

58. Rapin 2007, 50.

expected to offer new data to further explore these topics as well as less violent disruptions to settlement patterns over the *longue durée*.[59]

The smaller site of Koktepe, in particular, has yielded material from periods earlier and later than the Graeco-Bactrian occupation and shows how the various groups that held dominance in the Middle Zeravshan Valley in given periods used the same sites and structures in different ways. Koktepe is one of several sites on the edge of the irrigable plain where a preexisting fortified site of the mid-first millennium B.C.E. was repurposed as the site of a wealthy nomad tomb.[60] The layout of Koktepe IIIa, the fortified site of the Achaemenid period, deployed a format "characteristic of Central Asian urbanism near the steppe areas," where fortification walls enclosed and protected not just monumental architectural structures but large open areas suitable for the population of the settlement's hinterland to shelter with their livestock when necessary.[61] This format recurs at Samarkand, Ai Khanoum (chapter 2), and Taxila.[62] In the first century C.E., the tomb of a nomad princess was dug into the *tepe* (mound) left by the monumental platform of Achaemenid Koktepe.[63] Incoming groups might engage very closely with the remains of earlier settled occupation in this way. At Ai Khanoum and Tillya Tepe we also find later tombs dug into the mounds of settlements and monumental buildings.[64]

THE OXUS VALLEY

The archaeological evidence from Derbent, Samarkand, and Koktepe may therefore be situated within a common narrative of the periodic attempts by the Graeco-Bactrian kings and their Seleucid predecessors to assert control over regions to the north of the Surkhan-darya Valley and the Iron Gates. I have opted to discuss these regions before sites of the Bactrian heartland such as Ai Khanoum because the evidence from Sogdiana is altogether better: it offers a longer-term perspective on nomad-settled relations and antagonisms and Graeco-Bactrian successes and failures in establishing a secure political boundary (or at least a stable liminal zone) with peoples to the north. The incursions into the Oxus Valley of the mid-second century B.C.E. represented something more akin to a single, traumatic nomad invasion but must be situated within this longer history.

Eastern Bactria is, regrettably, a region where it is more difficult to explore the relationship between different economic strategies and the groups practicing them

59. Berdimuradov et al. 2007.
60. Stride, Rondelli, and Mantellini 2009, 81.
61. Rapin 2007, 36.
62. Sirkap: Fussman 1993b, 90–91.
63. Rapin 2007, 53; on the stratigraphy of Koktepe see most recently Isamiddinov 2010.
64. Sarianidi 1972.

over the *longue durée,* but the archaeological field survey of the 1970s has provided useful potential data on the movement of newcomers into eastern Bactria.[65] Bertille Lyonnet's treatment of the "period of the nomad invasions"[66] makes use of the ceramic data from the eastern Bactria survey to try to establish what if any material signature was left by mid-second-century-B.C.E. disturbances.

Chronological factors present the greatest problem in tracing the nomad invasions archaeologically in eastern Bactria. Sufficient chronological precision is not always possible to differentiate the distinctive material cultures of separate contemporary groups from those of successive groups within the same region.[67] Change in the ceramic record took place, but it did so over a long period of time. The ceramic assemblages of three nomadic groups identified by Lyonnet are very small, and at the same period when these new ceramic styles appeared, Greek-style ceramics continued to be produced throughout the region. Even in cemeteries, nomad vessels are frequently found associated with Graeco-Bactrian ceramic types.[68]

In the period of invasions there appears immediately to the north of the Oxus (Amu-darya) a certain number of large necropoleis that in their material and notably in their ceramics show close links to the sedentary milieu but still adhere to steppe-nomadic tradition in terms of the mode of inhumation (men are often accompanied by their weapons) and structure of tombs (mounds known in the literature as "kurgans").[69] All these burials are earlier than the more famous and spectacular nomad tombs of Tillya Tepe, in northern Afghanistan, which date from around the first century B.C.E. through the first century C.E. and contain material, such as gold jewelry, which in its style and techniques of manufacture belongs to the milieu of the Central Asian steppe.[70] Inevitably scholars have been tempted to relate such kurgan cemeteries to the nomad groups named in the historical sources. It is difficult, however, to identify specific and consistent variations in material culture and behavior that may be associated with the distinctive material repertoire of anything one may think of as an ethnic group. Cranial deformation, for example—such as that found among one of the later burials in the Ai Khanoum stone-vault mausoleum[71]—cannot be associated with a single nomadic group. Lyonnet's study of the nomads and the fall of the Graeco-Bactrian kingdom attempts to identify the kind of archaeological package that modern archaeologi-

65. Gentelle 1989, Lyonnet 1997, Gardin 1998.

66. Lyonnet 1997, 157–72.

67. Ibid. 165.

68. Ibid. 158–59.

69. Grenet 1984, 95, discusses a number from the valley of Bishkent, an affluent of the right bank of the Kafirnigan, and others to the north of the Amu-darya.

70. See, most recently, Mordvintseva 2010, Mairs 2014b.

71. Francfort and Liger 1976, 34 n. 1.

cal studies of migration emphasize as important, by considering specific artifact and ceramic types within their immediate archaeological context and by considering possible correspondences between particular assemblages and the orientation of graves in particular directions.[72] It is really only at much broader scales, however, that this analysis becomes most convincing. One particular vessel type, tripod vases, occurs in small numbers in the very latest phase of occupation of Ai Khanoum, associated with both Greek and Yuezhi ceramics. Tripod vases appear also in the kurgan cemeteries of Ksirov, Tup Khona, Tulkhar, and Aruktau, and at sites much further to the east, in the frontier region between the steppe and the Chinese sphere of influence.[73] Once again, the existence of a broad movement of peoples and their cultures from the northeast to the southwest in Central Asia is confirmed, though without our being able to say much more with confidence about the details.

The mid-second-century-B.C.E. nomad conquests were the culmination of a migratory process that took place over several decades, and also confirm that—a constant theme in this chapter—mobility comes in many forms and on many scales and may be reflected or not in the archaeological record in different ways, including invisibility.[74] Population movements may tentatively and critically be traced in the material culture of eastern Bactria, but the identification of tribes from surface sherds and the equation of these with historical groups is unjustified—a point that, unfortunately, it is still necessary to make. Long-term subtle changes in the material culture of eastern Bactria represent not the sudden arrival and sedentarization of hordes of mounted steppe true nomads but the appearance on the scene of groups who were already familiar with agriculture and who may well have entered or interacted with eastern Bactria during the period of the Graeco-Bactrian kingdom.[75] In the survey material it can be difficult to tell conquest from peaceful infiltration. As a counterpoint to this, I turn now to the evidence of direct military attack from settlement sites, and in particular Ai Khanoum.

THE FALL OF AI KHANOUM

Eastern Bactria is potentially an interesting place to watch the political upheavals of the early to mid-second century B.C.E. take shape. In the first half of the second century, Ai Khanoum and its region grew in importance during a period of factional dynastic conflicts (involving Demetrios, Eukratides, and others) and of

72. Lyonnet 1991, 153–54.
73. Lyonnet 1997, 166.
74. Gardin 1998, 157–66, who also discusses Anthony 1990.
75. Gardin 1998, 163.

changes in the power balance in neighboring regions. The wars in India and the nomad movements to the north gave eastern Bactria added strategic importance.[76] Tracing this in the archaeological record, however, is more difficult. The Indian coins and commodities in the treasury at Ai Khanoum and the immense citywide program of renovation of the first part of the second century B.C.E. (chapters 1 and 2) testify, certainly, to increasing wealth and contacts with India. But in eastern Bactria, which remained entirely under Greek control from Alexander's conquests through to the collapse of the Graeco-Bactrian kingdom, it is simply not possible to follow the ebb and flow of Graeco-Bactrian fortunes in the same level of detail as may be done for the Iron Gates and Zeravshan Valley, where territorial control fluctuated, and where the implications of the weakness or confidence of centralized authority at any particular period were potentially more extreme.

Although they were caught up in the same *longue-durée* processes of population movement, war, and political maneuvering, events at Samarkand and at Ai Khanoum in the mid-second century B.C.E. are less directly connected than may at first appear. Both cities and their regions were lost from Graeco-Bactrian control during the period at which the state as a whole bled to death. Both cities experienced a break in occupation and a discontinuity in population, with reoccupation in the periods immediately following the mid-second-century-B.C.E. destruction by groups with material cultures and relationships to the urban environment different from those that preceded them. But the same groups were not involved—the two cities lay along different prongs of nomadic advance from the north and east—and the nature of the destruction was more devastating at Ai Khanoum than at Samarkand.

Ai Khanoum was attacked and its territory occupied by populations whose material culture may, as I have already discussed, be linked to that from kurgan cemeteries such as Ksirov, in the Qizil Su region of southern Tajikistan.[77] The simple pit burials at Ksirov were accompanied by hand-worked ceramic vessels that are comparable to examples found in fairly large numbers in the post-Greek levels of Ai Khanoum. The more complete nomadic mortuary package may also be found in eastern Bactria and even within the city walls of Ai Khanoum. In Bactria, however, the typical such assemblage comes to contain material from the settled Greek milieu. At Ai Khanoum itself, five later tombs were dug into the remains of small houses on the acropolis.[78] These tombs contain both the northern tripod vessels that I have already mentioned and Graeco-Bactrian ceramic types. Among the other grave goods were weapons, another characteristic feature of some steppe kurgan burials. Other, later burials at Ai Khanoum include some modest tombs dug into the remains of the gymnasium.

76. Rapin 1992, 249.
77. Lyonnet 1998, 154–55.
78. Bernard et al. 1980, 71–72.

In chapter 1, I situated Ai Khanoum within its Bactrian and Near Eastern context. In the material discussed here, I have endeavored to do something similar in locating the city within a wide swath of Central Asia where population mobility over shorter and longer distances and symbiosis between mobile and settled populations and economic strategies were very much the norm. There were, however, episodes of more dramatic disruption to the status quo, such as those that we may illustrate more clearly in the archaeological record from the Samarkand region. My discussion of the arrival of new material-culture assemblages from southern Tajikistan—and their users—in eastern Bactria, and the subsequent modification that such assemblages underwent with the incorporation of Graeco-Bactrian ceramics, has thus far avoided direct reference to the historical event of the fall of Ai Khanoum. Is our impression of this fall as a traumatic and cataclysmic event an accurate one? My conclusion is yes, but with qualifications.

The fall of Ai Khanoum, certainly, was not a single event. The archaeological remains of the city reveal in many places the impact of both sudden attacks and longer-term decline and reappropriation of the site during the period in which Bactria was bleeding to death. In my discussion of the defenses of Ai Khanoum in chapter 2, I noted a number of points relevant to the mid-second-century-B.C.E. assaults on the city and their probable perpetrators. The mud-brick fortification walls were vulnerable to erosion and collapse and required constant maintenance, above and beyond what may have been necessitated by military attack. In several places where there is evidence of assault, the techniques used are not those that we may associate with steppe-nomad mounted archers: sapping and the use of heavy stone projectiles.[79] Establishing the chronology of attacks on the city's fortifications is difficult, but what is clear is that the final, decisive assault that ended the life of the Greek city around 145 B.C.E. was neither final nor decisive.[80] It was the first of two waves of attack.[81] A period of reoccupation followed, which ended with a devastating fire. The precise duration of the post-Greek occupation is not clear, but it was in the region of years rather than decades.[82]

In concluding, I would like to offer two further points about the fall of Ai Khanoum. One relates to the nature of the post-Greek occupation; the other, to the role that Graeco-Bactrian dynastic struggles may have played in the destruction of the city. Following on from the latter point, I shall round off my discussion of the second-century-B.C.E. political upheavals in Bactria by looking at the continuing

79. I shall consider the possible connections of this to Bactria's dynastic troubles below.

80. Holt 2012 reviews recent debates on the date of the fall of Ai Khanoum and concludes that the traditionally proposed date of the mid-second century B.C.E. withstands scrutiny.

81. Discussed by Rapin 2007, 50; and with specific reference to the pillaging of the treasury, Rapin 1992, 281–94.

82. Lyonnet 1997, 166.

influence of Graeco-Bactrian culture and forms of political authority into the first century B.C.E. and beyond.

Although the active life of the city in its existing form came to an end—and, it seems, a rather sudden end—around 145 B.C.E., it is still less than clear what happened in demographic rather than purely military terms at the fall of Ai Khanoum or what displacement of population may have taken place.[83] It is sometimes presented as the defeat and even subsequent exile of a Greek colonial population and the reoccupation of the city by local squatters.[84] But this supposes that there was a clear divide between a Greek colonial urban population and an indigenous Bactrian agricultural population in the countryside. Why should it not be the case that the city was reoccupied by some of the survivors—both city dwellers and country folk—of whatever event brought it to an end? The later reoccupation and reuse of the site certainly represents something more complex than simple squatting, and the architectural remains of this period merit further study.

The northern walls of Ai Khanoum with their towers and ditch were equipped to withstand siege warfare, and indeed excavations revealed attacks both by archers and by heavy artillery and sappers.[85] As well as external enemies—whether steppe nomads, or Seleucid or Parthian armies—we must consider the possibility that Ai Khanoum was attacked by the forces of rival Graeco-Bactrian kings.[86] The Indian invasions of the early second century B.C.E., as I have suggested, offered opportunities for social mobility: junior royals and victorious generals could make their own plays for political power. Euthydemos, as he reminded Antiochos at Bactra, had overthrown the Diodotids, the dynasty under whom Bactria had seceded from Seleucid control in the mid-third century B.C.E. Subsequently Eukratides rose to power at the expense of the family of Euthydemos and Demetrios, and he in turn was assassinated by his own son.

This brings us back to Justin and his account of Bactria's bloody demise. As a culmination to Eukratides' various troubles—war with Parthia, with Sogdians, Arachosians, Drancae, Arei, and Indians, and with a Demetrios "king of the Indians" who may be Demetrios son of Euthydemos or another king of the same name—he is finally killed by his own son and co-regent, who mutilates and discards his body unburied.[87] Justin does not name the son. One candidate is Heliok-

---

83. Fussman 1996, 247–48.

84. A term used in the French reports.

85. Lerner 2003–4, 397–99, argues in his reappraisal of the chronology of Ai Khanoum that some of these may be attributed to Antiochos III on his Eastern anabasis.

86. Leriche 1986, 82–84.

87. This notorious episode is mentioned by Boccaccio in his work *On the Downfalls of Famous Men,* making Eukratides one of the very few Graeco-Bactrian or Indo-Greek kings to be mentioned in a more popular medieval or modern European historical source (6.6: "Eucratides Bactrianorum Rex se a Demetrio Indorum rege obsessum et a filio demum occisum, ferisque lacerandum relictum

les I, the last Greek-named king known from his coins to have ruled in Bactria (fl. ca. 145–130 B.C.E.).[88] Eukratides' father—depicted on some of his coins—was also named Heliokles, making a family connection plausible.

Little or nothing else is known about King Heliokles; nor do we know how many Greek kinglets reigned in Bactria at around the same period or for how long. Heliokles' reign corresponds to the period after the first attack on Ai Khanoum but before its complete abandonment at the end of the brief period of reoccupation. None of his coins, however, was found at Ai Khanoum or in its environs, nor have any been found in southern Tajikistan;[89] there are a greater number from the Sur-khan-darya and other major northern tributaries of the Oxus. This pattern does not necessarily indicate directly the territories controlled by Heliokles: he is only known to have struck silver coinage, and bronzes are most common as stray finds.[90] The largest number of coins of Heliokles comes from the so-called Qun-duz hoard, actually found at Khisht Tepe, on the south bank of the Oxus between Ai Khanoum and Termez, and these themselves constitute by far the largest number of issues of any one king in the hoard.[91] Heliokles' coin type is, however, most frequently encountered somewhere else entirely: barbarized imitations of his coins were made and used after the fall of the Graeco-Bactrian kingdom by the incoming nomadic populations.[92]

In the copying of the "barbaric Heliokles" types, much is clearly misunder-stood.[93] The figure of Zeus is reworked, his thunderbolt reduced to a line. The Greek lettering of the legend is copied as image rather than script and becomes irregular. Just as the new groups that arrived in eastern Bactria in the course of the second and first centuries B.C.E. incorporated local Graeco-Bactrian ceramics into their funerary assemblages, however, the very production of these coins indicates some continuity in techniques of craft production, economic systems, and even administration. This must have facilitated the economic prosperity of post-Greek Bactria noted in the Chinese sources.

There are other areas in which we can explore socioeconomic, political, and administrative continuity from the days of the Graeco-Bactrian kingdom through the population movements and political changes of the second century into the period of the growth of the Kushan empire in the first century C.E. I do not intend

---

querebatur": ("Eukratides king of the Bactrians was himself besieged by Demetrios king of the Indians, and finally killed by his son and left to be torn apart by beasts"). See Bivar 1950.

88. Bopearachchi 1991, 222–25; MacDowall 2003–4.

89. Lyonnet 1997, 167.

90. MacDowall 2003–4, 37–38.

91. Curiel and Fussman 1965: 204 out of 627 coins.

92. Lyonnet 1997, 168.

93. MacDowall 2003–4, 32–33. See further Holt 1999a on "the fate of Greek culture on Bactrian coins."

FIGURE 9. Imitation coin of Heliokles. (© Trustees of the British Museum.)

to stray much further into the history and archaeology of the Kushan empire itself.[94] There are many archaeological sites, especially in the Surkhan-darya region, where we can see a long period of transition and cultural change from the Graeco-Bactrian period through into the Kushan but not any definitive break in occupation or serious disruption. An excellent example is Dalverzin-tepe, a small Graeco-Bactrian fortified site that in the first century B.C.E. develops into a larger town, then a fortified city under the Kushans.[95] Dalverzin-tepe's growing prominence is apparently as the capital of a new regional political player (the Yuezhi inevitably make an appearance in the scholarly literature). At Takht-i Sangin, recent excavations also suggest continuity in occupation throughout the second-century-B.C.E. period of struggles in Bactria.[96]

In many respects, the Kushans were the cultural and political heirs of their Graeco-Bactrian predecessors. Under the Kushan empire, Greek script was adapted to write the Bactrian language. A Bactrian inscription with the Greek signature "Through Palamedes" suggests the retention of a scribal class literate in Greek for at least a period of years.[97] In second-century-B.C.E. Greek writing on molds from a bronze-casting workshop at Takht-i Sangin, it has recently been suggested, we can already see the development of the local Bactrian Greek script in the direction of what would become the standard Kushan forms.[98] Kushan coins

94. On which see Staviskij 1986.

95. Pugachenkova 1978, Pugachenkova and Rtveladze 1978, Bernard 1980b, Abdullaev 2001, Tourgounov 2001.

96. Drujinina and Lindström 2013.

97. Fraser 1982.

98. Ivantchik 2011.

retain Greek iconography, and it is only in the first part of the second century C.E., under Kanishka the Great, that a new policy is introduced of replacing Greek names with the Iranian equivalents they had most probably represented all along (e.g., Helios-Mithra).[99] The population movements of the mid-second century B.C.E., and the political and cultural developments that came in their wake, profoundly altered the composition of the Graeco-Bactrian cultural *koinē*, but there was a degree of continuity as well as change.

The picture that I have sketched in this chapter is one of long-term political and cultural change within a dynamic zone of nomad-settled interaction in Central Asia. There were times and places where stable relations within this symbiosis were broken down or deliberately altered by the actions or policies of the settled states of Bactria and China, and by mobility of groups both from outside the mixed zone and from within it. In the mid-second century B.C.E., a long-distance domino effect of nomadic population movement from the borders of China southward and eastward into Central Asia contributed toward the collapse of the Greek state in the Oxus Basin.

The archaeological and the textual data sets on this period of change tell us slightly different things, both of great historical and cultural significance: the general trend of population movements and military expansions as revealed by changes in material culture and in the construction and destruction of defenses, and how these impacted on and were perceived by surrounding regions. The Chinese and Graeco-Roman historical sources, as it happens, give us rather more nuanced data on nomad lifestyles and nomad-settled interaction in Central Asia than may be assumed. Some historians both ancient and modern (Strabo is the worst offender) fall back on the cliché of the settled Greek civilization of Bactria overrun by nomadic hordes, but others, including Justin and Sima Qian, recognize the true complexity of the situation. Although incursions from Central Asia had a devastating impact on Bactria, the historical and archaeological evidence reveals that there was no single, sudden, decisive nomad invasion. Under the impact of a long series of such incursions, crippling wars with Parthia, and interdynastic fighting in Bactria and India, it still took Bactria some time to slowly bleed to death.

99. For epigraphic evidence of Kanishka's de-Hellenization policy, see Sims-Williams and Cribb 1996.

Conclusion

He took a Greek name, dressed like the Greeks,
learned, more or less, to behave like the Greeks;
and in his heart he dreaded that by some chance
he'd lose the goodish impression that he'd made
by speaking a terribly barbaric Greek
and that the Alexandrians would poke fun at him,
as is their wont, horrid people.

—C. P. CAVAFY, "POTENTATE FROM WESTERN LIBYA" (1928), TRANS.
MENDELSOHN 2012, 150

THE HELLENISTIC FAR EAST AND
THE HELLENISTIC WORLD

The Hellenistic Far East, as I argued in the introduction, demands to be considered as part of a wider Hellenistic world. I make no cultural assumptions here. By "Hellenistic" I do not mean Greek, and it is precisely the encounter of ethnic identities, languages, and cultures in the Hellenistic world that I think provides the best context for the material from the Hellenistic Far East. Politically, too, the Graeco-Bactrian and Indo-Greek kingdoms were very much part of the Hellenistic world. The periodic attempts of Seleucid monarchs to assert control over the region may have been rebuffed (chapter 4), but political ideologies and imagery were shared. The Indo-Greek king Agathokles (reigned ca. 190–180 B.C.E.) struck a series of pedigree coins, including one of Alexander the Great, making a play for legitimacy based on a connection to his illustrious Macedonian predecessor.[1] Various Graeco-Bactrian and Indo-Greek kings used royal epithets familiar from other Hellenistic dynasties, such as *dikaios,* "the Just," or *sōtēr,* "the Savior."[2] They also went in for both pre- and post-mortem deification. (See, for example, the regnal dating of Antimachos the God in the document discussed in chapter 1.) It is in

---

1. Holt 1984. On Alexander's image in Hellenistic politics, see Stewart 1993.
2. See Bopearachchi 1991 for numerous examples.

cultural and ethnic matters, however, that I think the Hellenistic context best serves studies of the Hellenistic Far East—and the Hellenistic Far East may, in turn, have things to offer Hellenistic studies.

The Greek question has dominated much of my discussion in the preceding chapters. I have sought to differentiate between the use of practices and material of ultimately Greek origin and the active assertion of a Greek identity. We may also make the point that people may feel and profess themselves to be Greek without this claim being recognized by others—as in the case of Cavafy's Libyan prince who goes about Alexandria in constant fear that his poor command of the Greek language, and thus his claim to a Greek identity, will be exposed. I have also suggested that Greek and non-Greek are not always the most important divisions in our evidence, especially in the analysis of material from a single site such as Ai Khanoum. For this, a wider perspective—geographically and historically—is necessary.

THE *LONGUE DURÉE*

My emphasis in chapters 1 and 4 was on the *longue durée* of Bactrian history, on the long process of development and evolution of society and administrative organization that accompanied apparently dramatic ruptures in Bactria's government. Thus, the incoming Greek regime did little, at least initially, to change an Achaemenid administration that had proved effective in managing the population and their affairs, and maximizing revenue from the land. Continuity in administration and management of resources can be a deliberate strategy as well as the result of a laissez-faire approach. The Achaemenid blueprint underlying the administration and economy of other Hellenistic kingdoms, at least in the early years of the new order, has increasingly been recognized in scholarship, as I discussed in chapter 1.

After the end of the period of Graeco-Bactrian rule, there also appears to have been some administrative continuity. The Greek language continued to be used as the main written medium until it was replaced by a deliberate policy of the Kushan king Kanishka the Great in the first half of the second century c.e.[3] Bactrian, however, was itself written in a modified form of the Greek script. In other regions, in the short term at least, an existing Greek administration and administrative titles were preserved. This is true for the Swat Valley, in Gandhāra, where we find the Greek titles *stratēgos* and *meridarchos* in some texts of the late centuries B.C.E. and early centuries C.E.[4]

---

3. This is attested by the Rabatak inscription (Fussman 2001), as well as numismatic evidence (Joe Cribb 2007).

4. A Buddhist reliquary of the first half of the first century B.C.E. contains the name Theodoros and the administrative title *meridarchos* (Konow 1929,1–4), a title that recurs in the Senavarma inscription, of the first half of the first century C.E. (Salomon 1986). *Stratēgos*, too, appears as an official title

Another area in which it makes sense to think of political and cultural evolution in the long term is in the relationship between settled and mobile populations. The Aramaic administrative documents from Achaemenid Bactria make some reference to the pastoral economy. As the evidence from field survey indicates, this continued to be important through the Hellenistic period. The best evidence comes from the valleys to the north of the Oxus, but the same is likely to have been true in eastern Bactria, around Ai Khanoum. This is one context in which we should view the contractions and expansions of Graeco-Bactrian power in Central Asia at the expense or to the advantage of nomadic populations. As well as indicating short-term conflicts with particular nomad groups and the periodic loss of territory beyond the Iron Gates at Derbent, in Samarkand, and in the Zeravshan Valley, what the evidence shows is a gradual process by which mobile populations moved south into Bactria, living for much of the Graeco-Bactrian period in symbiosis with settled populations, not in conflict with them.

AI KHANOUM

The city of Ai Khanoum has been a dominant presence throughout the preceding chapters. In the introduction, I discussed how the discovery of this city came about in the context of the history of European exploration and archaeological investigation in Central Asia. This discovery was reported in the popular press, including the *Kabul Times,* as well as in scholarly journals, but for a long time analysis of the remains appears to have stalled, with the ideas of a Greek city in Central Asia and an anomalous and bizarre mixture of different architectural traditions both persisting. In chapter 1 I tried to restore to Ai Khanoum something of its historical and geographical context. The city was located in a region heavily exploited in antiquity for its natural resources and agricultural potential, and was situated so as to control these. The administration of Ai Khanoum, which included individuals with Greek and Bactrian names, was the successor of an earlier Achaemenid administration, and we have evidence from the early years of Alexander's control of the region, at least, of some continuity in personnel and administrative practices. The remains of the city itself were discussed in chapter 2, and I argued that it must be considered more than the sum of its diverse parts. The urban landscape of the city made sense to those who lived and worked there, and the onus is on us to analyze its constituent parts together rather than separately. Finally, I proposed that there existed a Hellenistic-Bactrian architectural and cultural *koinē,* a set of practices and forms that must have been familiar to the population of the region, whatever their ethnic origin. (I will return to this idea below.) Chapter 4's discus-

on two objects, a silver saucer from Taxila and a reliquary: both postdate the Indo-Greeks and refer to officials who do not bear Greek names (Marshall 1951, 613, 777; Fussman 1980, 4, 25, 28).

sion of the fall of the Greek kingdom of Bactria also considered the fall of Ai Khanoum, and the evidence for the city's destruction and subsequent limited reoccupation.

In a Hellenistic context, there are several interesting parallels for the encounter
of different ethnic groups and cultural traditions at Ai Khanoum, and one that I
wish to pursue further is that of Babylon.[5] Unlike Ai Khanoum, Babylon had a
long pre-Hellenistic history, and it was not a major center of Greek settlement: this
was nearby at the new foundation of Seleucia-on-Tigris. There were, however,
some Greeks, and some form of Greek political organization,[6] alongside the persistence of separate native Babylonian structures and institutions, such as temple
complexes. There was also, as at Ai Khanoum, a Greek theater (an unfamiliar concept that was translated in Babylonian texts as *bīt tāmarti,* "house of observation").[7]
Greek literary and intellectual culture, too, were present at Babylon. The city had a
philosophical school, said to have been established by Archedemos of Tarsus.[8] It
was the home of the poet and grammarian Herodikos of Babylon, who lived at
Alexandria in Egypt for a period in the second century B.C.E., and who in an epi-
gram quoted by Athenaeus claims his attachment to both Greece and Babylon.[9]
Yet no Greek temple has yet been found at Babylon. Is this simply because it
remains to be excavated, or did Greeks also worship at the Babylonian temple of
Bel, perhaps interpreting him as a Greek god?[10] If they did so, they failed to leave
any recognizable evidence of Greek devotional practices. My point is not that Babylon presents a direct analogy for Ai Khanoum—the composition of their populations, one an ancient city and the other a Greek colony, was very different—but it
does show that there was room for Greek cultural foundations such as a theater in
an otherwise indigenous urban landscape, and that Greeks might incorporate
some unexpectedly local institutions into their everyday lives.

Ai Khanoum has, sadly, been heavily plundered during recent wars in Afghanistan.[11] Some material from the city appears to have emerged onto the antiquities
market, such as two golden bracelets with a Greek craftsman's signature and weight
marks.[12] A good portion of the site also remains to be fully published, such as the
public buildings to the south and east of the palace—although a new volume on
the domestic architecture has very recently appeared, too late to be taken into

5. See the important study by Boiy 2004, who considered the transition from Achaemenid to
Seleucid rule; on the installation of Seleucid rule in Babylonia as a whole, see Sherwin-White 1987.

6. Van der Spek 2009, 107–10.

7. Van der Spek 2001.

8. Plutarch, *De Exilio* 14.

9. Athenaeus, *Deipnosophistai* 5.222a.

10. Van der Spek 2009, 110–11.

11. Bernard 2001.

12. Bopearachchi and Bernard 2002.

account in this book.[13] In recent years, however, audiences in Europe and North America have been able for the first time to see material from the site in the international exhibition *Afghanistan: Les Trésors Retrouvés / Afghanistan: Hidden Treasures*, which contained many items from the National Museum of Afghanistan in Kabul that has survived three preceding decades of war and instability.[14] It is to be hoped that future research will do more to contextualize the finds from Ai Khanoum, both within their local Bactrian context and within Central Asia, and indeed the Hellenistic world as a whole.

ETHNIC IDENTITIES

As I noted in chapter 3, Heliodoros, the Greek ambassador from Taxila, is the only individual from the Hellenistic Far East for whom we have an explicit ethnic descriptor. This appears to contrast with the evidence from contemporary Egypt, where individuals were frequently classified as belonging to one ethnic group or another in both bureaucratic convention and in everyday social discourse. In Ptolemaic census documents, for example, we find listings of individuals and families as Greek, Arab, Jew, and the like.[15] There is also some evidence for ethnic discrimination and violence.[16]

Part of the reason why we do not have evidence of similar practices and forms of behavior in the Hellenistic Far East is that we do not have the same wealth of documentary texts as is available from Egypt. Should more finds be made in the future, this picture may well change. Even in the data available at present, we find some indication of the presence and differentiation of ethnic groups—in the section "The Siege of Bactra in 206 B.C.E. and the Nomad Threat," in chapter 4, I discussed a Greek documentary text that makes reference to Scythians. That the officials of the Ai Khanoum treasury are not given ethnic descriptors may simply be due to the facts that these are brief texts documenting financial transactions and that ethnicity was not salient in this context. We have little idea of how individuals of mixed descent and culture may have been classified in the Hellenistic Far East—or of whether the administration or society took an interest in such classifications—because we know so little about the family background (barring the occasional patronymic) of any of the individuals mentioned in our sources.

13. Lecuyot 2013.
14. Cambon and Jarrige 2006, Hiebert and Cambon 2008.
15. The Ptolemaic census documents are published by Clarysse and Thompson 2006.
16. In *PEnteux.* 79 (218 B.C.E.), a Greek named Herakleides complains that he has been assaulted by an Egyptian woman and that this assault is the more heinous because he is a Greek. Ptolemaios, a religious recluse, claims that he has been attacked specifically because he is a Greek. (See, e.g., UPZ 1, 7–8 and 15, from the 160s–150s B.C.E.)

Another way in which the material from the Hellenistic Far East differs from that from elsewhere in the Hellenistic world is in naming practices—or at least in the evidence that we have for naming practices. In places such as Egypt and Babylonia, we find double names in use, where an individual may be described using a Greek or an indigenous name according to context (or the language of the document) or may use both names together. This phenomenon has been much discussed for Egypt, where it was reasonably common, but it also occurred in other regions. In Babylonia, we find some Akkadian-Greek double naming.[17] The reasons why individuals might use double names are complex. The adoption of some of the trappings of Greek identity—and especially the Greek language—might allow a person to advance further in public life. Greek names might be granted as well as adopted: Anu-uballit, governor of Uruk, had the Greek name Nikarchos bestowed upon him by the first Seleucid emperor, Seleukos I.[18] As well as being adopted or bestowed, double names may reflect mixed descent and exposure to the language and customs of more than one ethnic community from birth. The children of interethnic marriages could and did move between communities and cultural spheres, whatever their official ethnicity. Double names may also reflect a very real attachment on the part of some individuals to both sides of their cultural identity.

In the Hellenistic Far East, in contrast, we find only single names. As I have already noted, this is at least in part a product of the kinds of evidence available to us. The concise, functional Ai Khanoum treasury texts have little room for subsidiary information on the transactions conducted, never mind any alternative names used by officials. We may suggest, however, that the adoption of a Greek name (with or without the Greek language or cultural practices) was not so common among the indigenous inhabitants of the Hellenistic Far East as it was in Hellenistic Egypt. The Ai Khanoum treasury is just the kind of context in which a Greek name may have been appropriate. Most telling, however, is the failure of Sōphytos the son of Naratos to use a Greek name. Given his otherwise careful cultivation of an educated Greek cultural identity, this suggests strongly to me that he did not have one. Although the appearance of a non-Greek name in such an overtly Greek inscription may strike us as jarring, however, it is by no means certain that this is the impression that it would have had on a contemporary observer. Acceptance could have been aided by a judicious choice of names. I have argued elsewhere that specific Greek names may have been adopted because of their local resonance. Heliodoros or Heliodotos, for example, could have been chosen because they were equivalents of the Iranian Mithradates.[19] Sōphytos, as I have

17. Boiy 2005a, Sherwin-White 1983.
18. On his family, see Boiy 2005b.
19. Mairs forthcoming (1).

already noted, although not a Greek name, was one that had been borne by an earlier dynast in the region.

In the introduction, I introduced some key theoretical approaches to thinking about ethnic identity. An ethnic identity is a constructed identity, predicated upon the selective mobilization of aspects of cultural behavior and material culture in the construction of a group identity, in which the delineation of a boundary between one's own group and others is an essential part of the process. What is important in the construction of an ethnic group and the maintenance of its boundaries is not that a group have any objective common culture but that groups take aspects of their cultural toolkit and invest these with ethnic significance. It is therefore impossible to identify an ethnic group in this sense solely in terms of observable behavior such as language use or material culture such as dress, ceramic forms, or architecture. It is also difficult in the archaeological record to identify what forms of material culture are being used ethnically and which are not.

In my discussion of Ai Khanoum in particular, I have aimed to identify some aspects of material culture and social practice that were ethnically salient in the Hellenistic Far East. Equally important, I believe that it is possible to identify other forms and practices that were not felt to compromise an individual's projected ethnic identity, whether as Greek or otherwise. At Ai Khanoum, temple architecture is perhaps the best example of an area in which ethnic resonance might be neutralized. There was no Greek-style temple in the city; therefore the non-Greek Temple with Indented Niches and the extramural temple were used by a broad constituency of the city's inhabitants, whether these considered themselves Greek or not. Areas in which we can see an overt assertion and celebration of Greekness are, in contrast, the sanctuary of Kineas with its Delphic inscription, the theater, and the gymnasium. It is significant that the first two of these were the findspots of some of the only Greek inscriptions from the city. Likewise, in death it seems that the inhabitants of Ai Khanoum were more inclined to resort to the Greek language, Greek motifs, and Greek tropes, with Greek funerary inscriptions and sculpture.[20]

The inscriptions of Sōphytos and Heliodoros offer further insights into forms of behavior that were and were not felt to compromise a Greek identity. As I have already noted, Sōphytos's non-Greek name does not from his perspective reduce the impact of his Greek education and cultural values. But then we do not know whether or not Sōphytos considered himself Greek or was considered such by others. Heliodoros is another matter. Here we find a clear indication that an individual who was considered Greek (by outsiders to his own community) could nevertheless be presented in Prākrit as the devotee of an Indian god. A great deal of further evidence would be necessary to explore the question of the material and

20. Mairs 2007; see also the newly published Greek funerary inscriptions from Ai Khanoum in Rougemont 2012, nos. 136, 137.

social bases of ethnic belonging in the Hellenistic Far East with any thoroughness, but with the evidence that we do have a certain amount can already be done.

CULTURE AND EDUCATION

Whichever cultural traits and models were invested with ethnic significance in the Hellenistic Far East, individuals must have acquired these somehow: in childhood from their families, through education or through acquisition later in life. Examples from elsewhere in the Hellenistic world show us some of the mechanisms by which people and communities acquired the building blocks of their identities or incorporated new practices into an old identity that they considered to remain unchallenged.

The Homeric flourishes given by Sōphytos to his verse inscription indicate that he had received the same kind of Greek education as students elsewhere in the Hellenistic world. Homer was by far the most commonly read and taught author at all levels of Greek education in Egypt, as can be seen from surviving papyri.[21] The philosophical and dramatic texts from Ai Khanoum, as well as the sundials in the gymnasium and the theater, also show that some of the city's inhabitants were both practitioners and consumers of Greek culture. So education and participation in cultural activities was one way in which a Greek identity might be inculcated or maintained—although Plutarch's assertion that "when Alexander was civilizing Asia, Homer was commonly read, and the children of the Persians, of the Susianians, and of the Gedrosians learned to sing the tragedies of Sophocles and Euripides"[22] is probably something of an overstatement.

Did a Greek education or attendance at the theater or gymnasium make a person Greek, by their, or their community's, own definition? In the preceding discussion, I have indicated that this was not necessarily so. But it is also important to emphasize the agency of individuals and communities in adopting the trappings of Greek culture, the reasons that they may have had for doing so, and the ways in which this might be perceived both by outsiders and by their own neighbors. The second book of Maccabees recounts how in 175 B.C.E. Jason, the Jewish high priest, established a gymnasium and ephebate and enrolled the inhabitants of Jerusalem as citizens of a new Antioch.[23] He encouraged his fellow Jews to adopt a Greek way of life in other areas, such as dress and participation in athletics, and to neglect sacrifices. All this brought Jason criticism and resentment—although it was another Hellenized Jew, Menelaos, who eventually deposed him as high priest. He died in exile in Greece. The example of Jason, the holder of a high office, shows that Greek culture could be adopted by individuals who in other respects adhered

---

21. Cribiore 1996, 46–49, and 2001.

22. *On the Fortune or Virtue of Alexander the Great* 1.328D.

23. II Maccabees 4, 10–17.

to their own ancestral traditions and that this might provoke a serious backlash. It also shows that Hellenization does not have to be thought of as top-down, something encouraged or imposed by Greek political authorities, but that people might for their own ends adopt Greek cultural practices, whether or not they considered that doing this actually went so far as to make them Greek.

THE POSTCOLONIAL HELLENISTIC FAR EAST

In the introduction I briefly noted some theoretical concepts from postcolonial studies that have been influential in the analysis of material from the Hellenistic world. A major problem with (perceived) earlier scholarly debates between Greek and Indian influence on the culture of the Hellenistic Far East is that they treat cultures as reified, bounded units, corporate entities that act in unison and may be isolated in our analysis. In response to similar problems, the postcolonial theoretical vocabulary for the spaces of interaction and negotiation between traditionally defined cultures has been enthusiastically taken up by archaeologists and historians of the Hellenistic world. The Hellenistic Far East is as good a testing ground as any for exploring how such theoretical concepts may—or may not—help us toward a better understanding of the ethnic and cultural dynamics of the region.[24]

Perhaps the most important—or at any rate most popular—of these concepts is that of hybridity, a biological metaphor adapted in, for example, the work of Homi Bhabha to describe the coming together and intermingling of cultures and the discourse and power dynamics that arise from this.[25] Hybridity and hybridization, however, have been adapted by classicists and archaeologists from postcolonial studies, not taken directly from the work of Bhabha and other scholars. There are ways in which hybridity in its postcolonial sense may not transfer well to historical contexts before modern European colonial enterprises. In particular, there is a potential clash between postcolonial hybridity's active, self-conscious negotiation between cultures (and the formation of new identities) and the efforts that we may observe in some populations of the Hellenistic Far East to defend monolithic old identities. Hybridity may therefore present a useful trope in analyzing the material culture of the Hellenistic Far East, but it may well have been a concept that was entirely alien to the cultural outlook of the people who created and used this material culture. The choice to call something hybrid is ours.[26]

24. Robert Young 2001 provides an accessible and comprehensive introduction to the postcolonial world and how it has shaped and been shaped by various political and cultural theories. On the application of some postcolonial theoretical tropes to the Hellenistic Far East, see Mairs 2011c.

25. Bhabha 1994. *The Location of Culture* has been criticized for its writing style and lack of accessibility (see, for example, Leo 1999), meaning that it is far more frequently cited than it is quoted.

26. Colonial Latin America: Dean and Leibsohn 2003. Hellenistic Far East: Mairs 2010c.

Other postcolonial memes, although they can generate productive approaches to our evidence, also require to be situated historically. Richard White's "middle ground," for example, originated as a literal description of a geographical territory in which Native Americans and European settlers interacted and by metaphorical extension the creative cultural dialogue instigated in this liminal space.[27] The middle ground's further metaphorical extension to refer to zones of cultural interaction in general was not something intended in White's original thesis, but this fact does not discredit the uses to which it has been put in other historical contexts.[28] The point, once again, is that theoretical evolution and reinterpretation does not invalidate a concept where it is found to be useful or evocative in ways beyond its original formulation. Tracing this evolution, however, may be extremely useful in allowing us to identify which aspects of the theory in question are historically contingent.

The archaeology of the Hellenistic Far East has thus far attracted only very limited analysis in the kinds of postcolonial theoretical veins outlined above. Instigating such analysis ought to be an important part of bringing the region into closer dialogue with scholarship on other regions of the Hellenistic world, and, indeed, neighboring regions of South and East Asia.[29]

What can the evidence considered in the preceding chapters bring to such debates? First, as I have already noted, we should be cautious in how we lift theoretical terminology from postcolonial studies, and indeed cultural studies more generally. Hybridity in many cases means something closer to the biological metaphor—of the mixing of two cultures to create a new one—in classical studies than it does to postcolonial hybridity, which focuses in addition on the discourse that arises from cultural contact and the further political implications of this discourse. The Hellenistic Far East, despite the architectural mélange that is Ai Khanoum and the mixed signals given out by the inscriptions of Heliodoros and Sōphytos, is not hybrid in the latter sense. A self-reflexive and open dialogue about cultural hybridity is not something I argue was happening in the Hellenistic Far East. Although, as discussed above, Heliodoros is the only individual in our evidence who is given an ethnic descriptor, there is evidence, too, from Ai Khanoum that a Greek identity was adhered to by many. We may find it useful on an abstract level to treat Ai Khanoum as hybrid, and the process of the intermixing of Greek, Persian, and Central Asian traditions that created its urban form as hybridization, but its inhabitants are unlikely to have described it as such—not least because, after the first generation, their points of comparison were few. As I outlined above in my discus-

27. White 1991

28. Deloria 2006.

29. The essays in Canepa 2010b provide a useful demonstration of the various uses to which theories of cultural interaction may be put in a Eurasian context.

sion of ethnicity, there is a potential disjuncture between the ethnic signals that we read from material culture, architecture, and even written documents, and those that may have been perceived or deliberately intended to be sent out as signals by the actors.

Does postcolonial theory and vocabulary have anything more positive to offer to the analysis of material from the Hellenistic Far East? Discussion of the "middle ground" emphasizes the process of creative misunderstanding: "A middle ground is the creation, in part through creative misunderstanding, of a set of practices, rituals, offices, and beliefs that although comprised of elements of the group in contact is as a whole separate from the practices and beliefs of all those groups."[30] This, I suggest, is one of the processes at work in the creation of the hybrid culture of the Hellenistic Far East: the creation of what in chapter 2 I called the Hellenistic-Bactrian cultural *koinē*. A structure such as the Temple with Indented Niches at Ai Khanoum could be understood in many ways by the people who used it and called by different names. But perhaps most important, as I argued in chapter 2, the shared practices and material environment, of diverse origins, that bound Hellen-istic Bactria together as such were important in allowing an accommodation and dialogue to come about between diverse ethnic and cultural constituencies. In this sense, I argue that closer attention to the original theoretical formulation of the middle ground, not interpretation in a generic sense, brings the most productive approach to evidence from the Hellenistic Far East.

FUTURE DIRECTIONS

Most of the buildings, artifacts, and texts discussed in this volume have come to light only within the last half-century, many only within the last decade. It is per-haps naive, or even unethical—given the provenance of many important pieces on the antiquities market—to hope that more material will soon come to light. With-out a site such as Ai Khanoum, we would know little about the material culture of the Graeco-Bactrian kingdom and would still be reliant on the numismatic record and on the few mentions of the kingdom in Greek, Roman, and Chinese historical accounts. Yet I hope to have demonstrated in the preceding chapters that much useful information can still be derived from the traditional sources, even on such apparently unlikely topics as interaction between mobile and settled populations.

Beyond the Bactrian cultural *koinē*, the material from the Hellenistic Far East has a wider relevance. Throughout this book, I have quoted from the work of the modern Alexandrian Greek poet Constantine P. Cavafy. For those with a taste for comparisons between the ancient and the modern world—as Cavafy had—the

---

30. White 1991, xiii. On the middle ground in classical archaeology see, for example, Antonaccio 2007, 201–2.

Hellenistic Far East is a potentially fascinating case study.[31] But it is in their Hellenistic context that the history and culture of the Graeco-Bactrian and Indo-Greek kingdoms has the greatest wider relevance. Instead of being an exotic aside to the history of the Hellenistic kingdoms, the Hellenistic Far East demands to be considered as Tarn imagined it in the 1930s: as an integral part of the Hellenistic *oikoumenē*. In this regard, the discussion of cultural interaction and ethnic identity in the Greek-ruled states of Central Asia and northwestern India has much to bring to wider debates on these issues in the Hellenistic world

31. The Hellenistic Far East is discussed alongside a variety of other, modern case studies of diaspora communities in Mairs 2013a.

APPENDIX

1. The Delphic inscription from the sanctuary of Kineas, Ai Khanoum (chapter 2):[1]

- - - ε[ὐλόγει πάντας]
φιλόσοφ[ος γίνου - - -]

Ἀνδρῶν τοι σοφὰ ταῦτα παλαιοτέρων ἀνάκει[τα]ι
ῥήματα ἀριγνώτων Πυθοῖ ἐν ἡγαθέαι·
ἔνθεν ταῦτ[α] Κλέαρχος ἐπιφραδέως ἀναγράψας
εἵσατο τηλαυγῆ Κινέου ἐν τεμένει.

Παίς ὢν κόσμιος γίνου,
ἡβῶν ἐγκρατής,
μέσος δίκαιος,
πρεσβύτης εὔβουλος,
τελευτῶν ἄλυπος.

. . . speak well of everyone; be a lover of wisdom. . . .
These wise sayings of men of old, the maxims of renowned men, are enshrined in
    the holy Pytho [i.e., at Delphi]. There Klearchos copied them conscientiously,
    and he set them up here in the sanctuary of Kineas, blazing them from afar.
As a child, be well behaved; as a young man, self-controlled; in middle age, be
    just; as an elder, be of good counsel; and when you come to the end, be
    without grief.

1. See above, chapter 2 note 55.

2. The Stele of Sōphytos, Old Kandahar (chapter 3, fig. 7):[2]

Σωφύτου στήλη

Δ	δηρόν ἐμῶγ κοκυῶν ἐριθηλέα ἐόντα
Ι	ἲς ἄμαχος Μοιρῶν ἐξόλεσεν τριάδος
Α	αὐτὰρ ἐγώ, τυννὸς κομιδῆι βιότοιό τε πατρῶν
Σ	Σώφυτος εὖνις ἐὼν οἰκτρὰ Ναρατιάδης,
Ω	ὡς ἀρετὴν Ἑκάτου Μουσέων τ᾽ ἤσχηκα σὺν ἐσθλῆι
Φ	φυρτὴν σωφροσύνηι, θῆμος ἐπεφρασάμην
Υ	ὑψώσαιμί κε πῶς μέγαρον πατρῴον αὖθις
Τ	τεκνοφόρον δὲ λαβὼν ἄλλοθεν ἀργύριον,
Ο	οἴκοθεν ἐξέμολον μεμαὼς οὐ πρόσθ᾽ ἐπανελθεῖν
Υ	ὕψιστον κτᾶσθαι πρὶμ μ᾽ ἀγαθῶν ἄφενος
Τ	τοὔνεκ᾽ ἐπ᾽ ἐμπορίηισιν ἰὼν εἰς ἄστεα πολλὰ
Ο	ὄλβον ἀλωβήτος εὐρὺν ἐληισάμην.
Υ	ὑμηντὸς δὲ πέλων πάτρην ἐτέεσιν ἐσῖγμαι
Ν	νηρίθμοις τερπνός τ᾽ εὐμενέταις ἐφάνην
Α	ἀμφοτέρους δ᾽ οἶκόν τε σεσηπότα πάτριον εἶθαρ
Ρ	ῥέξας ἐκ καινῆς κρέσσονα συντέλεσα
Α	αἰάν τ᾽ ἐς τύμβου πεπτωκότος ἄλλον ἔτευξα,
Τ	τὴν καὶ ζῶν στήλην ἐν ὁδῶι ἐπέθηκα λάλον.
Ο	οὕτως οὖν ζηλωτὰ τάδ᾽ ἔργματα συντελέσαντος
Υ	υἱέες υἱωνοί τ᾽ οἶκον ἔχοιεν ἐμοῦ.

STELE OF SŌPHYTOS

(Acrostic: Through Sōphytos the son of Naratos)

The irresistible force of the trio of Fates destroyed the house of my forefathers, which had flourished greatly for many years. But I, Sōphytos son of Naratos, pitiably bereft when quite small of my ancestral livelihood, after I had acquired the virtue of the Archer [i.e., Apollo] and the Muses, mixed with noble prudence, then did consider how I might raise up again my family house. Obtaining interest-bearing money from another source, I left home, keen not to return before I possessed wealth, the supreme good. Thus, by traveling to many cities for commerce, I acquired ample riches without reproach. Becoming celebrated, I returned to my homeland after countless years and showed myself, bringing pleasure to well-wishers. Straightaway I built afresh my paternal home, which was riddled with rot, making it better than before, and also, since the tomb had collapsed to the ground, I constructed another one and during my lifetime set upon it by the roadside this loquacious plaque. Thus may the sons and grandsons of myself, who completed this enviable work, possess my house.

2. See above, chapter 3 note 8.

3. The inscriptions of Paccius Maximus, Kalabsha, Lower Nubia (chapter 3):[3]

Μ	μακάριον ὅτ' ἔβην ἠρεμίης τόπον ἐσαθρῆσαι,	
Α	ἀέρι τὸ ποθεινὸν ψυχῆς πνεῦμ' ἐπανεῖναι,	
Ξ	ξένα μοι βιοτῇ περὶ φρένα πάντοθεν ἐδονεῖτο,	
Ι	ἵστορα κακίης ἐμαυτὸν οὐκ ἔχων ἔλεγχον,	
Μ	μύστην τότε κίκλησκε φύσις πόνον γεωργεῖν·	5
Ο	ὁ σοφὸς τότ' ἐγὼ ποικίλον ἥρμοζον ἀοιδήν,	
Σ	σεμνὸν ἀπὸ θεῶν κωτίλον ἐπιτυχὼν νόημα.	
Δ	δῆλον ὅτι θεοῖς ἀρεστὸν ἠργάζετο Μοῦσα,	
Ε	Ἑλίκωνι χλοῆς ἄνθεμον ἀπετίναξα κῶμον·	
Κ	καὶ τότε μέ τις ὕπνου μυχὸς ἠρέθισε φέρεσθαι,	10
Ο	ὀλίγον ἐπίφοβον φαντασίης ὄναρ τραπῆναι·	
Υ	ὕπνος δέ με λέ<ξας ταχὺν ἀπεκόμισε φί[λην γ]ῆν·	
Ρ	ῥείθροις ἐδόκουν γὰρ ποταμοῦ σῶμα ἀπο[λο]ύειν,	
Ι	ἱκανοῖς ἀπὸ Νίλου γλυκεροῦ ὕδασι προσ[η]νῶς·	
Ω	ᾠόμην δὲ σεμνὴν Μουσῶν Καλλιέπειαν	15
Ν	νυ[μ]φαῖς ἅμα πάσαις μέσ<σην κῶμον ἀείδειν·	
Ε	Ἑλλάδος τι κἀγὼ βραχὺ λείψανον νομίζων,	
Γ	γραπτὸν ἀπὸ σοφῆς ἔπνευσα ψυχῆς μου νόημα·	
Ρ	ῥάβδῳ δέ τις οἷα κατὰ μέλος δέμας δονηθείς,	
Α	ἁρμογὴν μέλει συνεργὸν ἐπεκάλουν χαράττειν,	20
Ψ	ψόγον ἀλλοτρίοις ἤθεσιν ἀπολιπὼν ἄδηλον.	
Α	ἀρχὴ δέ μ' ἔκληζεν τὸ σοφὸν πόημα λέξαι·	
	λαμπρὸς τότε Μάνδουλις ἔβη μέγας ἀπ' Ὀλύμπου,	
	θέλγων βαρβαρικὴν λέξιν ἀπ' Αἰθιόπων,	
	καὶ γλυκερὴν ἔσπευσεν ἐφ' Ἑλλάδα μοῦσαν ἀεῖσαι,	25
	λαμπρὰ παρεῖα φέρων καὶ δεξιὸς Ἴσιδι βαίνων,	
	Ῥωμαίων μεγέθει δόξαν ἀγαλλόμενος,	
	μαντικὰ πυθίων ἅτε δὴ θεὸς Οὐλύμποιο·	
	ὡς βίος ἀνθρώποις προορώμενος ἐξέθεν αὐχεῖ,	
	ὡς ἦμαρ καὶ νύξ σε σέβει, ὧραι δ' ἅμα πᾶσαι,	30
	καὶ καλέουσί σε Βρειθ καὶ Μάνδουλιν συνομαίμους,	
	ἄστρα θεῶν ἐπίσημα κατ' οὐρανὸν ἀντέλλοντα.	
	καὶ τάδε σοι στείχοντα χαράσσειν μ' αὐτὸς ἔλεξας	
	καὶ σοφὰ γράμματα πᾶσιν ἀθωπεύτως ἐσορᾶσθαι.	
	- - -	35
	[εἴκοσι] καὶ δυσὶ τοῖς πρώτοις γράμμασι πειθόμενος.	

(Acrostic: [I,] Maximus, a decurion, wrote [it])
When I had come to gaze on this blessed place of peace,
And to let wander free in the air the inspiration desired by my soul,
a way of life strange to me stirred my mind from all sides.

3. See above, chapter 3 note 143.

As I could not convict myself of any evil,
my nature urged me to cultivate mystic toil.
In my wisdom I then composed a complex song,
having received from the gods a holy and expressive idea.
When it was clear that the Muse had accomplished something pleasing to the gods,
I shook out my festival song, like the flower of a green shoot on Helicon.
Then a cave enticed me to enter and sleep,
although I was a little afraid to yield to a dream of fantasy.
Sleep picked me up and swiftly bore me away to a dear land.
I seemed to be gently washing my body in the flowing streams of a river
with the bountiful waters of the sweet Nile.
I imagined that Calliope, a holy member of the Muses,
sang together with all the nymphs a sacred song.
Thinking there still remained a bit of Greece,
I set down in written form the idea that my wise soul had inspired in me.
Just as one moving his body in time to music beaten by a staff,
I summoned rhythm as a partner for the inscription of my song,
leaving those of a critical bent little reason for blame.
The leader urged me to speak my clever poem.
Then great Mandoulis, glorious, came down from Olympus.
He charmed away the barbaric speech of the Aithiopians
and urged me to sing in sweet Greek verse.
He came with brilliant cheeks on the right hand of Isis,
exulting in his greatness and the glory of the Romans,
and uttering Pythian oracles like an Olympian god.
You declared how because of you men can look forward to a livelihood,
how day and night and all the seasons revere you
and call you Breith and Mandoulis, fraternal gods,
stars who rise as a sign of the gods in heaven.
And you yourself told me to inscribe these clever words,
in order that they be viewed by all without flattery.

. . . trusting in the first twenty-two letters.

(Acrostic: Paccius)

Π	Πάντοτέ σε ὑμνήσω (Λα)το[ῦ](ς) (γ)όνε, Π(ύ)θι(ε) Ἄπολλον,
Α	ἀθανάτων προκαθάγελμα κα(ὶ) χρυσόχελ(υ) Παιάν.
Κ	Καὶ γὰρ ἐγὼ παρὰ σοῖς προθύροις ἦλθον. (ἐ)π(ί)νεθσον
Κ	κύριε, τὰς προκ[πά]ς μ᾿ ἐν στρατιῇ μεγάλα[ς].
Ι	ἰ (γ)ὰρ μοι δοίης. κὰ(γ)ὼ λ(οι)βαῖς ἀποδώσω
Ο	οἷα θεῷ μεγάλῳ καὶἼσιδι τῇ βασιλίσσῃ.
Σ	Σπείσω πάντοτ᾿ ἐγὼ τοῖς δυσὶ τῶν προκοπῶν.

5

Ἰ δεῖ (ἀνα)γνῶναι καὶ τοὔνομα τοῦ γράψαντος
δὶς τὰς διακοσίας ψή(φ)ισον ἴκο(σι) μίαν.
Τὸ προσκύνημα τοῦ γράψαντος

10

καὶ τοῦ ἀναγνόντος σήμερον
παρὰ θεῷ Μάνδουλι.

(Acrostic: Paccius)
At all times I celebrate you, son of Leto, Pythian Apollo,
Guide of the immortals and Paean of the golden lyre.
For I have come before your gates. Give me,
Lord, great successes in the army.
For if you give me them, I will give you libations,
Such as those due to a great god and to Isis the queen.
I will always make libations to both for these successes.
To find out the name of the one who wrote this,
Count two times two hundred and twenty-one.
Act of dedication for the one who wrote it
And for the one who recognizes the sign
For the god Mandoulis.

4. A Greek document on skin, unprovenanced (chapters 1 and 4, fig. 4):

Βασιλεύοντος Ἀντιμάχου ἔτους τριακοστοῦ [μηνὸς - - -]
ἐν Ἀμφιπόλει τῆι πρὸς τῆι Ϙαρελοτηι εἰσηγεῖται[ι - - - τῶν]
ξένων μαγ ηεοχολλμηνον... τ ῶν τεσσαρά[κοντα - - -]
Σκυθῶν ἀργυρίου ἐπισήμου δ ρα χμῶν ἑκατὸν - - -
[. . . . . τοῦ. .] ε . . μενου πλήθους τ οῦ ἀργυρίου - - -
[ ]αρ ε . [traces of ink]

In the reign of Antimachos in year 30 [month + day]
in Amphipolis near Ḳarelote has introduced [NN of the]
mercenaries[(?) to NN] of the for[ty - - -]
Scythians, of one hundred drachmas of coined silver - - -
[ ] of [the above-mentioned(?)] sum of money [
[traces]

Abdullaev, Kazim. 2001. [Kazim Abdoullaev.] "La localisation de la capitale des Yüeh-chih." In P. Leriche, C. Pidaev, M. Gelin, K. Abdoullaev, and V. Fourniau, eds., *La Bactriane au carrefour des routes et des civilisations de l'Asie centrale: Termez et les villes de Bactriane-Tokharestan. Actes du colloque de Termez 1997.* La Bibliothèque d'Asie Centrale, vol. 1, 197–214. Paris: Maisonneuve et Larose.

———. 2007. "Nomad Migration in Central Asia." In Joe Cribb and Georgina Herrmann, eds., *After Alexander: Central Asia before Islam,* Proceedings of the British Academy, vol. 133, 73–98. Oxford: Oxford University Press for the British Academy.

Abdullaev, Kazim, et al. 2011. [Kazim Abdullaev, Bruno Genito, Fabiana Raiano, and Davide Lunelli.] "Trial Trenches at Koj Tepa, Samarkand Area (Sogdiana): Third Interim Report, 2011." *Newsletter di Archeologia CISA* 2, 7–72.

Abdullaev, Kazim, and Ladislav Stančo. 2003. "Djandavlattepa: Preliminary Report of the 2002 Excavation Season." *Studia Hercynia* 7, 165–68.

———. 2004. "Jandavlattepa: Preliminary Report of the 2003 Excavation Season." *Studia Hercynia* 8, 156–60.

———. 2005. "Jandavlattepa: Preliminary Report of the 2004 Excavation Season." *Studia Hercynia* 9, 273–75.

———. 2007. "Jandavlattepa 2006: Preliminary Excavation Report." *Studia Hercynia* 11, 157–59.

Adams, J. N. 1999. "The Poets of Bu Njem: Language, Culture and the Centurionate." *Journal of Roman Studies* 89, 109–34.

Alcock, S. E. 1993. "Surveying the Peripheries of the Hellenistic World." In P. Bilde, T. Engberg-Pedersen, L. Hannestad, J. Zahle, and K. Randsborg, eds., *Centre and Periphery in the Hellenistic World,* Studies in Hellenistic Civilization, vol. 4, 162–73. Aarhus: Aarhus University Press.

Allan, John. 1946. "A Tabula Iliaca from Gandhara." *Journal of Hellenic Studies* 66, 21–23.

Amiet, Pierre. 2010. "Le palais de Darius à Suse: Problèmes et hypothèses." *Arta* (www.achemenet.com/) 2010.001, 1–13.

Anthony, David. W. 1990. "Migration in Archaeology: The Baby and the Bathwater." *American Anthropologist*, n.s., 92, 895–914.

Antonaccio, Carla M. 2007. "Colonization: Greece on the Move, 900–480." In Harvey Alan Shapiro, ed., *The Cambridge Companion to Archaic Greece*, 201–24. Cambridge: Cambridge University Press.

Aperghis, G. G. 2004. *The Seleukid Royal Economy: The Finances and Financial Administration of the Seleukid Empire.* Cambridge: Cambridge University Press.

Asimov, M. S., et al., eds. 1985. *L'archéologie de la Bactriane ancienne: Actes du Colloque franco-soviétique, Dushanbe (U.R.S.S.), 27 octobre–3 novembre 1982.* Paris: Éditions du CNRS.

Audouin, R., and Paul Bernard. 1973. "Trésor de monnaies indiennes et indo-grecques d'Aï Khanoum (Afghanistan), I: Les monnaies indiennes." *Revue Numismatique* 5, 238–89.

———. 1974. "Trésor de monnaies indiennes et indo-grecques d'Aï Khanoum (Afghanistan), II: Les monnaies indo-grecques." *Revue Numismatique* 6, 7–41.

Banning, E. B. 1996. "Highlands and Lowlands: Problems and Survey Frameworks for Rural Archaeology in the Near East." *Bulletin of the American Schools of Oriental Research* 301, 25–45.

Barnard, H., and W. Wendrich, eds. 2008. *The Archaeology of Mobility: Old World and New World Nomadism.* Cotsen Advanced Seminar Series, vol. 4. Los Angeles: Cotsen Institute of Archaeology, University of California.

Barnett, L. D. 1909. "The Besnagar Inscription B." *Journal of the Royal Asiatic Society,* 1093–94.

Barth, F., ed. 1969a. *Ethnic Groups and Boundaries: The Organization of Cultural Difference.* Bergen and London: Universitetsforlaget and Allen and Unwin.

———. 1969b. "Introduction." In F. Barth, ed., *Ethnic Groups and Boundaries: The Organization of Cultural Difference,* 9–38. Bergen and London: Universitetsforlaget and Allen and Unwin.

Bavay, L. 1997. "Matière première et commerce à longue distance: Le lapis-lazuli et l'Égypte predynastique." *Archéo-Nil* 7, 79–100.

Bayer, Theophilus Siegfried. 1730. *Museum Sinicum in Quo Sinicae Linguae et Litteraturae Ratio Explicatur.* St. Petersburg: Ex Typographia Academiae Imperatoriae.

Bayly, S. 1999. *Caste, Society and Politics in India from the Eighteenth Century to the Modern Age.* Volume 4, part 3, of C. A. Bayly, Gordon Johnson, and John F. Richards, eds., *The New Cambridge History of India.* Cambridge: Cambridge University Press.

Bedal, Leigh-Ann. 2001. "A Pool Complex in Petra's City Center." *Bulletin of the American Schools of Oriental Research* 324 (Nabataean Petra), 23–41.

Benjamin, Craig R. 2007. *The Yuezhi: Origin, Migration and the Conquest of Northern Bactria.* Silk Road Studies, vol. 14. Turnhout: Brepols.

Benveniste, E. 1962. "Coutumes funéraires de l'Arachosie ancienne." In W. B. Henning and E. Yarshater, eds., *A Locust's Leg: Studies in Honour of S. H. Taqizadeh,* 39–43. London: Percy Lund, Humphreys and Co.

———. 1964. "Édits d'Asoka en traduction grecque." *Journal Asiatique* 252, 137–57.

Benveniste, E., and A. Dupont-Sommer. 1966. "Une inscription indo-araméenne d'Asoka provenant de Kandahar." *Journal Asiatique* 254, 437–65.

Berdimuradov, A., et al. 2007. [A. Berdimuradov, F. Franceschini, D. Giorgetti, Simone Mantellini, Bernardo Rondelli, and M. Tosi.] "Samarkand and Its Territory: From Archaeological Map to Cultural Landscape Management." *Bulletin of the International Institute for Central Asia Studies* 6, 22–33.

Bernand, André, and Étienne Bernand. 1969. *Les inscriptions grecques de Philae*. Vol. 1, *Époque ptolémaïque*. Paris: Editions du CNRS.

Bernand, Étienne. 1969. *Inscriptions métriques de l'Égypte gréco-romaine: Recherches sur la poésie épigrammatique des Grecs en Égypte*. Annales Littéraires de l'Université de Besançon, vol. 98. Paris: Les Belles Lettres.

Bernard, Paul. 1966. "Première campagne de fouilles d'Aï Khanoum." *Comptes-Rendus de l'Académie des Inscriptions et Belles-Lettres* 110, 127–33.

———. 1967a. "Ai Khanoum on the Oxus: A Hellenistic City in Central Asia." *Proceedings of the British Academy* 53, 71–95.

———. 1967b. "Deuxième campagne de fouilles d'Aï Khanoum." *Comptes-Rendus de l'Académie des Inscriptions et Belles-Lettres*, 306–24.

———. 1968a. "Chapiteaux corinthiens hellénistiques d'Asie centrale découverts à Aï Khanoum." *Syria* 45, 111–51.

———.1968b. "Troisième campagne de fouilles d'Aï Khanoum." *Comptes-Rendus de l'Académie des Inscriptions et Belles-Lettres*, 263–79.

———. 1969. "Quatrième campagne de fouilles à Aï Khanoum (Bactriane)." *Comptes-Rendus de l'Académie des Inscriptions et Belles-Lettres*, 313–55.

———. 1970a. "Campagne de fouilles 1969 à Aï Khanoum en Afghanistan." *Comptes-Rendus de l'Académie des Inscriptions et Belles-Lettres*, 301–49.

———. 1970b. "Sièges et lits en ivoire d'époque hellénistique en Asie centrale." *Syria* 47, 327–43.

———. 1971. "La campagne de fouilles de 1970 à Aï Khanoum (Afghanistan)." *Comptes-Rendus de l'Académie des Inscriptions et Belles-Lettres*, 385–452.

———. 1972. "Campagne de fouilles à Aï Khanoum (Afghanistan)." *Comptes-Rendus de l'Académie des Inscriptions et Belles-Lettres*, 605–32.

———, ed. 1973. *Fouilles d'Aï Khanoum*. Vol. 1, *Campagnes 1965, 1966, 1967, 1968*. Mémoires de la Délégation Archéologique Française en Afghanistan, vol. 21. Paris: Klincksieck.

———. 1974a. "Aï Khanoum, ville coloniale grecque." *Archeologia—Dossiers de l'Archéologie* 5, 99–114.

———. 1974b. "Fouilles de Aï Khanoum (Afghanistan): Campagnes de 1972 et 1973." *Comptes-Rendus de l'Académie des Inscriptions et Belles-Lettres*, 280–308.

———. 1975. "Campagne de fouilles 1974 à Aï Khanoum (Afghanistan)." *Comptes-Rendus de l'Académie des Inscriptions et Belles-Lettres*, 167–97.

———. 1976a. "Campagne de fouilles 1975 à Aï Khanoum (Afghanistan)." *Comptes-Rendus de l'Académie des Inscriptions et Belles-Lettres*, 287–322.

———. 1976b. "Les traditions orientales dans l'architecture gréco-bactrienne." *Journal Asiatique* 264, 245–75.

———. 1978. "Campagne de fouilles 1976–1977 à Aï Khanoum (Afghanistan)." *Comptes-Rendus de l'Académie des Inscriptions et Belles-Lettres*, 421–63.

———. 1979. "Pratiques financières grecques dans la Bactriane hellénisée." *Bulletin de la Société Française de Numismatique,* 517–20.

———. 1980a. "Campagne de fouilles 1978 à Aï Khanoum (Afghanistan)." *Comptes-Rendus de l'Académie des Inscriptions et Belles-Lettres,* 435–59.

———. 1980b. "Une nouvelle contribution soviétique à l'histoire des Kushans: La fouille de Dal'verzin-tépé (Uzbékistan)." *Bulletin de l'École Française d'Extrême Orient* 68, 313–48.

———. 1982a. "Aï Khanoum, une ancienne cité grecque d'Asie centrale." *Pour la Science* 53, 88–97.

———. 1982b. "An Ancient Greek City in Central Asia." *Scientific American* 246, 126–35.

———. 1985. *Fouilles d'Aï Khanoum.* Vol. 4, *Les monnaies hors trésors: Questions d'histoire gréco-bactrienne.* Mémoires de la Délégation Archéologique Française en Afghanistan, vol. 28. Paris: de Boccard.

———. 1987a. "Le Marsyas d'Apamée, l'Oxus et la colonisation séleucide en Bactriane." *Studia Iranica* 16, 103–15.

———. 1987b. "Les nomades conquérants de l'empire gréco-bactrien: Réflexions sur leur identité ethnique et culturelle." *Comptes-Rendus de l'Académie des Inscriptions et Belles-Lettres* 131, 758–68.

———. 1990. "L'architecture religieuse de l'Asie centrale à l'époque hellénistique." In *Akten des XIII Internationalen Kongresses für klassische Archäologie, Berlin 1988,* 51–59. Mainz am Rhein: von Zabern.

———. 1994. "Le temple de dieu Oxus à Takht-i Sangin en Bactriane: Temple du feu ou pas?" *Studia Iranica* 23, 81–121.

———. 2001. "Aï Khanoum en Afghanistan hier (1964–1978) et aujourd'hui (2001): Un site en peril." *Comptes-Rendus de l'Académie des Inscriptions et Belles-Lettres,* 971–1029.

———. 2002. "L'œuvre de la Délégation archéologique française en Afghanistan (1922–1982)." *Comptes-Rendus de l'Académie des Inscriptions et Belles-Lettres* 146, 1287–1323.

———. 2005. "Hellenistic Arachosia: A Greek Melting Pot in Action." *East and West* 55, 13–34.

Bernard, Paul, Roland Besenval, and Philippe Marquis. 2006. "Du 'mirage bactrien' aux réalités archéologiques: Nouvelles fouilles de la DAFA à Bactres (2004–2005)." *Comptes-Rendus de l'Académie des Inscriptions et Belles-Lettres,* 1175–1254.

Bernard, Paul, et al. 1976. [Paul Bernard, Henri-Paul Francfort, Jean-Claude Gardin, Jean-Claude Liger, Bertille Lyonnet, and Serge Veuve.] "Fouilles d'Aï Khanoum (Afghanistan): Campagne de 1974." *Bulletin de l'École Française d'Extrême Orient* 63, 5–51.

———. 1980. [Paul Bernard, Paul Garczinski, Olivier Guillaume, Frantz Grenet, Nader Ghassoulli, Pierre Leriche, Jean-Claude Liger, Claude Rapin, Axelle Rougeulle, Joël Thoraval, Régis de Valence, and Serge Veuve.] "Campagne de fouilles 1978 à Aï Khanoum (Afghanistan)." *Bulletin de l'École Française d'Extrême Orient* 68, 1–75.

Bernard, Paul, and Henri-Paul Francfort. 1978. *Études de géographie historique sur la plaine d'Aï Khanoum (Afghanistan).* Paris: Éditions du CNRS.

Bernard, Paul, and Frantz Grenet, eds. 1991. *Histoire et cultes de l'Asie centrale préislamique: Sources écrites et documents archéologiques. Actes du Colloque international du CNRS (Paris, 22–28 novembre 1988).* Paris: Éditions du CNRS.

Bernard, Paul, Frantz Grenet, and Muxammedzon Isamiddinov. 1990. "Fouilles de la mission franco-soviétique à l'ancienne Samarkand (Afrasiab): Première campagne, 1989." *Comptes-Rendus de l'Académie des Inscriptions et Belles-Lettres* 134, 356–80.

———. 1992. "Fouilles de la mission franco-ouzbèque à l'ancienne Samarkand (Afrasiab) en 1990 et 1991." *Comptes-Rendus de l'Académie des Inscriptions et Belles-Lettres* 136, 275–311.

Bernard, Paul, Marc Le Berre, and R. Stucki. 1973. "Architecture: Le téménos de Kinéas." In P. Bernard, ed., *Fouilles d'Aï Khanoum*, vol. 1, *Campagnes 1965, 1966, 1967, 1968*, Mémoires de la Délégation Archéologique Française en Afghanistan, vol. 21, 85–102. Paris: Klincksieck.

Bernard, Paul, Georges-Jean Pinault, and Georges Rougemont. 2004. "Deux nouvelles inscriptions grecques de l'Asie centrale." *Journal des Savants*, 227–356.

Bernard, Paul, and Claude Rapin. 1994. "Un parchemin gréco-bactrien d'une collection privée." *Comptes-Rendus de l'Académie des Inscriptions et Belles-Lettres*, 261–94.

Bernard, Paul, and Georges Rougemont. 2003. "Les secrets de la stèle de Kandahar." *L'Histoire* 280 (Oct.), 27–28.

Besenval, Roland, and Philippe Marquis. 2007. "Le rêve accompli d'Alfred Foucher à Bactres: Nouvelles fouilles de la DAFA 2002–2007." *Comptes-Rendus de l'Académie des Inscriptions et Belles-Lettres*, 1847–74.

Besenval, Roland, Philippe Marquis, and Pascal Mongne. 2009. "Le rêve accompli d'Alfred Foucher à Bactres: Premiers résultats des campagnes menées depuis 2004 par la Délégation archéologique française en Afghanistan et la Mission archéologique française en Bactriane d'Afghanistan en collaboration avec l'Institut afghan d'archéologie." In Pierre-Sylvain Filliozat and Jean Leclant, eds., *Bouddhismes d'Asie: Monuments et littératures. Journée d'étude en hommage à Alfred Foucher (1865–1952) réunie le vendredi 14 décembre 2007 à l'Académie des inscriptions et belles-lettres (Palais de l'Institut de France)*, 211–42. Paris: Académie des Inscriptions et Belles-Lettres.

Bhabha, Homi K. 1994. *The Location of Culture*. London: Routledge.

Bhandarkar, D. R. 1917. "Excavations at Besnagar." In *Archaeological Survey of India, Annual Report 1913–14*, 186–226. Calcutta: Government of India.

Bhattacharya, V. 1932. "The Besnagar Inscription of Heliodoros." *Indian Historical Quarterly* 8, 610.

Bivar, A. D. H. 1950. "The Death of Eucratides in Medieval Tradition." *Journal of the Royal Asiatic Society* 82, 7–13.

Boiy, Tom. 2004. *Late Achaemenid and Hellenistic Babylon*. Orientalia Lovaniensia Analecta. Leuven and Dudley, Mass.: Peeters.

———. 2005a. "Akkadian-Greek Double Names in Hellenistic Babylonia." In W. H. van Soldt, ed., *Ethnicity in Ancient Mesopotamia: Papers Read at the 48th Rencontre Assyriologique Internationale, Leiden, 1–4 July 2002*, 47–60. Leiden: Nederlands Instituut voor het Nabije Oosten.

———. 2005b. "The Fifth and Sixth Generation of the Nikarchos = Anu-Uballit Family." *Revue d'Assyriologie et d'Archéologie Orientale* 99, 105–10.

Bopearachchi, Osmund. 1991. *Monnaies gréco-bactriennes et indo-grecques: Catalogue raisonné*. Paris: Bibliothèque Nationale.

———. 1992. "Was Sagala Menander's Capital?" In C. Jarrige, J. P. Gerry, and R. H. Meadow, eds., *South Asian Archaeology 1989: Papers from the Tenth International Conference of South Asian Archaeologists in Western Europe*, 327–37. Madison: Prehistory Press.

———. 1993. *Indo-Greek, Indo-Scythian and Indo-Parthian Coins in the Smithsonian Institution*. Washington, D.C.: Smithsonian Institution.

————. 1996. "Sophytes, the Enigmatic Ruler of Central Asia." *Nomismatika Khronika* 15, 19–32.

————. 1998. *Sylloge Nummorum Graecorum: The Collection of the American Numismatic Society.* Part 9, *Graeco-Bactrian and Indo-Greek Coins.* New York: American Numismatic Society.

————. 2005. "Contribution of Greeks to the Art and Culture of Bactria and India: New Archaeological Evidence." *Indian Historical Review* 32, 103–25.

Bopearachchi, Osmund, and Paul Bernard. 2002. "Deux bracelets grecs avec inscriptions grecques trouvés dans l'Asie centrale hellénisée." *Journal des Savants,* 238–78.

Bopearachchi, Osmund, and Philippe Flandrin. 2005. *Le portrait d'Alexandre le Grand: Histoire d'une découverte pour l'humanité.* Paris: Éditions du Rocher.

Bosworth, A. B. 1996. *Alexander and the East: The Tragedy of Triumph.* Oxford: Clarendon Press.

Boucharlat, Rémy. 2001. "The Palace and the Royal Achaemenid City: Two Case Studies— Pasargadae and Susa." In Inge Nielsen, ed., *The Royal Palace Institution in the First Millennium BC: Regional Development and Cultural Interchange between East and West,* Monographs of the Danish Institute at Athens, 113–21. Athens and Aarhus: The Danish Institute at Athens and Aarhus University Press.

Bourdieu, Pierre. 1977. *Outline of a Theory of Practice.* Cambridge: Cambridge University Press.

————. 1998. *Practical Reason: On the Theory of Action.* Cambridge: Polity Press.

Boyce, Mary, and Frantz Grenet. 1991. *A History of Zoroastrianism.* Volume 3, *Zoroastrianism under Macedonian and Roman Rule.* Handbuch der Orientalistik, erste Abteilung: Der Nahe und Mittlere Osten, vol. 8.1.2.2.3. Leiden: E. J. Brill.

Bresciani, Edda. 1980. "I testi demotici della stele 'enigmistica' di Moschione e il bilinguismo culturale nell'Egitto greco-romano." *Egitto e Vicino Oriente* 3, 117–45.

Briant, Pierre. 1978. "Colonisation hellénistique et populations indigènes: La phase d'installation." *Klio* 60, 57–92.

————. 1982. *État et pasteurs au Moyen-Orient ancien.* Cambridge: Cambridge University Press.

————. 1984. *L'Asie centrale et les royaumes proche-Orientaux du premier millénaire (c. VIIIe—IVe siècles avant notre ère).* Éditions Recherche sur les Civilisations, mémoire 42. Paris: Éditions Recherche sur les Civilisations.

————. 1985a. "La Bactriane dans l'empire achéménide: L'état central achéménide en Bactriane." In M. S. Asimov et. al., eds., *L'archéologie de la Bactriane ancienne: Actes du Colloque franco-soviétique, Dushanbe (U.R.S.S.), 27 octobre–3 novembre 1982,* 243–51. Paris: Éditions du CNRS.

————. 1985b. "Les Iraniens d'Asie Mineure après la chute de l'empire achéménide: À propos de l'inscription d'Amyzon." *Dialogues d'Histoire Ancienne* 11, 167–95.

————. 1986. "Polythéismes et empire unitaire: Remarques sur la politique religieuse des Achéménides." In *Les grandes figures religieuses: Fonctionnement pratique et symbolique dans l'antiquité: Besançon, 25–26 avril 1984,* Lire les Polythéismes, vol. 1; Annales Littéraires de l'Université de Besançon, vol. 329; Centre de Recherches d'Histoire Ancienne, vol. 68, 425–43. Paris: Belles Lettres.

————. 1987. "Pouvoir central et polycentrisme culturel dans l'empire achéménide: Quelques réflexions et suggestions." In H. Sancisi-Weerderburg, ed., *Achaemenid History,* vol. 1,

Sources, Structures and Synthesis, 1–32. Leiden: Nederlands Instituut voor het Nabije Oosten.

———. 1988a. "Contingents est-iraniens et centre-asiatiques dans les armées achéménides." In *L'Asie centrale et ses rapports avec les civilisations orientales des origines à l'âge du fer*, 173–75. Paris: de Boccard.

———. 1988b. "Ethno-classe dominante et populations soumises dans l'empire achéménide: Le cas de l'Égypte." In Amélie Kuhrt and H. Sancisi-Weerderburg, eds., *Achaemenid History*, vol. 3, *Method and Theory: Proceedings of the London 1985 Achaemenid History Workshop*, 137–74. Leiden: Nederlands Instituut voor het Nabije Oosten.

———. 1997. "Notes d'histoire militaire achéménide: À propos des éléphants de Darius III." In Pierre Brulé and Jacques Oulhen, eds., *Esclavage, guerre, économie en Grèce ancienne: Hommages à Yvon Garlan*, 177–90. Rennes: Presses Universitaires de Rennes.

———. 2002. *From Cyrus to Alexander: A History of the Persian Empire*. Winona Lake: Eisenbrauns.

———. 2012. "From the Indus to the Mediterranean: The Administrative Organization and Logistics of the Great Roads of the Achaemenid Empire." In Susan E. Alcock, John P. Bodel, and Richard J. A. Talbert, eds., *Highways, Byways, and Road Systems in the Pre-Modern World*, 185–201. New York: Wiley-Blackwell.

Briant, Pierre, Wouter Henkelman, and Matthew W. Stolper. 2008. *L'archive des fortifications de Persépolis: État des questions et perspectives de recherches*. Persika, vol. 12. Paris: de Boccard.

Briant, Pierre, and Francis Joannès, eds. 2006. *La transition entre l'empire achéménide et les royaumes hellénistiques (vers 350–300 av. J.-C.)*. Persika, vol. 9. Paris: de Boccard.

Brosseder, Ursula, and Bryan K. Miller, eds. 2011. *Xiongnu Archaeology: Multidisciplinary Perspectives of the First Steppe Empire in Inner Asia*. Bonn Contibutions to Asian Archaeology, vol. 5. Bonn: Bonn Vor- und Frühgeschichtliche Archäologie.

Brunsch, W. 1979. "Die bilingue Stele des Moschion (Berlin Inv. Nr. 2135 + Cairo J.d'E Nr. 63160)." *Enchoria: Zeitschrift für Demotistik und Koptologie* 9, 5–32.

Buddhadatta Thero, A. P. 1923. *Sammoha-vinodanī: Abhidhamma-pitake Vibhangatthakathā*. Pali Text Society, Text Series. London: Pali Text Society.

Bulkin, V. A., Leo S. Klejn, and G. S. Lebedev. 1982. "Attainments and Problems of Soviet Archaeology." *World Archaeology* 13, 272–95.

Burn, Lucilla. 2004. *Hellenistic Art: From Alexander the Great to Augustus*. Los Angeles: J. Paul Getty Museum.

Burstein, Stanley M. 1985. *The Hellenistic Age from the Battle of Ipsos to the Death of Kleopatra VII*. Cambridge: Cambridge University Press.

———. 1993. "The Hellenistic Fringe: The Case of Meroë." In Peter Green, ed., *Hellenistic History and Culture*, Hellenistic Culture and Society, vol. 11, 38–54. Berkeley and Los Angeles: University of California Press.

———. 1997. *Ancient African Civilizations: Kush and Axum*. Princeton: Wiener.

———. 1998. "Paccius Maximus: A Greek Poet in Nubia or a Nubian Greek Poet?" In *Actes de la VIIIᵉ Conférence internationale des études nubiennes, Lille, 11–17 septembre 1994*, Cahiers de Recherches de l'Institut de Papyrologie et d'Égyptologie de Lille, vol. 17, 47–52. Villeneuve d'Ascq: Université Charles de Gaulle–Lille III.

———. 1999–2000. "A Soldier and His God in Lower Nubia: The Mandulis Hymns of Paccius Maximus." In *Graeco-Arabica*, vols. 7–8 (special number), *Proceedings of the Sixth*

International Congress of Graeco-Oriental and African Studies, Nicosia, 30 April–5 May 1996, 45–50.

———. 2003. "The Legacy of Alexander: New Ways of Being Greek in the Hellenistic Period." In W. Heckel and L. A. Tritle, eds., *Crossroads of History: The Age of Alexander*, 217–42. Claremont: Regina Books.

———. 2012. "Whence the Women? The Origin of the Bactrian Greeks." *Ancient West & East* 11, 97–104.

Butzer, Karl M. 1976. *Early Hydraulic Civilization in Egypt: A Study in Cultural Ecology.* Prehistoric Archeology and Ecology. Chicago: University of Chicago Press.

Cahill, N. 2002. *Household and City Organization at Olynthus.* New Haven: Yale University Press.

Callieri, Pierfrancesco. 1996. "Margiana in the Hellenistic Period: Problems of Archaeological Interpretation." In Enrico Acquaro, ed., *Alle soglie della classicità: Il Mediterraneo tra tradizione e innovazione*, vol. 2, *Archeologia e arte*, 569–78. Pisa: Istituti Editoriali e Poligrafici Internazionali.

Cambon, Pierre, and Jean-François Jarrige, eds. 2006. *Afghanistan, les trésors retrouvés: Collections du Musée National de Kaboul.* Paris: Réunion des Musées Nationaux and Musée National des Arts Asiatiques–Guimet.

Canali De Rossi, Filippo. 2004. *Iscrizioni dello Estremo Oriente greco: Un repertorio.* Inschriften griechischer Städte aus Kleinasien, vol. 65. Bonn: Dr. Rudolf Habelt.

Canepa, Matthew P. 2010a. "Achaemenid and Seleucid Royal Funerary Practices and Middle Iranian Kingship." In Henning Börm and Josef Wiesehöfer, eds., *Commutatio et Contentio: Studies in the Late Roman, Sasanian, and Early Islamic Near East in Memory of Zeev Rubin*, 1–21. Düsseldorf: Wellem Verlag.

———, ed. 2010b. *Theorizing Cross-Cultural Interaction among the Ancient and Early Medieval Mediterranean, Near East and Asia.* Ars Orientalis, vol. 38. Washington, D.C.: Smithsonian Institution.

Casella, Eleanor Conlin, and Chris Fowler, eds. 2004. *The Archaeology of Plural and Changing Identities: Beyond Identification.* New York: Kluwer Academic and Plenum Press.

Casson, Lionel. 1989. *The Periplus Maris Erythraei.* Princeton: Princeton University Press.

Chakrabarti, D. K. 1995. *The Archaeology of Ancient Indian Cities.* Oxford and Delhi: Oxford University Press.

Chalmers, R., ed. 1898. *The Majjhima-Nikāya.* Volume 2. London: Pali Text Society.

Chanda, R. P. 1920. *Archaeology and Vaishnava Tradition.* Memoirs of the Archaeological Survey of India, vol. 5. Calcutta: Superintendent of Government Printing.

Clarysse, Willy, and Dorothy J. Thompson. 2006. *Counting the People in Hellenistic Egypt.* 2 vols. Cambridge: Cambridge University Press. [Vol. 1, *Population Registers (P.Count)*; vol. 2, *Historical Studies.*]

———. 2007. "Two Greek Texts on Skin from Hellenistic Bactria." *Zeitschrift für Papyrologie und Epigraphik* 159, 273–79.

(Collectif). 1996. *La Bactriane, de l'hellénisme au bouddhisme.* Dossiers d'Archéologie 211.

Coloru, Omar. 2009. *Da Alessandro a Menandro: Il regno greco di Battriana.* Studi Ellenistici, vol. 21. Pisa and Rome: Fabrizio Serra Editore.

Coningham, Robin, and B. R. Edwards. 1997–98. "Space and Society at Sirkap, Taxila: A Re-Examination of Urban Form and Meaning." *Ancient Pakistan* 12, 47–75.

Coningham, Robin, and Ruth Young. 2007. "The Archaeological Visibility of Caste: An Introduction." In Timothy Insoll, ed., *The Archaeology of Identities: A Reader*, 250–64. London: Routledge.

Courtney, E. 1995. *Musa Lapidaria: A Selection of Latin Verse Inscriptions*. American Classical Studies, vol. 36. Atlanta: Scholars Press.

Cribb, Joe. 2007. "Money as a Marker of Cultural Continuity and Change in Central Asia." In Joe Cribb and Georgina Herrmann, eds., *After Alexander: Central Asia before Islam*, Proceedings of the British Academy, vol. 133, 333–76. Oxford: Oxford University Press for the British Academy.

Cribb, Roger. 1991. *Nomads in Archaeology*. New Studies in Archaeology. Cambridge: Cambridge University Press.

Cribiore, Raffaella. 1996. *Writing, Teachers, and Students in Graeco-Roman Egypt*. American Studies in Papyrology, vol. 36. Atlanta: Scholars Press.

———. 2001. *Gymnastics of the Mind: Greek Education in Hellenistic and Roman Egypt*. Princeton and Oxford: Princeton University Press.

Cunningham, Sir Alexander. 1880. *Archaeological Survey of India*. Volume 10, *Report of Tours in Bundelkhand and Malwa in 1874–75 and 1876–77*. Calcutta: Government of India.

Curiel, R., and G. Fussman. 1965. *Le trésor monétaire de Qunduz*. Memoires de la Délégation Archéologique Française en Afghanistan. Paris: Klincksieck.

Curto, Silvio, et al. 1965. [Silvio Curto, V. Maragioglio, C. Rinaldi, and L. Bongrani.] *Kalabsha*. Orientis Antiqui Collectio, vol. 5. Rome: Centro per le Antichità e la Storia dell'Arte del Vicino Oriente.

Dalton, O. M. 1964 [1905]. *The Treasure of the Oxus*. London: British Museum.

Danielsová, A., Ladislav Stančo, and A. Shaydullaev. 2010. "Preliminary Report of Archaeological Survey in Sherabad District, South Uzbekistan, in 2009." *Studia Hercynia* 14, 67–90.

Davis-Kimball, Jeannine, Vladimir A. Bashilov, and Leonid T. Yablonsky, eds. 1995. *Nomads of the Eurasian Steppe in the Early Iron Age*. Berkeley, Calif.: Zinat Press.

Dean, Carolyn, and Dana Leibsohn. 2003. "Hybridity and Its Discontents: Considering Visual Culture in Colonial Spanish America." *Colonial Latin American Review* 12, 5–35.

de Guignes, J. 1759. "Recherches sur quelques événements qui concernent l'Histoire des Rois Grecs de la Bactriane, et particulièrement la destruction de leur Royaume par les Scythes, l'établissement de ceux-ci le long de l'Indus, et les guerres qu'ils eurent avec les Parthes." *Mémoires de Littérature Tirés des Registres de l'Académie des Inscriptions et Belles-Lettres* 25, 17–33.

Deloria, Philip J. 2006. "What Is the Middle Ground, Anyway?" *The William and Mary Quarterly* 63, 15–22.

Deshayes, J., ed. 1977. *Le plateau iranien et l'Asie centrale des origines à la conquête islamique: Leurs relations à la lumière des documents archéologiques, Paris, 22–24 mars 1976*. Colloques Internationaux du Centre National de la Recherche Scientifique, vol. 567. Paris: Éditions du CNRS.

Di Cosmo, Nicola. 1994. "Ancient Inner Asian Nomads: Their Economic Basis and Its Significance in Chinese History." *The Journal of Asian Studies* 53, 1092–1126.

———. 2002. *Ancient China and Its Enemies: The Rise of Nomadic Power in East Asian History*. Cambridge: Cambridge University Press.

Doniger, Wendy, ed. and trans. 1991. *The Laws of Manu.* London: Penguin.

Downey, Susan B. 1986. "The Citadel Palace at Dura-Europos." *Syria* 63, 27–37.

———. 1988. *Mesopotamian Religious Architecture: Alexander through the Parthians.* Princeton: Princeton University Press.

Driver, Godfrey Rolles. 1957. *Aramaic Documents of the Fifth Century B.C.* Oxford: Clarendon Press.

Drujinina, Anjelina. 2001. "Die Ausgrabungen in Taxt-i Sangīn im Oxos-Tempelbereich (süd-Tadzikistan): Vorbericht der Kampagnen 1998–1999." *Archäologische Mitteilungen aus Iran und Turan* 33, 257–92.

———. 2004. [A. P. Druzhinina.] "A Stone Pyxis Lid Decorated with a Zoomorphic Frieze from the Tahti-Sangin Fort: A New Find from Ancient Bactria." *Archaeology, Ethnology & Anthropology of Eurasia* 3, 98–105.

Drujinina, Anjelina, and Gunvor Lindström. 2013. "Kultgefäße im Oxos-Tempel: Zur Frage der Kultkontinuität im unruhigen 2. Jh. v. Chr." *Archäologische Mitteilungen aus Iran und Turan* 14, 171–86.

Dubs, Homer H. 1938–55. *The History of the Former Han Dynasty (Ban Biao, Ban Gu, Ban Zhao).* 3 vols. Baltimore: Waverly Press.

Dupont-Sommer, A. 1966. "Une nouvelle inscription araméenne d'Asoka découverte à Kandahar (Afghanistan)." *Comptes-Rendus de l'Académie des Inscriptions et Belles-Lettres,* 440–51.

———. 1969. "Une nouvelle inscription araméenne d'Asoka trouvée dans la vallée du Laghman (Afghanistan)." *Comptes-Rendus de l'Académie des Inscriptions et Belles-Lettres,* 158–73.

Falk, H. 1991. "The Seven 'Castes' of Megasthenes." In U. P. Arora, ed., *Graeco-Indica: India's Cultural Contacts with the Greek World,* 48–56. New Delhi: Ramanand Vidya Bhawan.

Fenet, Annick. 2010. *Documents d'archéologie militante: La mission Foucher en Afghanistan (1922–1925).* Mémoires de l'Académie des Inscriptions et Belles-Lettres, vol. 42. Paris: Académie des Inscriptions et Belles-Lettres.

Fleet, J. F. 1909. "An Inscription from Besnagar." *Journal of the Royal Asiatic Society,* 1087–92.

———. 1910. "The Besnagar Inscription A." *Journal of the Royal Asiatic Society,* 141–42, 815–17.

Foucher, Alfred. 1927. "La Délégation archéologique française en Afghanistan (octobre 1922–novembre 1925)." *Comptes-Rendus des Séances de l'Académie des Inscriptions et Belles-Lettres,* 117–23.

Foucher, Alfred, and Eugénie Bazin-Foucher. 1942–47. *La vieille route de l'Inde de Bactres à Taxila.* Mémoires de la Délégation Archéologique Française en Afghanistan, vol. 1. Paris: Les Éditions d'Art et d'Histoire.

Frachetti, Michael D. 2008. "Variability and Dynamic Landscapes of Mobile Pastoralism in Ethnography and Prehistory." In H. Barnard and W. Wendrich, eds., *The Archaeology of Mobility: Old World and New World Nomadism,* Cotsen Advanced Seminar Series, vol. 4, 366–96. Los Angeles: Cotsen Institute of Archaeology, University of California.

Francfort, Henri-Paul. 1976. "Les modèles gréco-bactriens de quelques reliquaires et palettes à fard gréco-bouddhiques." *Arts Asiatiques* 32, 91–98.

———. 1977. "Le plan des maisons gréco-bactriennes et le problème des structures de type 'megaron' en Asie centrale et en Iran." In J. Deshayes, ed., *Le plateau iranien et l'Asie centrale des origines à la conquête islamique: Leurs relations à la lumière des documents archéologiques,* Colloques Internationaux du Centre National de la Recherche Scientifique, vol. 567, 267–80. Paris: Éditions du CNRS.

———. 1979. *Les fortifications en Asie centrale de l'age du bronze à l'époque kouchane.* Paris: CNRS, Centre de Recherches Archéologiques.

———. 1983. "Excavations at Shortughaï in Northeast Afghanistan." *American Journal of Archaeology* 87, 518–19.

———. 1984a. "The Early Periods of Shortughaï (Harappan) and the Western Bactrian Culture of Dashly." In B. Allchin, ed., *South Asian Archaeology 1981: Proceedings of the Sixth International Conference of the Association of South Asian Archaeologists in Western Europe, Held in Cambridge University, 5–10 July 1981,* University of Cambridge Oriental Publications, vol. 34, 170–75. Cambridge: Cambridge University Press.

———. 1984b. *Fouilles d'Aï Khanoum.* Vol. 3, *Le sanctuaire du temple à niches indentées.* Part 2, *Les trouvailles.* Mémoires de la Délégation Archéologique Française en Afghanistan, vol. 27. Paris: de Boccard.

———. 1984c. "The Harappan settlement of Shortughaï (N-E Afghanistan) and Some Aspects of Central Asia in the Bronze Age." In B. B. Lal and S. P. Gupta, eds., *Frontiers of the Indus Civilization: Sir Mortimer Wheeler Commemoration Volume,* 301–10. New Delhi: Books and Books on Behalf of Indian Archaeological Society Jointly with Indian History and Culture Society.

———. 1989. *Fouilles de Shortughaï: Recherches sur l'Asie centrale protohistorique.* Mémoires de la Mission Archéologique Française en Asie Centrale, vol. 2. Paris: Mission Archéologique Française en Asie Centrale and Diffusion de Boccard.

———, ed. 1990. *Nomades et sédentaires en Asie centrale: Apports de l'archéologie et de l'ethnologie. Actes du Colloque franco-soviétique, Alma Ata (Kazakhstan) 17–26 octobre 1987.* Paris: Éditions du CNRS.

———. 1993. "Mission archéologique française en Asie centrale (MAFAC)." *Bulletin de l'École Française d'Extrême Orient* 80, 281–85.

———. 2005. "Asie centrale." In Pierre Briant and Rémy Boucharlat, eds., *L'archéologie de l'empire achéménide: Nouvelles recherches,* Persika, vol. 6, 313–52. Paris: de Boccard.

———. 2013. *L'art oublié des lapidaires de la Bactriane aux époques achéménide et hellénistique.* Persika, vol. 17. Paris: de Boccard.

Francfort, Henri-Paul, and Olivier Lecomte. 2002. "Irrigation et société en Asie centrale des origines à l'époque achéménide." *Annales: Histoire, Sciences Sociales* 57, 625–63.

Francfort, Henri-Paul, and Jean-Claude Liger. 1976. "L'hérôon au caveau de pierre." In Paul Bernard, Henri-Paul Francfort, Jean-Claude Gardin, Jean-Claude Liger, Bertille Lyonnet, and Serge Veuve, "Fouilles d'Aï Khanoum (Afghanistan): Campagne de 1974," *Bulletin de l'École Française d'Extrême Orient* 63, 5–51.

Fraser, P. M. 1979. "The Son of Aristonax at Kandahar." *Afghan Studies* 2, 9–21.

———. 1982. "Palamedes at Bağlan." *Afghan Studies* 3–4, 77–78.

Frye, Richard N. 1966. "A Greek City in Afghanistan." *American Journal of Archaeology* 70, 286.

Fussman, G. 1980. "Nouvelles inscriptions saka: Ère d'Eucratide, ère d'Azès, ère Vikrama, ère de Kaniska." *Bulletin de l'École Française d'Extrême Orient* 67, 1–44.

———. 1982. "Pouvoir central et régions dans l'Inde ancienne: Le problème de l'empire maurya." *Annales: Économies, Sociétés, Civilisations* 37, 621–47.

———. 1989. "Gāndhārī écrite, Gāndhārī parlée." In C. Caillat, ed., *Dialectes dans les littéra-tures indo-aryennes*, Publications de l'Institut de Civilisation Indienne, série in 8°, vol. 55, 433–99. Paris: Collège de France, Institut de Civilisation Indienne.

———. 1993a. "L'Indo-Grec Ménandre; ou, Paul Demiéville revisité." *Journal Asiatique* 281, 61–138.

———. 1993b. "Taxila: The Central Asian Connection." In H. Spodek and D. M. Srinivasan, eds., *Urban Form and Meaning in South Asia: The Shaping of Cities from Prehistoric to Precolonial Times*, Studies in the History of Art, vol. 31, 83–100. Washington D.C.: National Gallery of Art.

———. 1996. "Southern Bactria and Northern India before Islam: A Review of Archaeo-logical Reports." *Journal of the American Oriental Society* 116, 243–59.

———. 2001. "L'inscription de Rabatak, la Bactriane et les Kouchans." In P. Leriche, C. Pidaev, M. Gelin, K. Abdoullaev, and V. Fourniau, eds., *La Bactriane au carrefour des routes et des civilisations de l'Asie centrale: Termez et les villes de Bactriane-Tokharestan. Actes du Colloque de Termez 1997*, La Bibliothèque d'Asie Centrale, vol. 1, 251–91. Paris: Maisonneuve et Larose and IFEAC.

Gardin, Jean-Claude. 1977. "The Study of Central Asiatic Pottery: Some Reflections on Pub-lication." *American Journal of Archaeology* 81, 80–81.

———. 1980. "L'archéologie du paysage bactrien." *Comptes-Rendus de l'Académie des Inscrip-tions et Belles-Lettres* 124, 480–501.

———. 1984. "Canal Irrigation in Bronze Age Eastern Bactria." In B. B. Lal and S. P. Gupta, eds., *Frontiers of the Indus Civilization: Sir Mortimer Wheeler Commemorative Volume*, 311–20. New Delhi: Indian Archaeological Society.

———. 1985. "Les relations entre la Méditerranée et la Bactriane dans l'antiquité, d'après des données céramologiques inédites." In J.-L. Huot, M. Yon, and Y. Calvet, eds., *De l'Indus aux Balkans: Recueil à la mémoire de Jean Deshayes*, 447–60. Paris: Editions Recherche sur les Civilisations.

———. 1990a. "La céramique hellénistique en Asie centrale: Problèmes d'interpretation." In *Akten des XIII. Internationalen Kongresses für klassische Archäologie, Berlin 1988*, 187–93. Mainz am Rhein: von Zabern.

———. 1990b. "Indicateurs archéologiques du nomadisme : Études de cas en Bactriane." In H.-P. Francfort, ed., *Nomades et sédentaires en Asie centrale: Apports de l'archéologie et de l'ethnologie. Actes du Colloque franco-soviétique, Alma Ata (Kazakhstan,) 17–26 octobre 1987*, 131–40. Paris: Éditions du CNRS.

———. 1998. *Prospections archéologiques en Bactriane orientale (1974–1978)*. Vol. 3, *Descrip-tion des sites et notes de synthèse*. Mémoires de la Mission Archéologique Française en Asie Centrale, vol. 9. Paris: Éditions Recherche sur les Civilisations.

Gardin, J.-C., and Pierre Gentelle. 1976. "Irrigation et peuplement dans la plaine d'Aï Kha-noum, de l'époque achéménide à l'époque musulmane." *Bulletin de l'École Française d'Extrême Orient* 63, 59–110.

———. 1979. "L'exploitation du sol en Bactriane antique." *Bulletin de l'École Française d'Extrême Orient* 66, 1–29.

Gardin, Jean-Claude, and Bertille Lyonnet. 1979. "La prospection archéologique de la Bac-triane orientale (1974–1978): Premiers résultats," *Mesopotamia* 13–14, 99–154

Gauthier, Henri. 1911–14. *Le temple de Kalabchah.* 2 vols. Les Temples Immergés de la Nubie. Cairo: Imprimerie de l'Institut Français d'Archéologie Orientale.

Gelin, Mathilde. 2010. *Daniel Schlumberger: L'Occident à la rencontre de l'Orient.* Damascus and Beirut: Institut Français du Proche-Orient.

Genito, Bruno, et al. 2009. [Bruno Genito, Alexej Gricina, Luciano Rendina, and Maria D'Angelo.] "The Achaemenid Period in the Samarkand Area (Sogdiana)." *Newsletter di Archeologia CISA,* 122–41.

———. 2010. [Bruno Genito, Alexej Gricina, Rahimov Kamill, and Luciano Rendina.] "The Achaemenid Period in the Samarkand Area (Sogdiana): Trial Trenches at Koj Tepa, 2009 Campaign." *Newsletter di Archeologia CISA* 1, 113–61.

Genito, Bruno, and Fabiana Raiano. 2011. "Ceramics from Koj Tepa (Samarkand Area, Uzbekistan): A Preliminary Study Report (2009–2010)." *Newsletter di Archeologia CISA* 2, 103–77.

Gentelle, Pierre. 1978. *Étude géographique de la plaine d'Aï Khanoum et de son irrigation depuis les temps antiques.* Publications de l'URA, vol. 10; Centre de Recherches Archéologiques, mémoire 2. Paris: Éditions du CNRS.

———. 1989. *Prospections archéologiques en Bactriane orientale (1974–1978).* Vol. 1, *Données paléogéographiques et fondements de l'irrigation.* Mémoires de la Mission Archéologique Française en Asie Centrale, vol. 3. Paris: de Boccard.

Ghosh, A. 1948. "Taxila (Sirkap), 1944–45," *Ancient India* 4, 41–84.

Gillie, Darsie. 1964. "A Coin That the Pillagers Missed." *Guardian* (11 July), 9.

———. 1965. "Site of Greek City Found in Central Asia." *Guardian* (22 Feb.), 13.

———. 1966. "Discoveries at Ancient Greek City." *Guardian* (14 Mar.), 21.

———. 1969. "Ai Khanoum God with Feet of Marble." *Guardian,* 30 July, 3.

Gombrich, R. F. 1988. *Theravāda Buddhism: A Social History from Ancient Benares to Modern Colombo.* Library of Religious Beliefs and Practices. London: Routledge and Kegan Paul.

Good, Irene. 2010. "Exploring Inner Asia's High Alpine Frontier: High Alpine Transhumant Pastoralism, Vertical Cultivation and Environmental Archaeology in the Lower Vakhsh-Panj Confluence and Gorno-Badakhshan Regions, Southern Tajikistan." In D. Frenez and M. Tosi, eds., *South Asian archaeology 2007: Proceedings of the 19th Meeting of the European Association of South Asian Archaeology in Ravenna, Italy, July 2007,* 107–16. Oxford: Archaeopress.

Gorshenina, Svetlana. 1999. [Svetlana Goršenina.] "Premiers pas des archéologues russes et français dans le Turkestan russe (1870–1890): Méthodes de recherche et destin des collections." *Cahiers du Monde Russe* 40, 365–84.

———. 2003. *Explorateurs en Asie centrale: Voyageurs et aventuriers de Marco Polo à Ella Maillart.* Geneva: Olizane.

———. 2004. *The Private Collections of Russian Turkestan in the Second Half of the 19th and Early 20th Century.* Berlin: Klaus Schwarz.

Gorshenina, Svetlana, and Claude Rapin. 2001. *Les archéologues en Asie centrale: De Kaboul à Samarcande.* Collection Découvertes Gallimard, série Archéologie, vol. 411. Paris: Gallimard.

Gosden, Chris, and Y. Marshall. 1999. "The Cultural Biography of Objects." *World Archaeology* 33, 169–78.

Goudriaan, Koen. 1988. *Ethnicity in Ptolemaic Egypt.* Dutch Monographs on Ancient History and Archaeology, vol. 5. Amsterdam: J. C. Gieben.

Graves-Brown, P., Sian Jones, and Clive Gamble, eds. 1996. *Cultural Identity and Archaeology: The Construction of European Communities.* London: Routledge.

Green, Peter, 1990. *Alexander to Actium: The Historical Evolution of the Hellenistic Age.* Berkeley and Los Angeles: University of California Press.

Grenet, Frantz. 1984. *Les pratiques funéraires dans l'Asie centrale sédentaire: De la conquête grecque à l'islamisation.* Publications de l'U.R.A., vol. 29; Centre de Recherches Archéologiques, mémoire 1. Paris: CNRS.

———. 1991. "Mithra au temple principal d'Aï Khanoum?" In P. Bernard and F. Grenet, eds., *Histoire et cultes de l'Asie centrale préislamique: Sources écrites et documents archéologiques. Actes du Colloque international du CNRS (Paris, 22–28 novembre 1988),* 147–51. Paris: Éditions du CNRS.

———. 1996. "Ασαγγωρνοις, Ασκισαγγοραγο, Sangchârak." *Topoi* 6, 470–74.

Grenet, Frantz, and Claude Rapin. 1998a. "Alexander, Aï Khanum, Termez: Remarks on the Spring Campaign of 328." *Bulletin of the Asia Institute* 12, 79–89.

———. 1998b. "De la Samarkand antique à la Samarkand islamique: Continuités et ruptures." In Roland-Pierre Gayraud, ed., *Colloque international d'archéologie islamique, IFAO, Le Caire, 3–7 février 1993,* Textes Arabes et Études Islamiques, vol. 36, 387–402. Cairo: Institut Français d'Archéologie Orientale.

Gruen, Erich S. 2001. "Jewish Perspectives on Greek Culture and Ethnicity." In Irad Malkin, ed., *Ancient Perceptions of Greek Ethnicity,* Center for Hellenic Studies, Colloquia, vol. 5, 347–73. Washington, D.C.: Center for Hellenic Studies and Trustees for Harvard University.

Guardian. 1953. "The Bactrian Greeks: Discoveries in Afghanistan." *Manchester Guardian* (Jan. 31).

———. 1958. "Greek Letter in Afghanistan: Valuable Archaeological Discovery." *Manchester Guardian* 7 (July 23).

Gubaev, A., G. Koshelenko, and M. Tosi, eds. 1998. *The Archaeological Map of the Murghab Delta: Preliminary Reports, 1990–95.* Istituto Italiano per l'Africa e l'Oriente, Centro Scavi e Richerche Archeologiche, Reports and Memoirs, series minor, vol. 3. Rome: Istituto Italiano per l'Africa e l'Oriente.

Guillaume, Olivier. 1983. *Fouilles d'Aï Khanoum.* Vol. 2, *Les propylées de la rue principale.* Mémoires de la Délegation Archéologique Française en Afghanistan, vol. 26. Paris: de Boccard.

———. 1990. *Analysis of Reasonings in Archaeology: The Case of Graeco-Bactrian and Indo-Greek Numismatics.* French Studies in South Asian Culture and Society, vol. 4. Delhi: Oxford University Press.

———. 1991. *Graeco-Bactrian and Indian Coins from Afghanistan.* French Studies in South Asian Culture and Society, vol. 5. Delhi: Oxford University Press.

Guillaume, Olivier, and Axelle Rougeulle. 1987. *Fouilles d'Aï Khanoum.* Vol. 7, *Les petits objets.* Mémoires de la Délegation Archéologique Française en Afghanistan, vol. 31. Paris: de Boccard.

Gurt, Josep Maria, et al. 2007. [Josep Maria Gurt, Shakir Pidaev, Anna Maria Rauret, and Sebastian Stride.] *Preliminary Report of the First Season of Work of the International Pluridisciplinary Archaeological Expedition to Bactria, 2006.* Barcelona: ERAUB.

————. 2008a. *Preliminary Report of the Work of the International Pluridisciplinary Archae-ological Expedition to Bactria, 2007.* Volume 2. Barcelona: ERAUB.

————. 2008b. *Preliminary Report of the Work of the International Pluridisciplinary Archae ological Expedition to Bactria, 2008.* Volume 3. Barcelona: ERAUB.

Gurt, Josep Maria, and Shakir Pidaev. 2009. *Preliminary Report of the Work of the Interna-tional Pluridisciplinary Archaeological Expedition to Bactria, 2009.* Volume 5. Barcelona: ERAUB.

Hackin, J. 1939. *Recherches archéologiques à Begram.* Mémoires de la Délégation Archéologique Française en Afghanistan, vol. 9. Paris: Les Éditions d'Art et d'Histoire.

————. 1940a. "The 1939 Dig at Begram, I." *Asia* 40, 525–28.

————. 1940b. "The 1939 Dig at Begram, II." *Asia* 40, 608–12.

————. 1954. *Nouvelles recherches archéologiques à Begram.* Mémoires de la Délégation Archéologique Française en Afghanistan, vol. 11. Paris: Imprimerie Nationale–Presses Universitaires.

Hakenbeck, Susanne. 2008. "Migration in Archaeology: Are We Nearly There Yet?" *Archae-ological Review from Cambridge* 23, 9–26.

Hall, Edith, and Phiroze Vasunia, eds. 2010. *India, Greece, and Rome, 1757 to 2007.* Bulletin of the Institute of Classical Studies, supplement 108. London: Institute of Classical Stud-ies, School of Advanced Study, University of London.

Hall, Jonathan M. 1997. *Ethnic Identity in Greek Antiquity.* Cambridge: Cambridge Univer-sity Press.

————. 2002. *Hellenicity: Between Ethnicity and Culture.* Chicago: University of Chicago Press.

Hallock, Richard T. 1969. *Persepolis Fortification Tablets.* University of Chicago Oriental Institute Publications, vol. 92. Chicago: University of Chicago Press.

Hannestad, L., and D. Potts. 1990. "Temple Architecture in the Seleucid Kingdom." In P. Bilde et al., eds., *Religion and Religious Practice in the Seleucid Kingdom,* Studies in Hel-lenistic Civilization, vol. 1, 91–124. Aarhus: Aarhus University Press.

Hardwick, Lorna, and Carol Gillespie, eds. 2007. *Classics in Post-Colonial Worlds.* Classical Presences. Oxford: Oxford University Press.

Harmatta, J. 1994. "Languages and Scripts in Graeco-Bactria and the Saka Kingdoms." In J. Harmatta, B. N. Puri, and G. F. Etemadi, eds., *History of the Civilizations of Central Asia,* vol. 2, *The Development of Sedentary and Nomadic Civilizations: 700 B.C. to A.D. 250,* 386–406. Paris: UNESCO.

Härtel, H. 1993. *Excavations at Sonkh: 2500 Years of a Town in Mathura District.* Monogra-phien zur indischen Archäologie, Kunst und Philologie, vol. 9. Berlin: D. Reimer. [With contributions by H.-J. Paech and R. Weber.]

Heckel, Waldemar, and J. C. Yardley. 2008. *Alexander the Great: Historical Sources in Trans-lation.* Blackwell Sourcebooks in Ancient History. Oxford: Blackwell.

Helms, S. W. 1979. "Old Kandahar Excavations, 1976: Preliminary Report." *Afghan Studies* 2, 1–8.

————. 1982. "Excavations at 'the City and the Famous Fortress of Kandahar, the Foremost Place in all of Asia.'" *Afghan Studies* 3–4, 1–24.

————. 1997. *Excavations at Old Kandahar in Afghanistan 1976–1978 Conducted on Behalf of the Society for South Asian Studies (Society for Afghan Studies): Stratigraphy, Pottery and*

Other Finds. BAR International Series, no. 686; Society for South Asian Studies, monograph 2. Oxford: Archaeopress.

Henning, W. B. 1949. "The Aramaic Inscription of Asoka Found in Lampāka." *Bulletin of the School of Oriental and African Studies* 13, 80–88.

Herrmann, Georgina, V. M. Masson, and K. Kurbansakhatov. 1993. "The International Merv Project: Preliminary Report on the First Season, 1992." *Iran* 31, 39–62.

Hiebert, Fredrik, and Pierre Cambon, eds. 2008. *Afghanistan: Hidden Treasures from the National Museum, Kabul.* Washington, D.C.: National Geographic Society.

———. 2011. *Afghanistan: Crossroads of the Ancient World.* London: British Museum Press.

Hollis, Adrian S. 1996. "Addendum to J. R. Rea, R. C. Senior and A. S. Hollis, 'A Tax Receipt from Hellenistic Bactria,' ZPE 104, 1994, 261–280." *Zeitschrift für Papyrologie und Epigraphik* 110, 164.

———. 2011. "Greek Letters in Hellenistic Bactria." In Dirk Obbink and Richard Rutherford, eds., *Culture in Pieces: Essays on Ancient Texts in Honour of Peter Parsons,* 104–18. Oxford: Oxford University Press.

Holt, Frank L. 1984. "The So-Called 'Pedigree Coins' of the Bactrian Greeks." In Waldemar Heckel and Richard Sullivan, eds., *Ancient Coins of the Graeco-Roman World: The Nickle Numismatic Papers,* 69–91. Waterloo, Ont.: Wilfrid Laurier University Press for the Calgary Institute for the Humanities.

———. 1987. "Hellenistic Bactria: Beyond the Mirage." *Ancient World* 15, 3–15.

———. 1988. *Alexander the Great and Bactria: The Formation of a Greek Frontier in Central Asia.* Mnemosyne Supplements, vol. 104. Leiden and New York: E. J. Brill.

———. 1993. "Response to S. M. Burstein." In Peter Green, ed., *Hellenistic History and Culture,* Hellenistic Culture and Society, vol. 11, 54–64. Berkeley and Los Angeles: University of California Press.

———. 1999a. "Mimesis in Metal: The Fate of Greek Culture on Bactrian Coins." In F. B. Titchener and R. F. Moorton, eds., *The Eye Expanded: Life and the Arts in Greco-Roman Antiquity,* 93–104. Berkeley and Los Angeles: University of California Press.

———. 1999b. *Thundering Zeus: The Making of Hellenistic Bactria.* Hellenistic Culture and Society, vol. 32. Berkeley and Los Angeles: University of California Press.

———. 2005. *Into the Land of Bones: Alexander the Great in Afghanistan.* Hellenistic Culture and Society, vol. 47. Berkeley and Los Angeles: University of California Press.

———. 2012. "When Did the Greeks Abandon Aï Khanoum?" *Anabasis: Studia Classica et Orientalia* 3, 161–72.

Horner, I. B. 1954–59. *The Collection of the Middle Length Sayings (Majjhima-nikāya).* 3 vols. Pali Text Society, Translation Series, vols. 29–31. London: Pali Text Society.

Inagaki, Hajime. 2002. *Treasures of Ancient Bactria: Catalog of an Exhibition Held at the Miho Museum, Aug. 18–Sept. 1, 2002.* Shigaraki: Miho Museum.

Irwin, J. 1975–76. "The Heliodorus Pillar at Besnagar." *Purātattva* 8, 166–76.

Isamiddinov, Muhammadjon. 2010. "Стратиграфия городища Коктепа и некоторые вопросы истории и культуры Согдианы Эллинистического периода." In Kazim Abdullaev, ed., *Традиции Востока и Запада в Античной Культуре Средней Азии: Сборник Статей в Честь Поля Бернара,* Институт Археологии Имени Я. Гулямова Академии Наук Республикии Узбекистан, 131–40. Tashkent: Noshirlik yog'dusi. ["Stratigraphy of the Koktepa Site and Certain Aspects of History and Culture of Sogdia in the Hellenistic Period." In Kazim Abdullaev, ed., *The Traditions of East and West in the Antique Cultures of Central Asia: Papers in Honor of Paul Bernard*, Institute of Archaeology, Academy of Sciences of the Republic of Uzbekistan, 131–40.]

Ivantchik, Askold I. 2011. "Новые греческие надписи из Тахти-Сангина и проблема возникновения бактрийской письменности." *Вестник Древней Истории*, 110-31. ["A New Greek Inscription and the Problem of Bactrian Writing." *Vestnik Drevnei Istorii*, 110–31.]

Jaiswal, S. 1967. *The Origin and Development of Vaiṣṇavism: Vaiṣṇavism from 200 B.C. to A.D. 500*. Delhi: Munshiram Manoharlal.

Jones, Sian. 1998. *The Archaeology of Ethnicity: Constructing Identities in the Past and Present*. London: Routledge.

Kabul Times. 1964. "Archaeologists Find 2300 Year Old Greek City in Northern Afghanistan." *Kabul Times* (20 Dec.), 3.

Karttunen, K. 1989. *India in Early Greek Literature*. Studia Orientalia, vol. 65. Helsinki: Finnish Oriental Society.

———. 1994. "Yonas, Yavanas, and Related Matter in Indian Epigraphy." In A. Parpola and P. Koskikallio, eds., *South Asian Archaeology 1993: Proceedings of the Twelfth International Conference of the European Association of South Asian Archaeologists*, Annales Academiae Scientiarum Fennicae, series B, vol. 271, 329–36. Helsinki: Suomalainen Tiedeakatemia.

———. 1997. *India and the Hellenistic World*. Studia Orientalia, vol. 83. Helsinki: Finnish Oriental Society.

Khan, N. A. 1990. "A New Relief from Gandhāra Depicting the Trojan Horse." *East and West* 40, 315–19.

Khare, M. D. 1966. "Discovery of a Vishṇu Temple near the Heliodoros Pillar, Besnagar, Dist. Vidisha (M.P.)." *Lalit Kalā* 13, 21–27.

———. 1975-76. "Comments on Irwin (1975–76)." *Purātattva* 8, 176–78.

———. 1989. "Besnagar." In A. Ghosh, ed., *An Encyclopaedia of Indian Archaeology*, 62. New Delhi: Munshiram Manoharlal.

Killingley, D. 1997. "*Mlecchas*, Yavanas and Heathens: Interacting Xenologies in Early Nineteenth-Century Calcutta." In E. Franco and K. Preisendanz, eds., *Beyond Orientalism: The Work of Wilhelm Halbfass and Its Impact on Indian and Cross-Cultural Studies*, 123–40. Amsterdam and Atlanta: Rodopi.

Klejn, Lev S. 1997. *Das Phänomen der sowjetischen Archäologie: Geschichte, Schulen, Protagonisten*. Gesellschaften und Staaten im Epochenwandel, vol. 6. Frankfurt am Main and New York: P. Lang.

Kohl, Philip L. 2002. "Archaeological Transformations: Crossing the Pastoral/Agricultural Bridge." *Iranica Antiqua* 37, 151–90.

———. 2007. *The Making of Bronze Age Eurasia*. Cambridge World Archaeology. Cambridge: Cambridge University Press.

Konow, Sten. 1929. *Corpus Inscriptionum Indicarum*. Vol. 2, part 1, *Kharoshthi Inscriptions: Inscriptions with the Exception of Those of Aśoka*. Calcutta: Government of India.

Kopsacheili, Maria. 2011. "Hybridisation of Palatial Architecture: Hellenistic Royal Palaces and Governors' Seats." In Anna Kouremenos, Sujatha Chandrasekaran, and Roberto Rossi, eds., *From Pella to Gandhara: Hybridisation and Identity in the Art and Architecture of the Hellenistic East*, BAR International Series, no. 2221, 17–34. Oxford: BAR.

Kopytoff, Igor. 1986. "The Cultural Biography of Things: Commodotization as Process." In Arjun Appadurai, ed., *The Social Life of Things: Commodities in Cultural Perspective*, 64–91. Cambridge: Cambridge University Press.

Kristiansen, Kristian. 2005. "Theorising Diffusion and Population Movements." In Colin Renfrew and Paul Bahn, eds., *Archaeology: The Key Concepts*, 56–59. London: Routledge.

Kruglikova, I. T., ed. 1976. *Древняя Бактия: Материалы Советско-Афганской экспедиции 1969–1973 гг.* Moscow: Nauka. [*Ancient Bactria: Material from the Soviet-Afghan Archaeological Expedition / Drevnyaya Baktriya: Materialy Sovetsko-Afganskoi arkheologicheskoi ekspeditsii, 1969–1973.*]

———. 1977. "Les fouilles de la mission archéologique soviéto-afghane sur le site gréco-kushan de Dilberdjin en Bactriane (Afghanistan)." *Comptes-Rendus de l'Académie des Inscriptions et Belles-Lettres*, 407–27.

———. 1979. *Древняя Бактия.* Vol. 2, *Материалы Советско-Афганской археологической экспедиции.* Moscow: Nauka. [*Ancient Bactria.* Vol. 2, *Material from the Soviet-Afghan Archaeological Expedition / Drevnyaya Baktriya: Materialy Sovetsko-Afganskoi arkheologicheskoi ekspeditsii.*]

———. 1984. *Древняя Бактия.* Vol. 3, *Материалы Советско-Афганской археологической экспедиции.* Moscow: Nauka. [*Ancient Bactria.* Vol. 3, *Material from the Soviet-Afghan Archaeological Expedition / Drevnyaya Baktriya: Materialy Sovetsko-Afganskoi arkheologicheskoi ekspeditsii.*]

Kruglikova, I. T., and G. A. Pugachenkova. 1977. *Дильберджин (раскопки 1970–1973 гг).* Часть 2. Матерналы к археологической карте Северного Афганистана, выпуск 3. Moscow: Nauka. [*Dil'berdzhin: Finds 1970–1973*, part 2. Materials for an Archaeological Map of Northern Afghanistan, vol. 3.]

Kuhrt, Amélie. 2007. *The Persian Empire: A Corpus of Sources from the Achaemenid Period.* London: Routledge.

Kuz'mina, E. E. 1976. "The 'Bactrian Mirage' and the Archaeological Reality: On the Problem of the Formation of North Bactrian Culture." *East and West* 26, 111–31.

Lecuyot, Guy, ed. 2013. *Fouilles d'Aï Khanoum.* Vol. 9, *L'habitat.* Mémoires de la Délégation Archéologique Française en Afghanistan, vol. 34. Paris: de Boccard.

Leo, John. 1999. "Tower of Pomobabble." *U.S. News & World Report* (15 Mar.), 16.

Leriche, Pierre. 1986. *Fouilles d'Aï Khanoum.* Vol. 5, *Les remparts et les monuments associés.* Mémoires de la Délégation Archéologique Française en Afghanistan, vol. 29. Paris: de Boccard.

Leriche, P., et al., eds. 2001. [C. Pidaev, M. Gelin, K. Abdoullaev, and V. Fourniau.] *La Bactriane au carrefour des routes et des civilisations de l'Asie centrale: Termez et les villes de Bactriane-Tokharestan. Actes du Colloque de Termez 1997.* La Bibliothèque d'Asie Centrale, vol. 1. Paris: Maisonneuve and Larose and IFEAC.

Leriche, Pierre, and Chakirjan Pidaev. 2008. *Termez sur Oxus: Cité-capitale d'Asie centrale.* Publication AURORHE 3. Paris: Maisonneuve et Larose.

Leriche, Pierre, and Shakir Pidaev. 2001. "L'action de la Mission Archéologique Franco-Ouzbèque de Bactriane." *Cahiers d'Asie Centrale* 9, 243–48.

———. 2007. "Termez in Antiquity." In Joe Cribb and Georgina Herrmann, eds., *After Alexander: Central Asia before Islam,* Proceedings of the British Academy, vol. 133, 179–211. Oxford: Oxford University Press for the British Academy.

Leriche, Pierre, and Joël Thoraval. 1979. "La fontaine du rempart de l'Oxus à Aï Khanoum." *Syria* 56, 171–205.

Lerner, Jeffrey D. 2003. "The Aï Khanoum Philosophical Papyrus." *Zeitschrift für Papyrologie und Epigraphik* 142, 45–51.

———. 2003–4. "Correcting the Early History of Ay Kanom." *Archäologische Mitteilungen aus Iran und Turan* 35–36, 373–410.

———. 2011. "A Re-Appraisal of the Economic Inscriptions and Coin Finds from Ai Khanoum." *Anabasis: Studia Classica et Orientalia* 2, 103–47.

Lézire, A. 1964. "Hérat: Notes de voyage." *Bulletin d'Études Orientales* 18, 127–45.

Liger, J.-C. 1979. "La physionomie urbaine d'une cité hellénistique en Asie centrale." Unpublished maîtrise thesis, Département d'Urbanisme, Université de Paris VIII.

Litvinskii, Boris A. 1998. [Boris A. Litvinskij.] *La civilisation de l'Asie centrale antique.* Archäologie in Iran und Turan, vol. 3. Rahden: Leidorf.

———. 2001. *Храм Окса в Бактрии (Южный Таджикистан).* Vol. 2, *Бактрийское Вооружение в Древневосточном и Греческом Контексте.* Moscow: Vostochnaya Literatura. [*The Temple of the Oxus in Bactria (Southern Tadzhikistan). Vol. 2, Bactrian Arms in the Ancient Eastern and Greek Context.*]

Litvinskii, B. A., and K. Mukhitdinov. 1969. "Античное Городище Саксанохур (Южный Таджикистан)." *Советская Археология,* 160–78. ["The Ancient Site of Saksanokhur (Southern Tadzhikistan)." *Sovyetskaya Arkheologiya,* 160–78.]

Litvinskii, B. A., and I. R. Pichikiyan. 1981. [B. A. Litvinskiy and I. R. Pichikiyan.] "The Temple of the Oxus." *Journal of the Royal Asiatic Society,* 133–67.

———. 1995. "River-Deities of Greece Salute the God of the River Oxus-Vaksh: Achelous and the Hippocampess." In A. Invernizzi, ed., *In the Land of the Gryphons: Papers on Central Asian Archaeology in Antiquity,* Monografie di Mesopotamia, vol. 5, 129–49. Florence: Casa Editrice Le Lettere.

———. 2000. [B. A. Litvinskij and I. R. Pičikian.] *Эллинистический Храм Окса в Бактрии (Южный Таджикистан).* Vol. 1, *Раскопки, Архитектура, Религиозная Жизнь.* Moscow: Vostochnaya Literatura. [*The Hellenistic Temple of the Oxus in Bactria (Southern Tadzhikistan). Vol. 1, Excavations, Architecture, Religious Life.*]

———. 2002. *Taxt-i Sangin, der Oxus-Tempel: Grabungsbefund, Stratigraphie und Architektur.* Archäologie in Iran und Turan, vol. 4. Mainz am Rhein: von Zabern.

Litvinskii, B. A., Y. G. Vinogradov, and I. R. Pichikyan. 1985. "Вотив Атросока из Храма Окса в Северной Бактрии." *Вестник Древней Истории,* 85–110. ["The Votive Offering of Atrosokes from the Temple of the Oxus in Northern Bactria." *Vestnik Drevnei Istorii,* 85–110.]

Lougovaya, Julia. 2009. "Review of A. Chaniotis, T. Corsten, R. S. Stroud, R. A. Tybout, eds., *Supplementum Epigraphicum Graecum, Volume LIV (2004).* Leiden/Boston: Brill, 2008." *Bryn Mawr Classical Review* 2009.11.24.

Lundbæk, Knud. 1986. *T. S. Bayer, 1694–1738: Pioneer Sinologist.* Scandinavian Institute of Asian Studies Monograph Series, vol. 54. London: Curzon Press.

Lunin, Boris Vladimirovich. 1958. *Из истории русского востоковедения и археологии в Туркестане: Туркестанский кружок любителей археологии (1895—1917 гг.).* Tashkent: Izdvo Akademiya Nauk Uzbekskoi SSR. [*From the History of Russian Oriental Studies and Archaeology in Turkestan: The Turkestan Circle of Amateurs of Archaeology (1895-1917).*]

Lyonnet, Bertille. 1991. "Les nomades et la chute du royaume gréco-bactrien: Quelques nou-veaux indices en provenance de l'Asie centrale orientale. Vers l'identification des Tokhares—Yueh-Chi?" In Paul Bernard and Frantz Grenet, eds., *Histoire et cultes de l'Asie centrale préislamique: Sources écrites et documents archéologiques. Actes du Colloque international du CNRS (Paris, 22–28 novembre 1988)*, 153–61. Paris: Éditions du CNRS.

———. 1993. "The Problem of the Frontiers between Bactria and Sogdiana: An Old Discus-sion and New Data." In A. J. Gail and G. J. R. Mevissen, eds., *South Asian Archaeology 1991*, 195–208. Stuttgart: Franz Steiner.

———. 1997. *Prospections archéologiques en Bactriane orientale (1974–1978)*. Vol. 2, *Céramique et peuplement du chalcolithique à la conquête arabe*. Mémoires de la Mission Archéologique Française en Asie Centrale. Paris: Éditions Recherche sur les Civilisa-tions.

———. 1998. "Les Grecs, les nomades et l'indépendance de la Sogdiane, d'après l'occupation comparée d'Aï Khanoum et de Marakanda au cours des derniers siècles avant notre ère." *Bulletin of the Asia Institute* 12, 141–59.

———. 2010. "D'Aï Khanoum à Koktepe: Questions sur la datation absolue de la céramique hellénistique d'Asie centrale." In Kazim Abdullaev, ed., Традиции Востока и Запада в Античной Культуре Средней Азии: Сборник Статей в Честь Поля Бернара, Институт Археологии Имени Я. Гулямова Академии Наук Республики Узбекистан, 141–53. Tashkent: Noshirlik Yog'dusi. [In Kazim Abdullaev, ed., *The Tradi-tions of East and West in the Antique Cultures of Central Asia: Papers in Honor of Paul Bernard*, Institute of Archaeology, Academy of Sciences of the Republic of Uzbekistan, 141–53.]

MacDowall, David W. 2003–4. "Heliocles I the Greek King of Bactria." *Numismatic Digest* 27–28, 31–38.

Mairs, Rachel. 2006a. "Ethnic Identity in the Hellenistic Far East." Unpublished PhD thesis, Faculty of Classics, University of Cambridge.

———. 2006b. "Hellenistic India." *New Voices in Classical Reception* 1, 19–30.

———. 2007. "Ethnicity and Funerary Practice in Hellenistic Bactria." In H. Schroeder, P. Bray, P. Gardner, V. Jefferson, and E. Macaulay-Lewis, eds., *Crossing Frontiers: The Opportunities and Challenges of Interdisciplinary Approaches to Archaeology*, Oxford University School of Archaeology Monographs, vol. 63, 111–24. Oxford: School of Archaeology.

———. 2008. "Greek Identity and the Settler Community in Hellenistic Bactria and Ara-chosia." *Migrations and Identities* 1, 19–43.

———. 2009. "The 'Greek Grid-Plan' at Sirkap (Taxila) and the Question of Greek Influence in the North West." In Michael Willis, ed., *Migration, Trade and Peoples: European Asso-ciation of South Asian Archaeologists, Proceedings of the Eighteenth Congress, London, 2005*, 135–47. London: The British Association for South Asian Studies and The British Academy.

———. 2010. "An 'Identity Crisis'? Identity and Its Discontents in Hellenistic Studies." In Jennifer E. Gates-Foster, ed., "Beyond Identity in the Hellenistic East," in M. Dalla Riva, ed., *Meetings between Cultures in the Ancient Mediterranean: Proceedings of the 17th International Congress of Classical Archaeology, Rome, 22–26 Sept. 2008*. Rome. [Availa ble at *Bolletino di Archeologia* online.]

——. 2011a. "Acrostich Inscriptions at Kalabsha (Roman Talmis): Cultural Identities and Literary Games." *Chronique d'Égypte* 86, 281–97.

——. 2011b. *The Archaeology of the Hellenistic Far East, a Survey: Bactria, Central Asia and the Indo-Iranian Borderlands, c. 300 BC–AD 100.* British Archaeological Reports, International Series, no. 2196. Oxford: BAR.

——. 2011c. "The Places in Between: Model and Metaphor in the Archaeology of Hellenistic Arachosia." In Anna Kouremenos, Sujatha Chandrasekaran, and Roberto Rossi, eds., *From Pella to Gandhara: Hybridisation and Identity in the Art and Architecture of the Hellenistic East,* BAR International Series, no. 2221, 177–89. Oxford: BAR.

——. 2012. "*Sopha Grammata*: Greek Acrostichs in Inscriptions from Arachosia, Nubia and Libya." In Jan Kwapisz, David Petrain, and Mikołaj Szymański, eds., *The Muse at Play: Riddles and Wordplay in Greek and Latin Poetry,* Beiträge zur Altertumskunde, vol. 305, 279–306. Berlin: De Gruyter.

——. 2013a. "Greek Settler Communities in Central and South Asia, 323 BC–AD 10." In Girish Daswani and Ato Quayson, eds., *A Companion to Diaspora and Transnationalism,* 443–54. Oxford: Blackwell.

——. 2013b. "The Hellenistic Far East: From the *Oikoumene* to the Community." In Eftychia Stavrianopoulou, ed., *Shifting Social Imaginaries in the Hellenistic Period: Narratives, Practices, and Images,* Mnemosyne Supplements, vol. 363, 365–85. Leiden: Brill.

——. 2013c. "The 'Temple with Indented Niches' at Ai Khanoum: Ethnic and Civic Identity in Hellenistic Bactria." In Richard Alston, Onno M. van Nijf, and Christina G. Williamson, eds., *Cults, Creeds and Identities in the Greek City after the Classical Age,* Groningen–Royal Holloway Studies on the Greek City after the Classical Age, vol. 3, 85–111. Leuven: Peeters.

——. 2014a. "The Founder Shrine and the 'Foundation' of Ai Khanoum." In Naoíse Mac Sweeney, ed., *Foundation Myths in Dialogue: Discourses about Origins in Ancient Societies,* 103–28. Philadelphia: University of Pennsylvania Press.

——. 2014b. "Models, Moulds and Mass Production: The Mechanics of Stylistic Influence from the Mediterranean to Bactria." *Ancient West & East* 13, 175–95.

——. 2014c. "The Reception of T. S. Bayer's *Historia Regni Graecorum Bactriani* (1738)." *Anabasis: Studia Classica et Orientalia* 4, 255–62.

——. Forthcoming 1. "Heliodotos and Heliodoros: Identity and Ambiguity in Two Inscriptions from the Hellenistic Far East." In *Cultural Encounters in Near Eastern History,*. Copenhagen.

——. Forthcoming 2. "Heroes and Philosophers? Greek Personal Names and Their Bearers in Hellenistic Bactria." In *The Silk Road: Interwoven History,* vol. 1, *Long-Distance Trade, Culture and People.*

——. Forthcoming 3. "The Indo-Greek Cultural Encounter: Comparative Approaches." In Nawaz Mody, ed., *Indo-Hellenic Cultural Transactions.* Mumbai: K. R. Cama Institute.

——. Forthcoming 4. "'Proclaiming It to Greeks and Natives, along the Rows of the Chequer-Board': Readers and Viewers of Greek, Latin and Demotic Acrostich Inscriptions." In Niv Allon and Julia Hseih, eds., *Double Stories, Double Lives: Contextualizing Inscribed Objects in the Pre-Print World.* New York: Gorgias Press.

Malkin, Irad, ed. 2001. *Ancient Perceptions of Greek Ethnicity.* Center for Hellenic Studies, Colloquia, vol. 5. Washington, D.C.: Center for Hellenic Studies and Trustees for Harvard University.

Mandelbaum, D. G. 1970. *Society in India.* Berkeley and Los Angeles: University of California Press.

Marshall, J. H. 1909. "Notes on Archaeological Exploration in India, 1908–9." *Journal of the Royal Asiatic Society,* 1053–56.

———. 1951. *Taxila: An Illustrated Account.* Cambridge: Cambridge University Press.

———. 1960. *A Guide to Taxila.* Cambridge: Cambridge University Press.

McNicoll, A. 1978. "Excavations at Kandahar, 1975: Second Interim Report." *Afghan Studies* 1, 41–66.

McNicoll, A., and W. Ball. 1996. *Excavations at Kandahar 1974 and 1975: The First Two Seasons at Shahr-i Kohna (Old Kandahar) Conducted by the British Institute of Afghan Studies.* BAR International Series, no. 641. Society for South Asian Studies Monograph 1. Oxford: Tempus Reparatum.

Mendelsohn, Daniel, trans. 2012. *C. P. Cavafy: Complete Poems.* New York: Alfred A. Knopf.

Millard, Alan. 2003. "Aramaic Documents of the Assyrian and Achaemenid Periods." In Maria Brosius, ed., *Ancient Archives and Archival Traditions: Concepts of Record-Keeping in the Ancient World,* Oxford Studies in Ancient Documents, 230–40. Oxford: Oxford University Press.

Millett, Martin. 1990. *The Romanization of Britain: An Essay in Archaeological Interpretation.* Cambridge: Cambridge University Press.

Mongait, A. L. 1961. *Archaeology in the U.S.S.R.* Harmondsworth: Penguin.

Mordvintseva, Valentina. 2010. "Tillya-Tepe Gold Jewellery and Its Relation to the Sarmatian Animal Style of the Northern Black Sea Area." In *Studies in Memory of Józef Wolski,* ed. M. J. Olbrycht, *Anabasis: Studia Classica et Orientalia* 1, 175–207.

Mukhitdinov, K. 1968. "Гончарный квартал городища Саксанохур." *Известия Академии Наук Таджикской ССР: Серия общественных наук* 3, 53. ["The Potters' Quarter at the Site of Saksanokhur." *Izvestiya Akademii Nauk Tadzhikskoi SSR, Social Sciences Series,* 3, 53.]

Nagle, D. Brendan, and Stanley M. Burstein. 2006. *Readings in Greek History: Sources and Interpretations.* Oxford: Oxford University Press.

Ñānamoli, B., ed. 1991. *The Dispeller of Delusion (Sammohavinodanī).* Part 2. Sacred Books of the Buddhists, vol. 41. Oxford: Pali Text Society.

Narain, A. K. 1957. *The Indo-Greeks.* Oxford: Clarendon Press.

———. 1987. "On the Foundation and Chronology of Ai-Khanum, A Greek-Bactrian City." In Gilbert Pollet, ed., *India and the Ancient World: History Trade, and Culture before A.D. 650,* Orientalia Lovaniensia Analecta, vol. 25, 115–30. Leuven: Departement Oriëntalistiek.

Naveh, Joseph, and Shaul Shaked. 2012. *Aramaic Documents from Ancient Bactria (Fourth Century B.C.E.) from the Khalili Collections.* Studies in the Khalili Collection. London: The Khalili Family Trust.

Nehru, Lolita. 1999–2000. "Khalchayan Revisited." *Silk Road Art and Archaeology* 6, 217–39.

Nielsen, I. 1994. *Hellenistic Palaces: Tradition and Renewal.* Studies in Hellenistic Civilization, vol. 5. Aarhus: Aarhus University Press. [2nd ed. 1999.]

———. 2001a. "The Gardens of Hellenistic Palaces." In Inge Nielsen, ed., *The Royal Palace Institution in the First Millennium BC: Regional Development and Cultural Interchange between East and West,* Monographs of the Danish Institute at Athens, 165–87. Athens and Aarhus: The Danish Institute at Athens and Aarhus University Press.

———, ed. 2001b. *The Royal Palace Institution in the First Millennium BC: Regional Development and Cultural Interchange between East and West.* Monographs of the Danish Institute at Athens. Athens and Aarhus: The Danish Institute at Athens and Aarhus University Press.

The Observer. 1966. "Desert Booty." *The Observer* 40 (Feb. 20).

Oikonomides, A. N. 1984. "A Little-Known Poem by C. P. Cavafy: *Coins with Indian Inscriptions.*" *Ancient World* 9, 35–37.

Olivelle, Patrick. 2004. *Manu's Code of Law: A Critical Edition and Translation of the Mānava-Dharmaśāstra.* South Asia Research. Cary, N.C.: Oxford University Press.

Olivier-Utard, F. 1997. *Politique et archéologie: Histoire de la Délégation archéologique française en Afghanistan (1922–1982).* Paris: Éditions Recherche sur les Civilisations.

Parasher, A. 1991. *Mlecchas in Early India: A Study in Attitudes towards Outsiders up to AD 600.* New Delhi: Munshiram Manoharlal.

Parasher-Sen, Aloka. 2006. "Naming and Social Exclusion: The Outcast and the Outsider." In Patrick Olivelle, ed., *Between the Empires: Society in India, 300 BCE to 400 CE,* 415–55. Oxford: Oxford University Press.

Picard, O. 1984. "Sur deux termes des inscriptions de la trésorerie d'Aï Khanoum." In Hélène Walter, ed., *Hommages à Lucien Lerat,* vol. 2, Annales Littéraires de l'Université de Besançon, vol. 294; Centre de Recherches d'Histoire Ancienne, vol. 55, 679–90. Paris: Les Belles lettres.

Pidaev, S. R. 1974. "Материалы к изучению древних памятников Северной Бактрии." In V. M. Masson, ed., *Древняя Бактрия: Предварительные сообщения об археологических работах на юге Узбекистана,* 32–41. Leningrad: Nauka. ["Materials for the Study of Ancient Monuments in Northern Bactria." *Drevnyaya Baktriya: Predvaritel'nye soobshcheniya ob arkheologicheskikh rabotakh na yuge Uzbekistana,* 32–41.]

———. 1984. "Керамика Джига-тепе (из раскопок 1976 г.)." In I. T. Kruglikova, ed., *Древняя Бактия,* vol. 3, *Материалы Советско-Афганской археологической экспедиции,* 112–24. Moscow: Nauka. ["Ceramics of Dzhiga-tepe (from the 1976 Excavations)." In I. T. Kruglikova, ed., *Drevnyaya Baktriya,* vol. 3, *Materialy Sovetsko-Afganskoi arkheologicheskoi ekspeditsii,* 112–24.]

Pinault, Georges-Jean. 2005. "Remarques sur les noms propres d'origine indienne dans la stèle de Sôphytos." In Osmund Bopearachchi and Marie-Françoise Boussac, eds., *Afghanistan: Ancien carrefour entre l'est et l'ouest,* Indicopleustoi: Archaeologies of the Indian Ocean, vol. 3, 137–42. Turnhout: Brepols.

Pitschikjan, I. R. 1992. *Oxos-Schatz und Oxus-Tempel: Achämenidische Kunst in Mittelasien.* Antike in der Moderne, vol. 1. Berlin: Akademie Verlag.

Pitts, Martin. 2007. "The Emperor's New Clothes? The Utility of Identity in Roman Archaeology." *American Journal of Archaeology* 111, 693–713.

Porten, Bezalel, and Ada Yardeni. 1986–. *Textbook of Aramaic Documents from Egypt.* Winona Lake: Eisenbrauns.

Porter, Anne. 2011. *Mobile Pastoralism and the Formation of Near Eastern Civilizations: Weaving Together Society.* Cambridge: Cambridge University Press.

Posch, Walter. 1995. *Baktrien zwischen Griechen und Kuschan: Untersuchungen zu kulturellen und historischen Problemen einer Übergangsphase, mit einem textkritischen Exkurs zum Shiji 123*. Wiesbaden: Harrassowitz.

Pugachenkova, G. A. 1965. [G. A. Pougatchenkova.] "La sculpture de Khaltchayan." *Iranica Antiqua* 5, 116–27.

———. 1971. *Скульптура Халчаяна*. Moscow: Iskusstvo. [*The Sculpture of Khalchayan*.]

———. 1978. [G. A. Pougatchenkova.] *Les trésors de Dalverzine-Tépé*. Leningrad: Éditions d'Art Aurore.

———. 1979. "Жига-тепе (раскопки 1974 г.)." In I. T. Kruglikova, ed., *Древняя Бактия*, vol. 2, *Материалы Советско-Афганской Археологической Экспедиции*, 63–94. Moscow: Nauka. ["Zhiga-tepe (Excavations 1974)." In I. T. Kruglikova, ed., *Drevnyaya Baktriya*, vol. 2, *Materialy Sovetsko-Afganskoi arkheologicheskoi ekspeditsii*, 63–94.]

———. 1990. [G. A. Pougatchenkova.] "La culture de la Bactriane du nord." In E. Kiessling and M. A. Rupprecht, eds., *Akten des XIII. Internationalen Kongresses für klassische Archäologie, Berlin, 1988*, 61–66. Mainz am Rhein: von Zabern.

———. 2001a. [G. A. Pougatchenkova.] "C'était hier; c'était il y a longtemps: Souvenirs d'une participante à l'expédition archéologique de Termez en 1938." In P. Leriche, C. Pidaev, M. Gelin, K. Abdoullaev, and V. Fourniau, eds., *La Bactriane au carrefour des routes et des civilisations de l'Asie centrale: Termez et les villes de Bactriane-Tokharestan. Actes du Colloque de Termez 1997*, La Bibliothèque d'Asie Centrale, vol. 1, 37–46. Paris: Maisonneuve et Larose.

———. 2001b. [G. A. Pougatchenkova.] "Histoire des recherches archéologiques en Bactriane septentrionale: Région du Sourkhan Darya, Ouzbékistan (jusqu'à la création de la MAFOuz B)." In P. Leriche, C. Pidaev, M. Gelin, K. Abdoullaev, and V. Fourniau, eds., *La Bactriane au carrefour des routes et des civilisations de l'Asie centrale: Termez et les villes de Bactriane-Tokharestan. Actes du Colloque de Termez 1997*, La Bibliothèque d'Asie Centrale, vol. 1, 23–34. Paris: Maisonneuve et Larose.

Pugachenkova, G. A., et al. 1994. [G. A. Pugachenkova, S. R. Dar, R. C. Sharma, M. A. Joyenda, and H. Siddiqi.] "Kushan Art." In J. Harmatta, B. N. Puri, and G. F. Etemadi, eds., *History of the Civilizations of Central Asia*, vol. 2, *The Development of Sedentary and Nomadic Civilizations: 700 B.C. to A.D. 250*, 323–85. Paris: UNESCO.

Pugachenkova, G. A., and V. A. Germanov. 1996. "Туркестанский кружок любителей археологии и домусульманские древности Средней Азии (К 100-летию Туркестанского кружка любителей археологии)." *Vestnik Drevnei Istorii*, 189–95. ["The Turkestan Circle of Archaeology Amateurs and Pre-Moslem Antiquities in Middle Asia: Centenary of the Turkestan Circle of Archaeology Amateurs."]

Pugachenkova, G. A., and E. V. Rtveladze. 1978. *Дальверзинтепе—Кушанский город на юге Узбекистана*. Tashkent: Fan. [*Dal'verzin-tepe—A Kushan Town in Southern Uzbekistan*.]

Pugliese Carratelli, Giovanni, and Giovanni Garbini. 1964. *A Bilingual Graeco-Aramaic Edict by Asoka: The First Greek Inscription Discovered in Afghanistan*. Serie Orientale Roma, vol. 29. Rome: Istituto Italiano per il Medio ed Estremo Oriente.

Rangarajan, L. N. 1987. *The Arthashastra*. New Delhi: Penguin Books India.

Rapin, Claude. 1983. "Les inscriptions économiques de la trésorerie hellénistique d'Aï Khanoum (Afghanistan)." *Bulletin de Correspondance Hellénique* 107, 315–81.

———. 1987. "La trésorerie hellénistique d'Aï Khanoum." *Revue Archéologique*, 41–70.

————, ed. 1992. *Fouilles d'Aï Khanoum.* Vol. 8, *La trésorerie du palais hellénistique d'Aï Khanoum: L'apogée et la chute du royaume grec de Bactriane.* Mémoires de la Délégation Archéologique Française en Afghanistan, vol. 33. Paris: de Boccard.

————. 1995. "Hinduism in the Indo-Greek Area: Notes on Some Indian Finds from Bactria and on Two Temples in Taxila." In A. Invernizzi, ed., *In the Land of the Gryphons: Papers on Central Asian Archaeology in Antiquity,* Monografie di Mesopotamia, vol. 5, 275–91. Florence: Casa Editrice Le Lettere.

————. 1996a. *Indian Art from Afghanistan: The Legend of Śakuntalā and the Indian Treasure of Eucratides at Ai Khanum.* New Delhi: Manohar.

————. 1996b. "Nouvelles observations sur le parchemin gréco-bactrien d'Asangôrna." *Topoi* 6, 458–69.

————. 1998. "L'incompréhensible Asie centrale de la carte de Ptolémée: Propositions pour un décodage." *Bulletin of the Asia Institute* 12, 201–25.

————. 2005. "L'Afghanistan et l'Asie centrale dans la géographie mythique des historiens d'Alexandre et dans la toponymie des géographes gréco-romains: Notes sur la route d'Herat à Begram." In Osmund Bopearachchi and Marie-Françoise Boussac, eds., *Afghanistan: Ancien carrefour entre l'est et l'ouest,* Indicopleustoi: Archaeologies of the Indian Ocean, vol. 3, 143–72. Turnhout: Brepols.

————. 2007. "Nomads and the Shaping of Central Asia: From the Early Iron Age to the Kushan Period." In Joe Cribb and Georgina Herrmann, eds., *After Alexander: Central Asia before Islam,* Proceedings of the British Academy, vol. 133, 29–72. Oxford: Oxford University Press for the British Academy.

Rapin, Claude, and P. Hadot. 1987. "Les textes littéraires grecs de la trésorerie d'Aï Khanoum." *Bulletin de Correspondance Hellénique* 111, 225–66.

Rapin, Claude, Muxammedzon Isamiddinov, and Mutalib Khasanov. 2001. "La tombe d'une princesse nomade à Koktepe près de Samarkand." *Comptes-Rendus de l'Académie des Inscriptions et Belles-Lettres* 145, 33–92.

Rapin, Claude, and S. A. Rakhmanov. 1999. "Les 'Portes de Fer' près de Derbent." *Dossiers d'Archéologie* 243, 18–19.

Raschke, M. G. 1974. "The Office of Agoranomos in Ptolemaic and Roman Egypt." In E. Kiessling and M. A. Rupprecht, eds., *Akten des XIII. Internationalen Papyrologenkongresses: Marburg/Lahn, 2.–6. August 1971,* Münchener Beiträge zur Papyrusforschung und antiken Rechtsgeschichte, vol. 66, 349–56. Munich: Beck.

Rawlinson, H. G. 1909. *Bactria: From the Earliest Times to the Extinction of Bactrio-Greek Rule in the Punjab (Being the Hare University Prize Essay, 1908).* Bombay: The "Times of India" Office.

Ray, Himanshu P. 1988. "The Yavana Presence in Ancient India." *Journal of the Economic and Social History of the Orient* 31, 311–25.

Raychaudhuri, H. C. 1922. "The Mahābhārata and the Besnagar Inscription of Heliodoros." *Journal and Proceedings, Asiatic Society of Bengal,* n.s., 18, 269–71.

Rea, John, R. C. Senior, and Adrian S. Hollis. 1994. "A Tax Receipt from Hellenistic Bactria." *Zeitschrift für Papyrologie und Epigraphik* 104, 261–80.

Reiss-Engelhorn-Museen. 2009. *Alexander der Grosse und die Öffnung der Welt: Asiens Kulturen im Wandel.* Publikationen der Reiss-Engelhorn-Museen, vol. 36. Regensburg: Schnell und Steiner GmbH.

Rhys-Davids, T. W., trans. 1890. *The Questions of King Milinda.* 2 vols. Sacred Books of the East, vols. 35 and 36. Oxford: Oxford University Press.

Robert, Louis. 1968. "De Delphes à l'Oxus: Inscriptions grecques nouvelles de la Bactriane." *Comptes-Rendus de l'Académie des Inscriptions et Belles-Lettres,* 416–57.

Rougemont, Georges. 2005. "Nouvelles inscriptions grecques de l'Asie centrale." In Osmund Bopearachchi and Marie-Françoise Boussac, eds., *Afghanistan: Ancien carrefour entre l'est et l'ouest,* Indicopleustoi: Archaeologies of the Indian Ocean, vol. 3, 127–36. Turnhout: Brepols.

———. 2012. *Inscriptions grecques d'Iran et d'Asie centrale.* Corpus Inscriptionum Iranicarum, series 2, Inscriptions of the Seleucid and Parthian Periods and of Eastern Iran and Central Asia, vol. 1, Inscriptions in Non-Iranian Languages. London: School of Oriental and African Studies.

Rtveladze, E. V. 1990. "On the Historical Geography of Bactria-Tokharistan." *Silk Road Art and Archaeology* 1, 1–33.

———. 1999. "Kampyr Tepe–Pandokheïon." *Dossiers d'Archéologie* 247, 56–57.

Sachs, A. J., and H. Hunger. 1988. *Astronomical Diaries and Related Texts from Babylonia.* Vol. 1, *Diaries from 652 B.C. to 262 B.C.* Denkschriften der Österreichischen Akademie der Wissenschaften, philosophisch-historische Klasse, vol. 195. Vienna: Österreichische Akademie der Wissenschaften.

Saidel, Benjamin A., and E. J. van der Steen. 2007. *On the Fringe of Society: Archaeological and Ethnoarchaeological Perspectives on Pastoral and Agricultural Societies.* BAR International Series, no. 1657. Oxford: Archaeopress.

Salomon, Richard. 1986. "The Inscription of Senavarma, King of Oḍi." *Indo-Iranian Journal* 29, 261–93.

———. 1998. *Indian Epigraphy: A Guide to the Study of Inscriptions in Sanskrit, Prakrit, and the Other Indo-Aryan Languages.* South Asia Research. New York and Oxford: Oxford University Press.

Salvatori, Sandro, Maurizio Tosi, and Barbara Cerasetti, eds. 2008. *The Archaeological Map of the Murghab Delta.* Vol. 2, *The Bronze Age and Early Iron Age in the Margiana Lowlands: Facts and Methodological Proposal for a Redefinition of the Research Strategies.* BAR International Series, no. 1806; The Archaeological Map of the Murghab Delta, Studies and Reports, vol. 2. Oxford: Archaeopress.

Sancisi-Weerderburg, H. 2001. "*Yaunā* by the Sea and Across the Sea." In Irad Malkin, ed., *Ancient Perceptions of Greek Ethnicity.* Center for Hellenic Studies, Colloquia, vol. 5. Washington, D.C.: Center for Hellenic Studies and Trustees for Harvard University.

Sancisi-Weerderburg, H., and Amélie Kuhrt, eds. 1987. *Achaemenid History.* Vol. 2, *The Greek Sources: Proceedings of the Groningen 1984 Achaemenid History Workshop.* Leiden: Nederlands Instituut voor het Nabije Oosten.

Sarianidi, V. I. 1972. *Раскопки Тилля-тепе в Северном Афганистане.* Volume 1. Материалы к Археологической Карте Северного Афганистана. Moscow: Nauka. [*Finds at Tillya-tepe in Northern Afghanistan,* vol. 1. Materials for an Archaeological Map of Northern Afghanistan.]

Sayce, A. H. 1894. "Inscriptions et papyrus grecs d'Égypte." *Revue des Études Grecques* 7, 284–304.

Scerrato, U. 1980. "Due tombe ad incinerazione del Museo di Kandahar." *Annali dell'Istituto Orientale di Napoli* 40, 627–50.

Schlumberger, Daniel. 1946. "Rapport sur une mission en Afghanistan." *Comptes-Rendus de l'Académie des Inscriptions et Belles-Lettres*, 169–77.

———. 1949. "La prospection archéologique de Bactres (printemps 1947): Rapport sommaire." *Syria* 26, 173–90.

———. 1960. "Descendants non-méditerranéens de l'art grec." *Syria* 37, 131–66.

———. 1961. "Excavations at Surkh Kotal and the Problem of Hellenism in Bactria and India." *Proceedings of the British Academy* 47, 77–95.

———. 1964. "Une nouvelle inscription grecque d'Açoka." *Comptes-Rendus de l'Académie des Inscriptions et Belles-Lettres*, 126–40.

———. 1965. "Aï Khanoum, une ville hellénistique en Afghanistan." *Comptes-Rendus de l'Académie des Inscriptions et Belles-Lettres*, 36–46.

Schlumberger, Daniel, and Paul Bernard. 1965. "Ai Khanoum." *Bulletin de Correspondance Hellénique* 89, 590–657.

Schlumberger, Daniel, et al. 1958. [Daniel Schlumberger, Louis Robert, A. Dupont-Sommer, and E. Benveniste.] "Une bilingue gréco-araméenne d'Asoka." *Journal Asiatique* 246, 36–48.

Schmidt, E. F. 1953. *Persepolis*. Vol. 1, *Structures, Reliefs, Inscriptions*. Oriental Institute Publications, vol. 68. Chicago: University of Chicago Press.

Schmitt, R. 1990. "Ex Occidente Lux: Griechen und griechische Sprache im hellenistischen Fernen Osten." In P. Steinmetz, ed., *Beiträge zur hellenistischen Literatur und ihrer Rezeption in Rom*, Palingenesia, vol. 28, 41–58. Stuttgart: Franz Steiner.

Seldeslachts, E. 2004. "The End of the Road for the Indo-Greeks?" *Iranica Antiqua* 39, 249–96.

Senior, R. C., and D. MacDonald. 1998. *The Decline of the Indo-Greeks: A Re-Appraisal of the Chronology from the Time of Menander to That of Azes*. Monographs of the Hellenic Numismatic Society, vol. 2. Athens: Hellenic Numismatic Society.

Shaked, Shaul. 2003. "De Khulmi à Nikhšapaya: Les données des nouveaux documents araméens de Bactres sur la toponymie de la région (IVe siècle av. n. è.)." *Comptes-Rendus de l'Académie des Inscriptions et Belles-Lettres*, 1517–35.

———. 2004. *Le satrape de Bactriane et son gouverneur: Documents araméens du IVe s. avant notre ère provenant de Bactriane*. Persika, vol. 4. Paris: de Boccard.

Shanks, Michael. 1996. *Classical Archaeology of Greece: Experiences of the Discipline*. Experiences of Archaeology. London: Routledge.

Sharma, G. R. 1980. *Reh Inscription of Menander and the Indo-Greek Invasion of the Gaṅgā Valley*. Studies in History, Culture and Archaeology, vol. 1. Allahabad: Abinash Prakashan.

Shenkar, Michael. 2011. "Temple Architecture in the Iranian World in the Hellenistic Period." In Anna Kouremenos, Sujatha Chandrasekaran, and Roberto Rossi, eds., *From Pella to Gandhara: Hybridisation and Identity in the Art and Architecture of the Hellenistic East*, BAR International Series, no. 2221, 117–40. Oxford: BAR.

Sherwin-White, S. M. 1983. "Aristeas Ardibelteios: Some Aspects of the Use of Double Names in Seleucid Babylonia." *Zeitschrift für Papyrologie und Epigraphik* 50, 209–21.

———. 1987. "Seleucid Babylonia: A Case-Study for the Installation and Development of Greek Rule." In Amélie Kuhrt and Susan Sherwin-White, eds., *Hellenism in the East: The Interaction of Greek and Non-Greek Civilizations from Syria to Central Asia after Alexander*, 1–31. London: Duckworth.

Sims-Williams, Nicholas. 2000. *Bactrian Documents from Northern Afghanistan.* Part 1, *Legal and Economic Documents.* Studies in the Khalili Collection, vol. 3, part 1; Corpus Inscriptionum Iranicarum, part 2, Inscriptions of the Selucid and Parthian Periods and of Eastern Iran and Central Asia, vol. 6, Bactrian. Oxford: Nour Foundation in Association with Azimuth Editions and Oxford University Press.

———. 2007. *Bactrian Documents from Northern Afghanistan.* Part 2, *Letters and Buddhist Texts.* Studies in the Khalili Collection, vol. 3, part 2; Corpus Inscriptionum Iranicarum, part 2, Inscriptions of the Selucid and Parthian Periods and of Eastern Iran and Central Asia, vol. 6, Bactrian. London: Nour Foundation in Association with Azimuth Editions.

Sims-Williams, Nicholas, and Joe Cribb. 1996. "A New Bactrian Inscription of Kanishka the Great." *Silk Road Art and Archaeology* 4, 75–142.

Sircar, D. C. 1965a. *Indian Epigraphy.* Delhi: Motilal Banarsidass.

———. 1965b. *Select Inscriptions Bearing on Indian History and Civilization.* Vol. 1, *From the Sixth Century BC to the Sixth Century AD.* Calcutta: University of Calcutta Press.

———. 1966. *Indian Epigraphical Glossary.* Delhi: Motilal Banarsidass.

Skydsgaard, J. E. 1993. "The Greeks in Southern Russia: A Tale of Two Cities." In P. Bilde, T. Engberg-Pedersen, L. Hannestad, J. Zahle, and K. Randsborg, eds., *Centre and Periphery in the Hellenistic World,* Studies in Hellenistic Civilization, vol. 4, 124–31. Aarhus: Aarhus University Press.

Smith, Stuart Tyson. 2003. *Wretched Kush: Ethnic Identities and Boundaries in Egypt's Nubian Empire.* London: Routledge.

———. 2008. "Crossing Boundaries: Nomadic Groups and Ethnic Identities." In H. Barnard and W. Wendrich, eds., *The Archaeology of Mobility: Old World and New World Nomadism,* Cotsen Advanced Seminar Series, vol. 4, 343–65. Los Angeles: Cotsen Institute of Archaeology, University of California.

Stančo, Ladislav. 2009. "The Activities in Uzbekistan in the 2008 Season: Testing the Google Earth Programme as a Tool for Archaeological Prospecting." *Studia Hercynia* 13, 115–22.

Stančo, Ladislav, et al. 2006. [Ladislav Stančo in cooperation with Petra Belaňová, Libor Grmela, Jakub Halama, Jan Kysela, Lucie Šmahelová, and Kristýna Urbanová.] "Jandavlattepa 2005: Preliminary Excavation Report." *Studia Hercynia* 10, 167–72.

Staviskij, B. J. 1986. *La Bactriane sous les Kushans: Problèmes d'histoire et de culture.* Paris: Maisonneuve.

Stevenson, Alice. 2007. "Ethnicity and Migration? The Predynastic Cemetery of el-Gerzeh." In B. Midant-Reynes and Y. Tristant, eds., *Origins,* vol. 2, *Proceedings of the Second International Conference on Predynastic and Early Dynastic Egypt, Toulouse, France, September 2005,* Orientalia Lovaniensia Analecta, vol. 172, 543–60. Leuven: Peeters.

Stewart, A. 1993. *Faces of Power: Alexander's Image and Hellenistic Politics.* Berkeley and Los Angeles: University of California Press.

Stride, Sebastian. 2001. "Le programme de prospection de la MAFOuz B dans la région du Sourkhan Darya." In P. Leriche, C. Pidaev, M. Gelin, K. Abdoullaev, and V. Fourniau, eds., *La Bactriane au carrefour des routes et des civilisations de l'Asie centrale: Termez et les villes de Bactriane-Tokharestan. Actes du Colloque de Termez 1997,* La Bibliothèque d'Asie Centrale, vol. 1, 173–83. Paris: Maisonneuve et Larose and IFEAC.

———. 2004. "An Archaeological GIS of the Surkhan Darya Province (Southern Uzbekistan)." *The Silk Road* 2, 30–35.

———. 2007. "Regions and Territories in Southern Central Asia: What the Surkhan Darya Province Tells Us about Bactria." In Joe Cribb and Georgina Herrmann, eds., *After Alexander: Central Asia before Islam,* Proceedings of the British Academy, vol. 133, 99–117. Oxford: Oxford University Press for the British Academy.

Stride, Sebastian, Bernardo Rondelli, and Simone Mantellini. 2009. "Canals versus Horses: Political Power in the Oasis of Samarkand." *World Archaeology* 41, 73–87.

Stronach, David. 2001. "From Cyrus to Darius: Notes on Art and Architecture in Early Achaemenid Palaces." In Inge Nielsen, ed., *The Royal Palace Institution in the First Millennium BC: Regional Development and Cultural Interchange between East and West,* Monographs of the Danish Institute at Athens, 95–111. Athens and Aarhus: The Danish Institute at Athens and Aarhus University Press.

Sverchkov, Leonid M. 2008. "The Kurganzol Fortress: On the History of Central Asia in the Hellenistic Era." *Ancient Civilizations from Scythia to Siberia* 14, 123–91.

Szuchman, Jeffrey, ed. 2009. *Nomads, Tribes, and the State in the Ancient Near East: Cross-Disciplinary Perspectives.* Oriental Institute Seminars, vol. 5. Chicago: Oriental Institute.

Tarn, Sir William Woodthorpe. 1951 [1938]. *The Greeks in Bactria and India.* Cambridge: Cambridge University Press.

Tarzi, Zemaryalli. 1996. "Jules Barthoux: Le découvreur oublié d'Aï Khanoum." *Comptes-Rendus de l'Académie des Inscriptions et Belles-Lettres* 140, 595–611.

Thapar, Romila. 1971. "The Image of the Barbarian in Early India." *Comparative Studies in Society and History* 13, 408–36.

———. 1974. "Social Mobility in Ancient India, with Special Reference to Elite Groups." In R. S. Sharma, ed., *Indian Society: Historical Probings,* 95–123. New Delhi: People's Publishing House.

———. 1997. *Aśoka and the Decline of the Mauryas.* Rev. ed. Delhi and Oxford: Oxford University Press.

Theuns–de Boer, G. 1999. "Ritual Life of the Heliodorus Pillar: Photographic Prints at the Kern Institute, Leiden." *International Institute for Asian Studies Newsletter* 20. [Online.]

Tourgounov, Bakhadir. 2001. "Nouvelles données sur le site de Dalverzine-Tepe." In P. Leriche, C. Pidaev, M. Gelin, K. Abdoullaev, and V. Fourniau, eds., *La Bactriane au carrefour des routes et des civilisations de l'Asie centrale: Termez et les villes de Bactriane-Tokharestan. Actes du Colloque de Termez 1997,* La Bibliothèque d'Asie Centrale, vol. 1, 241–44. Paris: Maisonneuve et Larose and IFEAC.

Trigger, Bruce G. 2006. *A History of Archaeological Thought.* 2nd ed. Cambridge: Cambridge University Press.

Tripathi, K. K. 2002. *Archaeology of Vidiśā (Daśārṇa) Region.* Delhi: Sharada.

Tušlová, Petra. 2011. "Systematical Field Survey in Sherabad District, South Uzbekistan." *Studia Hercynia* 15, 27–38.

van der Spek, R. J. 2001. "The Theatre of Babylon in Cuneiform." In W. H. van Soldt, ed., *Veenhof Anniversary Volume: Studies Presented to Klaas R. Veenhof on the Occasion of His Sixty-Fifth Birthday,* 444–56. Leiden: Brill.

———. 2005. "Ethnic Segregation in Hellenistic Babylon." In W. H. van Soldt, ed., *Ethnicity in Ancient Mesopotamia: Papers Read at the 48th Rencontre Assyriologique Internationale, Leiden, 1–4 July 2002,* 393–408. Leiden: Nederlands Instituut voor het Nabije Oosten.

———. 2009. "Multi-ethnicity and Ethnic Segregation in Hellenistic Babylon." In Ton Derks and Nico Roymans, eds., *Ethnic Constructs in Antiquity: The Role of Power and Tradition*, Amsterdam Archaeological Studies, vol. 13, 101–15. Amsterdam: Amsterdam University Press.

van Dommelen, Peter. 2005. "Colonial Interactions and Hybrid Practices: Phoenician and Carthaginian Settlement in the Ancient Mediterranean." In Gil J. Stein, ed., *The Archaeology of Colonial Encounters: Comparative Perspectives*, 109–41. Santa Fe: School of American Research Press.

Vassiliades, D. T. 2000. *The Greeks in India: A Survey in Philosophical Understanding*. New Delhi: Munshiram Manoharlal.

Venis, A. 1910. "A Note on the Two Besnagar Inscriptions." *Journal of the Royal Asiatic Society*, 813–15.

Veuve, Serge. 1982. "Cadrans solaires gréco-bactriens à Aï Khanoum (Afghanistan)." *Bulletin de Correspondance Hellénique* 106, 23–51.

———. 1987. *Fouilles d'Aï Khanoum*. Vol. 6, *Le gymnase: Architecture, céramique, sculpture*. Mémoires de la Délégation Archéologique Française en Afghanistan, vol. 30. Paris: de Boccard.

Vinogradova, Natalia M., and Giovanna Lombardo. 2002. "Farming Sites of the Late Bronze and Early Iron Ages in Southern Tajikistan." *East and West* 52, 71–125.

Vleeming, S. P. 2001. *Some Coins of Artaxerxes and Other Short Texts in the Demotic Script Found on Various Objects and Gathered from Many Publications*. Studia Demotica 5. Leuven: Peeters.

Vogel, J. P. 1912. "The Garuda Pillar of Besnagar." In *Archaeological Survey of India Annual Report, 1908–9*, 126–29. Calcutta: Government of India.

Wagner, Guy. 1993. "Le décurion Paccius Maximus, champion de l'acrostiche." *Zeitschrift für Papyrologie und Epigraphik* 95, 147–48.

Walleser, M., and H. Kropp, eds. 1967. *Manorathapūranī: Buddhaghosa's Commentary on the Anguttara-nikāya*. Pali Text Society Text Series. London: Pali Text Society.

Watson, Burton. 1993. *Records of the Grand Historian by Sima Qian: Han Dynasty*. Volume 2. Records of Civilization, vol. 65. Hong Kong and New York: Research Centre for Translation, the Chinese University of Hong Kong, and Columbia University Press.

Webster, Jane. 2001. "Creolizing the Roman Provinces." *American Journal of Archaeology* 105, 209–25.

Webster, Jane, and Nicholas Cooper, eds. 1996. *Roman Imperialism: Post-Colonial Perspectives*. Leicester Archaeological Monograph 3. Leicester: University of Leicester, School of Archaelological Studies.

Wheeler, Mortimer. 1962. *Chārsada: A Metropolis of the North-West Frontier*. Oxford: Oxford University Press.

———. 1968. *Flames over Persepolis: Turning Point in History*. London: Weidenfeld and Nicolson.

White, Richard. 1991. *The Middle Ground: Indians, Empires, and Republics in the Great Lakes Region, 1650–1815*. Cambridge Studies in North American Indian History. Cambridge: Cambridge University Press.

Whitehouse, David. 1978. "Excavations at Kandahar, 1974: First Interim Report." *Afghan Studies* 1, 9–39.

Widemann, François. 2009. *Les successeurs d'Alexandre en Asie centrale et leur héritage culturel: Essai.* 2nd ed. Paris: Riveneuve.

Will, Edouard. 1985. "Pour une 'anthropologie coloniale' du monde hellénistique." In J. W. Eadie and J. Ober, eds., *The Craft of the Ancient Historian: Essays in Honor of Chester G. Starr,* 273–301. Lanham: University Press of America.

Wood, John. 1841. *A Personal Narrative of a Journey to the Source of the River Oxus, by the Route of the Indus, Kabul, and Badakhshan, Performed under the Sanction of the Supreme Government of India, in the Years 1836, 1837, and 1838.* London: John Murray.

Woolf, Greg. 1998. *Becoming Roman: The Origins of Provincial Civilization in Gaul.* Cambridge: Cambridge University Press.

Yardley, J. C., and R. Develin, eds. 1994. *Justin: Epitome of the Philippic History of Pompeius Trogus.* Classical Resources Series, vol. 3. Atlanta: Scholars Press.

Young, R. S. 1955. "The South Wall of Balkh-Bactra." *American Journal of Archaeology* 59, 267–76.

Young, Robert J. C. 2001. *Postcolonialism: An Historical Introduction.* Oxford: Blackwell.

Zadneprovskiy, Y. A. 1994. "The Nomads of Northern Central Asia after the Invasion of Alexander." In J. Harmatta, B. N. Puri, and G. F. Etemadi, eds., *History of the Civilizations of Central Asia,* vol. 2, *The Development of Sedentary and Nomadic Civilizations: 700 B.C. to A.D. 250,* 448–63. Paris: UNESCO.

Zandee, J. 1966. *An Ancient Egyptian Crossword Puzzle: An Inscription of Neb-wenenef from Thebes.* Mededelingen en Verhandelingen van het Vooraziatisch-Egyptisch Genootschap "Ex Oriente Lux" / Mémoires de la Société d'Études Orientales "Ex Oriente Lux," vol. 15. Leiden: Ex Oriente Lux.

Printed in Great Britain
by Amazon